The New America

Also by Mark Little

Turn Left at Greenland
Zulu Time

The New America
And the Rise of the Obama Generation

Mark Little

**NEW
ISLAND**

The New America – And the Rise of the Obama Generation
First published 2009
by New Island
2 Brookside
Dundrum Road
Dublin 14

www.newisland.ie

ISBN 978-1-84840-039-9

British Library Cataloguing Data. A CIP catalogue record for this book is
available from the British Library.

Book design by Inka Hagen.
Typeset by TypeIT, Dublin.
Index by John Ryan.
Printed in Ireland by Colourbooks Ltd.

10 9 8 7 6 5 4 3 2 1

Acknowledgments

I would like to offer my eternal gratitude to Tara Peterman for being my guiding light during the writing of this book, and apologise to Tommie, Daisy and Sorcha for my absences during the past year.

Once again, I owe a great debt to literary agent Jonathan Williams for his clarity and warmth. All at New Island have done a tremendous job in bringing this book to life, in particular Deirdre Nolan.

I would also like to acknowledge the guidance and support of my colleagues and editors at RTÉ during my travels through the 'New America', especially Ed Mulhall, Noel Curran and David Nally. Adrian Lynch of Animo Productions and Ruan Magan played a key role in developing some of the central themes of this book. They also taught me that there is a lot more to communicating big ideas than writing them down.

Friends and family have helped shape this book. In particular, I would like to thank Tom Little and Neil Leyden for offering game-changing advice at critical moments.

Mark Little

Gatsby believed in the green light, the orgastic future that year by year recedes before us. It eluded us then, but that's no matter – tomorrow we will run faster, stretch our arms farther . . . And one fine morning – So we beat on, boats against the current, borne back ceaselessly into the past.

F. Scott Fitzgerald, *The Great Gatsby*

Contents

Preface
Washington DC – Yes, We Did

In years to come, we may look back at Barack Obama's victory in 2008 as preordained. That is not how it felt at the time.

Even hard-core believers struggled to process the collision of hope and history on election night. A senior Obama adviser told me that she greeted the president-elect that evening with the words: 'Does not compute.'

The networks called Florida, Pennsylvania, Ohio, Michigan, but the unfolding outcome still seemed profoundly unlikely. When the TV screen flashed the news that Obama would be the next president, it felt like a sensational shift in the plot of a Hollywood thriller, not an actual statement of fact.

Obama himself would need to confirm it before they would believe it; before they could take a breath and let out a roar.

'This is our moment. This is our time …'

With those words, spoken by the president-elect in Chicago's Grant Park, the banks of the river finally gave way and a torrent of hope-mongers flooded city streets from LA to DC.

A few minutes after Obama thanked America, and asked God to bless it, CNN carried footage of a small group of flag-waving celebrants outside the northwest gate of the White House. The pictures triggered an uncommon stampede of common purpose. Thousands raced out of bars and dormitories and apartments around Washington to join the impromptu party outside Obama's new home. With sudden,

1

spontaneous clarity, their mutual joy had a blindingly obvious destination.

And yet, even then, in the opening minutes of a new era, as they raced towards the White House, something stirred in the dark corners of the American capital. Perhaps it was just the drumbeat of rain – churlish and defiant – reminding members of the Obama generation that some things would forever be outside their control.

But they seem determined to ignore the warnings. The plum-faced juvenile drunk on the corner of 16th and K screamed at a couple across the road from him, 'Yes, we can.'

As I passed, I muttered, 'Yes, you did.'

The young man heard me and swivelled his head in a slow, pronounced motion as if sizing up a threat. He stared at me with widening eyes, unsure what to do next.

He repeated the words in a reverent, ponderous whisper. 'Yes. We. Did.'

Then, remembering his initial purpose, he turned back to the couple across the road and bellowed the good news. 'Yes, we did.'

Indeed they did; all of them, all the bright young things now walking, striding, running in an unplanned advance on the White House, a surge of realised dreams set free by Barack Obama just a few minutes earlier.

'If there is anyone out there who still doubts that America is a place where all things are possible ... tonight is your answer.'

Trickle became flood, swishing about the fringes of Lafayette Square, surging toward Andrew Jackson on a horse, past a temporary wire fence before finally washing up at the gates to 1600 Pennsylvania Avenue. I paused to get my bearings before joining the crowd and as I wiped the film of rain from my hair, a passing young man let out a scream borne of rage and relief: 'We're taking it back.'

At the centre of the crowd, pots and pans were being bashed together. A rolling serenade swept through the crowd in the direction of the darkened living quarters of the White House: 'Hey, hey, goodbye.' Two uniformed Secret Service men stood silently in silhouette on the roof of the building. They didn't need to worry. There was no threat in that crowd, only youth and promise and – occasionally – the sweet and sour scent of exhaled alcohol.

A shirtless boy with a shiny hairless chest danced inside a semi-circle of elated black women like a victorious warrior claiming his prize. Two women in pyjamas staggered by arm-in-arm with rictus grins on their faces. Another walked by in a tight red cocktail dress on unfeasibly high heels, grasping at imaginary supports in the damp, livid air.

Even in that shallow stream of juvenile abandon, you could feel an undercurrent of maturity. Burning in the eyes of those old enough to remember past nightmares was the incandescent promise of that fabled American dream. Heads turned to listen to the proud, resolute baritone of an elderly black lady.

'I'm a 66-year-old woman,' she announced, 'coloured, negro, black, African American.'

As a small group gathered around, she placed her closed fist on her chest.

'But in here, I am an American, and I am living to see something I never thought I would live to see.'

The lady was speaking for her generation, those forged by the unfulfilled struggles of an unforgiving era, and for people of colour, who were about to see a black man occupy the White House, a mansion which slaves helped build. She was speaking for all Americans of her age and background, for whom Obama's election was a beautiful but bewildering event. They loved their country but never believed it had the potential to change quite this much.

Some will tell you the result of this election was never in doubt, but they are wrong. As I followed the campaign, I could sense that appetite for change, but I also heard the fear of change, a yearning for security. Right to the end, there was a real possibility that American voters would recoil from the leap of faith required to elect a black man called Barack Hussein Obama.

Yet, as I travelled beyond the manufactured drama of the campaign trail, I discovered something else: the United States had already started to change, election or no election. Obama was trying to harness the energy of this unfolding reinvention, but he did not create it. America was going to be a very different nation, no matter who became the next president.

The New America was first published before the election of Barack Obama. It argued that the United States was being transformed by an explosive combination of people and places. I had doubts about the speed of that transformation and avoided firm predictions about the outcome of the race for the White House. With the benefit of hindsight, I was too cautious. When I looked closely at the voting patterns in the 2008 election, particularly the geographic and demographic spread of Obama's winning coalition, I saw the new America was no longer an emerging trend – it was a political reality.

In one sense, I didn't need to wait for the election post-mortems. I could see the new America in the crowd gathered outside the White House on election night, in the many faces of the Obama generation: the Arab American boys with *kaffiyehs* around their necks waving the Stars and Stripes; a pair of West African immigrants wearing matching T-shirts featuring Martin Luther King and Obama side by side; black fraternity boys from Howard University step-dancing across Lafayette Park; a gaggle of Muslim girls with long modest coats and oval faces framed by the *hijab*; a dreadlocked young white man banging out a rhythm on the bottom of a plastic bin; voices calling out the old slogan of Latino activists, '*Sí, se puede*' – yes, we can.

My eye was drawn to something in the middle of the crowd. It was an arrow on a red T-shirt pointing to the face of the young, beautiful woman wearing it. The slogan underneath said, 'This is what democracy looks like.' It is also what the new America looks like.

My story begins and ends with the Millennial generation: Americans born in the last two decades of the 20th century. The 2008 election was their coming-out party. In their first act as a substantial voting bloc, they embraced change by an unprecedented margin. Obama won the support of two-thirds of voters between the ages of 18 and 29. That is a remarkable shift when you consider that in every election for the past 30 years, young voters have backed Republican and Democratic presidential candidates in almost equal numbers.

It's not enough to say American youngsters are shifting to the political left. Part of the reason the Millennials backed Obama in such big numbers is because of his talk of a 'new spirit of patriotism and responsibility'. All the evidence suggests the Millennials are uniquely civically minded and politically engaged, tending towards collective action rather than individualism. This is reflected in the numbers who actually voted. Back in 1996, a little more than one in three young Americans turned out at the polls. In 2008, more than half of them did (it was not the record-breaking levels some had expected but represented a steady shift in the tectonic plates of American politics nonetheless).

The Obama campaign also showed a keen understanding of the social technology that frames the Millennial world view. Young Americans live by the YouTube ethic, which values self-starting, autonomous forms of expression and disdains mainstream media filters and traditional political institutions. By

5

copying the ethos of social platforms such as Facebook, the Obama campaign has changed the political landscape forever.

Perhaps the most potent characteristic of the Millennial generation is its diversity, stunning to behold. More than four out of ten Americans born since the early 1980s are part of an ethnic or racial minority, and if current trends persist the majority of Americans under the age of 18 will be non-white by 2023. As the population of the new America becomes more diverse, so does its electorate. In the presidential election of 2000, 80 per cent of voters were white. Eight years later, it was 74 per cent. The fastest-growing component of the new America is the Latino community, and its political allegiance has shifted dramatically in the last two election cycles. In 2004, George Bush won a very respectable 44 per cent of Latino votes. In 2008, Barack Obama got 67 per cent.

As well as being the most diverse in American history, the Millennial generation is also one of the most dynamic and mobile, which brings us to the other great force for change in the new America: a surge in migration to the sprawling cities and big skies of the Sunbelt states.

The population of southern and western states such as Florida, California, Arizona and Texas has expanded at a mind-numbing rate since the 1960s and 1970s, when they were a powerbase for conservative revolutionaries such as Barry Goldwater and Ronald Reagan. In 2008, the Sunbelt threw its new-found electoral muscle behind a very different kind of political revolution. Florida, Colorado, Nevada and New Mexico had all lined up behind George Bush in 2004 but in 2008 they backed Obama (Arizona might well have followed had Republican candidate John McCain not lived there). New Mexico is of particular note: Bush won the state by a few thousand votes in 2004; Obama's winning margin was a whopping 15 per cent of the vote.

The Sunbelt states are the new centre of political gravity in the new America because they are growing fastest, staying young and becoming more diverse. But they also matter because they are overwhelmingly suburban. In recent decades, as young families drifted out of America's decaying cities, millions of them chose to live in the sprawling 'boomburbs' that thrive around established metropolises in desert states such as Nevada and Arizona. These voters played a pivotal role in the creation of America's new political order. Obama's victory in states such as Nevada is largely due to his stunning performance in Clark County, which encompasses Las Vegas and surrounding boomburbs such as Henderson (which we will visit a little later). His margin of victory in the county was five times the surplus enjoyed by John Kerry in 2004.

The importance of these cities may come as a surprise to you. There's a good reason for that. Boomburbs have been completely ignored by the media, even as they reshape the landscape of American life. Around the time Obama was inaugurated, *Forbes* magazine published a list of the ten 'most boring' cities in America. The snarky title was misleading since the poll actually rated the major cities with the fewest mentions in major newspapers and magazines. All ten of the most ignored cities in the US were Sunbelt boomburbs, including Henderson and North Las Vegas in Nevada, and Gilbert, Mesa and Chandler, which encircle Phoenix, Arizona. If there was ever a demonstration of how detached American journalism had become from American reality, this *Forbes* poll was it.

They may bore the pants off the media, but suburban voters have become arguably the single most important voting bloc in US politics, making up 49 per cent of the electorate in 2008 (up from 43 per cent in 2000). They are also unerringly accurate barometers of America's political climate. As you will see later in this book, suburban communities tend to moderate their politics as they settle. They seek out new civic and communal activities

7

which offset the deadening impact of sprawl and lay the foundation for a new type of suburban cosmopolitanism.

The shift to Obama was most pronounced in what many are calling the 'monied burbs' which have grown up around the high-tech and high-paying industries that have moved away from old cities. Obama became the first Democrat to win Colorado since 1992, in large measure because of his success in wealthy suburbs around Denver. He became the first Democrat to win North Carolina since 1976 because he did so well in the suburbs of Raleigh/Durham and Charlotte, which have attracted thousands of finance, medical and technology jobs.

It's worth stopping at this point to just take stock of all these component parts of new America. Any one of them – the Millennial generation, the rise of Latinos, the surge to the Sunbelt suburbs – could have shifted US politics, but added together, they become more than the sum of the parts. They combine to form a new nation, a new America.

In the pages that follow, I will take you to places that have been transformed by the collision of all these forces. This, by and large, is a story of hope. But I also want to explore what I saw stirring in the dark shadows on that joyous night in Washington. If the first edition of *The New America* was far too cautious in some ways, in others, it was not cautious enough.

I am particularly mindful that the breathtaking, technicolour detail of this American reinvention has been obscured by the cult of personality which formed around Barack Obama. The story of the new America is not the story of one man, just as this book is not an assessment of the policies he might pursue. The transformation of the United States did not begin with one election and will not end if Obama does not live up to his promise. If he truly lives up to his potential to be a great president, it will be because he understands the many dimensions of change and the hidden rhythms of reinvention.

And this brings me to my second fear and my primary reason for writing the second edition of this book. *The New America* was published before Lehman Brothers collapsed and just as the US property market went from decline into white-knuckle free-fall, therefore it didn't capture the epic challenges posed by economic crisis. The communities which helped drive the transformation you are about to witness – the Sunbelt boomburbs – have been worst affected by the collapse of the property market and the wider recession and, in the conclusion of this book, I'll show you what happens when the engine of the new America apparently runs out of fuel.

In case you think I am predicting doom and gloom for the Obama era, that is not my intention. I set out to write a book about America's greatest strength: its talent for constant reinvention. 'For that is the true genius of America,' Obama said on election night, 'that America can change.'

Yet, I am a realist about America, as well as an idealist. When I look to the history of the United States, I see that transformation doesn't always move in a straight line. It is always difficult and sometimes violent. The journey progresses in fits and starts, and never quite ends. Above all, change is scary, especially for those who stand to lose from it.

In August 2008, two days before Obama accepted the Democratic nomination, I met former presidential candidate and senator Gary Hart. In the interview in his office in downtown Denver, he articulated the contradiction of change in American society far better than I ever could.

> Our self-image is of being progressive, experimental, of being on the cutting edge of all kinds of things. But deep down, culturally and socially, this is a conservative country that is afraid of moving to a future that causes people to lose the values of the

> past. People sense we are living in a revolutionary age and that we must adapt – as Thomas Jefferson said over 200 years ago – to those new realities. But in the process, they don't want to lose what they feel is unique about this society. So, in a way, there is schizophrenia. We must change, but we don't want change to make us somebody that we're not.

I see the potential for conflict in the new America. I see a generational tension which seemed to grow even more pronounced as the presidential election campaign progressed (when the ballots were counted, they found the young and old voters had expressed different preferences to a greater extent than any time since Nixon's re-election in 1972). Even within the Millennial generation, I have discovered the potential for conflict, between those who still cling to the notion of small towns not suburbs, to American values not universal principles and to security not change.

Forty-eight hours after that scene of celebration outside the White House, I boarded a commuter flight at Reagan National Airport in Washington bound for Philadelphia. In the seat next to me was a young soldier in uniform. His name was Brandon Beaster and he grew up on a farm near the town of Jackson, Michigan.

When he joined the army, he became a military mortician, one of just 300 in the US armed forces. Then he was sent to Iraq. His job was to recover bodies from major combat operations or serious ambushes. Often the combat was still continuing. 'I was flown into Hot LZs five or six times a week,' he explained casually. 'Sometimes I could hear the ping-ping off the metal plates on the Blackhawk.'

Brandon's luck ran out in July 2008, not in a Blackhawk but while he was taking out the rubbish in his barracks at the US army base in Belad. A mortar exploded beside him and nearly blew his head off. He was shipped home and spent five months recovering in the Walter Reed military hospital. He had been discharged just hours before boarding our flight and was on his way back to his unit.

'I still have scar tissue and some ringing in my ears. The only way I can get to sleep at night is to leave the TV on.'

Doctors told him severe headaches would be a permanent feature of his life. Yet Brandon considered himself lucky. While at Walter Reed, he met Travis, a friend from high school, who lost both his legs when his Humvee hit a landmine.

He figured he'd be sent off to Afghanistan once he rejoined his unit. He had been offered a medical discharge from the army, which he had refused. 'I suppose I'm a gung-ho kind of guy.'

Brandon looked down at the portrait of Obama on the front of the magazine on my lap and shook his head. His country no longer felt like home. When he got out of the army, he planned to make a life for himself somewhere other than Obama's America.

Brandon was barely out of his teenage years. He was a Millennial. He knew all about the spirit of responsibility and patriotism that enlivens the Obama generation. But he was simultaneously wedded to an America that has ceased to exist. He was a living symbol of the hidden code of US history: the everlasting struggle between the sanctuary of a mythical yesterday and the promise of a better tomorrow. Out of that tension comes the energy that powers the new America.

Introduction:
The Game

Scottsdale – Sunset in the Shining City

The towering columns of thundercloud circling the stadium are dark with the promise of rain but no one pays them much heed.

'That's one of the things you discover living here,' says the school official. 'The rainstorms never seem to make it beyond the edge of the city. Must be something to do with all that concrete and asphalt.'

The last storm of summer will send nothing more than a brisk warm breeze across the playing fields of Saguaro High School tonight. Tonight, the opening game of the football season will kick off in front of a golden sunset. This is Scottsdale, Arizona. It could be no other way.

The Saguaro Sabercats are defending state champions. In tonight's game, the team will face the Prescott Badgers. Not the fiercest opposition they can expect this year. Truth be told, the biggest obstacles the players will face this season are their own expectations. Here and now, in the late golden hour of a desert evening, what you hear through gritted teeth is the sound of young men straining to keep their demons in check.

The Sabercats are on the field now, with just over a half-hour to game time. They play in black and gold: boys in men's uniforms.

A coach in khaki pants and a white golf shirt directs a series of exercise routines. Three parallel lines of players are crouched down on the pitch as if profoundly constipated, their shiny black helmets on the ground beside them. They keep that position for what seems like an age, until a coach lets out a guttural grunt.

'Up.'

They rise, limber, unblocked. The coach shouts out a question which is audible only to a football player's ear.

'Dropmedownsareyouallright?'

The boys respond from the back of their throats.

'Igh.'

There is much crying out and high-fiving, but there are also moments of solitude as players come to rest on the sidelines. One stands slightly aloof, his face obscured by his helmet, thinking deep thoughts behind layers of plastic and styrofoam. Still breathless from the warm-up, his mouth hangs open as his chest rises and falls. Absentmindedly, he adjusts the metal grid on the front of the helmet as if looking for some karmic balance between heavily protected head and pounding heart. Then he is at rest. Static. Unsmiling. Pumped.

The loudspeakers pour out the bass-laden drone of death-metal and rap music, breaking the tranquillity of the evening, guarding the young men against the complacency of calm.

The boys of defence begin to drift toward the sideline. A voice in the developing huddle barks: 'Bring it up.'

The defensive coach addresses his boys, now gathered around him in a tight circle of brawn and congested aggression.

'Lot of work. Spring. Summer. Lifting. Push-ups. Sit-ups. Lifting. Everything you worked for. Everything you worked for. This here's where the fun starts.'

He delivers the words in a monotone, stripped of emotion. The boys are like ravenous birds picking at a carcass. Glass-eyed. Determined.

'Got to be prepared. Mentally prepared and you will be fine.'

Sensing the pep talk has run its course, deep, young voices in the huddle trade snippets of inspirational gibberish.

'Stay in it. Let's go.'

'This is where the VO2s pay off.'

'Atta boy. Here we go. Watch the hop.'

It's over now. The boys of defence have one last ritual to observe. They come closer and clasp hands and call out a single word as they do: 'Intensity!'

Saguaro is the rule, not the exception. The lowliest American town will turn out on a Friday night to celebrate their juvenile heroes, in playing fields with big stands seating many hundreds, if not thousands, of fans. Local TV crews are often there to record the action (as they are at Saguaro on opening night) and, at the very least, there is a commentator to call the plays on the PA system. The action will unfold against a backdrop of beautiful noise created by marching bands and cheerleaders.

High-school football exists in a separate universe from the schoolboy leagues of an Irish childhood. The players will never know what it is like to be outnumbered by a handful of dutiful parents shivering on a blustery sideline. They will never change hurriedly in a tin hut smelling of cowshit and Deep Heat. There's no chance that they will travel home from an away game knee-to-mucky-knee in the back of a borrowed Hiace van. We live our schoolboy dreams in stark, brutal prose. They preen themselves with epic, inflated poetry.

Mike Garcia is responsible for all the equipment that the Sabercats will use tonight. To everyone at Saguaro, he is known as Tug. His big round face, framed by a neat goatee beard, is moist from the last rays of the fading sun.

'You really breathe this. Friday night. From a very young age. It's Friday night and there's thousands at a game. You live for a Friday night.'

Tug drives away with one leg hanging out the side of his golf cart, his eyes darting around in search of an unresolved detail.

The big stand framing the playing field is filling up with the

17

home crowd. The track just in front is alive with the colour and sensual promise of cheerleaders. Their uniforms are also black and gold, absorbing and reflecting the glow of the evening sun.

Five girls move clear of their friends to practise their human pyramid. One young woman is lifted skyward by the hands of others. She reaches maximum altitude with her right arm pushed into the sky at the very same angle as her left leg.

The pose is held for not more than a couple of seconds before the young woman on top begins to fall. As she goes from vertical to horizontal, her body executes a perfect twirl before her four friends catch her. She is at rest. Pristine. Controlled. Incorruptible.

It's getting near floodlight time as the cheerleaders finish their warm-up. The sun has left behind just enough light to illuminate an approaching blanket of twilight cloud. The Sabercats and their coaches look like they have already lived through hours of physical combat. Beads of sweat have gathered around the thick black marks smeared beneath the eyes of their biggest players.

The anthem is over. Heads disappear into helmets again. Sabercats are on the move. Time for one last huddle, one final burst of inspirational jargon only the boys will understand.

'Here we go, baby. Let's kick off.'

'You show me some kick-off, you show me some, boys.'

Sabercats win the toss.

The players dance through the early plays, skipping over the grass as if it were red-hot embers, moving their heads vertically and horizontally in momentary spasms. The ball disappears into a car-crash of colour. Gold and black for Saguaro, blue and white for Prescott. Number 46 emerges from the wreckage of bodies and pushes his fist into the warm air, jumping and twirling, swinging his hand as if he were slapping an imaginary backside. Sabercats have retaken control of the game. They have taken one step closer to their destiny.

At an American-football game, you are surrounded on all sides by agitation. Unrest spreads like a pandemic from band-members and cheerleaders to spectators and from coaches to players. Even when there is a pause in the action, there are the frenetic gymnastics of the cheerleaders and the music, urging you to move. For God's sake, just move.

Perhaps because of that perpetual frenzy, American football doesn't travel well. It has to be consumed on the spot, as a spectacle, wrapped up in a ribbon of beautiful noise, magnified by thousands of spectators watching young men being transformed into storybook heroes.

On Friday nights, in towns and suburbs across America, high-school football does the impossible: it reminds people why a country with a manic devotion to the individual survives as a nation. Football offers reinvention, but also sanctuary.

Up in the stands, thousands of supporters have come together to worship the civic creed of football. One of them is Herman Serignese, who was principal of Saguaro High for ten years. He speaks gruffly, with an east-coast accent, suggesting a life-story shaped by an immigrant experience of America. If not his, then his family's.

'I moved to Arizona 30 years ago to improve life for me and my kids and it's worked out great. You get up and work hard and do your best and things work out for you.'

'And you get to watch Friday-night football, right?'

'You come to Friday-night football coz it represents the whole American spirit. It embodies everything that America is about.'

Herman points to the field now. The Sabercats are rolling over Prescott and he is warming to his theme.

'They work hard and have a lot of pride and they have a lot of discipline.'

Pride is everywhere. Oozing from every pore. The type of pride that forgives all division and repels all doubt.

'People criticise, but I will be truthful ... I don't really care what other people think about America.'

'After all the problems of the last eight years ...?'

'What problems ... what problems we got? Sure, we had to deal with a terrorist attack and got involved in a war in Iraq but that's just the way it has been.'

In the eyes of a patriotic man such as Herman, those calamities were like natural disasters, they come with the territory. When the aftershocks subside, this will still be the shining city.

'America is the greatest country in the world. No doubt about it in my mind. People fight to get in this country. Name me another country people fight to get into. People dying to get in this country. Literally dying.'

He gestures with both hands to the pitch, almost laughs, as if it would be ridiculous not to see this.

'You won't get me to change my mind. It's great. It's like being in heaven.'

—•—

Pride. Dynamism. Destiny. Words that enchant Americans at their moments of greatest opportunity and deepest difficulty.

When Herman Serignese told us that he was living in heaven, he was speaking for a majority of Americans. In virtually every global survey of happiness, Americans are more satisfied with their lives than people in almost any other nation. The great observer of early American life, Alexis de Tocqueville, put this optimism down to 'a lively faith in the perfectibility of man'.

It has been that way ever since the Puritan preacher John Winthrop set the earliest American settlers a momentous challenge in 1630: 'For we must consider that we shall be as a city upon a hill. The eyes of all people are upon us.' Winthrop borrowed this image from the Sermon on the Mount in which

Jesus said: 'A city set on a hill cannot be hid.' Jesus compared that city to a lamp: 'Let your light so shine before men, that they may see your good works …' So was born the shining city, a vision of the earthly paradise America is destined to be.

Not everyone will end up at rest in their own personal Garden of Eden, but that's not the point. Belief in the American dream creates an actual pursuit of happiness. It may be inspired by a myth, but it is a noble myth which sparks movement on a breath-taking scale.

American history is the story of this transition from fairy tale to fact. However, it is a tale of contradictions and contrasts; like all fairy tales there is darkness as well as light. The greatest contrast of all is between hope and fear. American optimism is nowhere near as absolute as the good people at Saguaro High lead you to believe. Hope is the engine of the American dream, but fear is the fuel.

What is often overlooked is the central role of failure in the American dream. To begin with, there is the doctrine of virtuous failure: when you chase its grandiose ambitions, it is accepted that you will stumble along the way. That kind of failure is simply proof that you are trying.

There is also a greater existential fear that America will turn out to be an illusion. Americans have battled that profound doubt since the Puritans made landfall in the New World. Right after those inspiring lines about the 'city on the hill', John Winthrop cautioned 'that if we shall deal falsely with our God in this work we have undertaken … we shall shame the faces of many of God's worthy servants, and cause their prayers to be turned into curses upon us til we be consumed out of the good land whither we are a-going'. Don't say he didn't warn you.

Broken dreams are a constant theme in American history. Perhaps the most literate of the founding fathers, Benjamin Franklin, once warned his countrymen: 'He that lives on hope, dies farting.' (Some scholars claim that Franklin was the victim of an unfortunate misprint and the word should have read fasting. Either way, you get the point.)

American literature is bursting with stories of broken dreams. One of the most powerful themes in American writing is the poisonous effect of constant change, the angry void at the core of plenty.

Once more, football is a powerful metaphor, captured beautifully in the story of 'Swede' Levov, the tragic hero of Philip Roth's *American Pastoral*. A former high-school football and baseball star, Levov's beautiful life is torn apart by the social upheaval of the 1960s and the bitterness of those around him: 'It was as though while their lives were rich and full they were secretly sick of themselves and couldn't wait to dispose of their sanity and their health and all sense of proportion so as to get down to that other self, the true self, who was a wholly deluded fuckup.'

The battle between hope and fear feeds into a much broader American tension between the individual and the collective. On the face of it, the United States is nothing more than an enormous celebration of personal achievement. Look at American football and the pedestal on which those star players are placed. Their prestige extends far beyond the playing field. They are masters of the high-school universe. They are walking, talking reminders of the difference between individual failure and success.

The cult of the individual reminds every outsider, nerd and oddball that they too can excel. One of the classic American tales is of a misfit maverick who emerges from the frontier and faces down the close-minded establishment. The modern classic is the story of the Internet pioneer. In the words of Steve Wozniak, the man who co-designed the first Apple computer, 'All the ideas that mattered to me came from outsiders.'

The celebration of the individual explains the powerful grip of a free-market ideology on the American psyche. More so than people in any other Western nation, Americans are convinced that each person is responsible for his or her destiny. Among forty-four nations surveyed by the prestigious Pew Research Center, America believed most strongly that failure is about the individual and not society.

Belief is one thing, but historical fact is another. Americans may think of themselves as a nation of individuals but their way of life has been shaped by the collective. Take another look at our football team. The star player is the quarterback: the lonely, vulnerable hero who throws the winning pass into wide-open spaces. But he would be pulverised were it not for the blocking tackles of others. He would be nothing without that vast back-room team.

It is one of the great unspoken realities of American life that the path to every individual's destiny is paved by a bureaucracy. Consider the explosion of migration that followed the Second World War: returning veterans who had fought for their country now demanded their own personal slice of the American dream. As the old song says, 'How you gonna keep 'em down on the farm after they've seen Paris?'

It was the federal government which enabled them to chase their dreams by expanding the highway network in the post-war years. Through the 1940s and 1950s, one in five Americans changed homes every year, taking to the road to perform what Jack Kerouac described as 'our one and noble function of the time, move'.

They could not have moved without team players such as Sam Schoen, who founded U-Haul in 1945 and began hiring out distinctive orange and white trucks and trailers to migrating Americans. As one of Schoen's colleagues would later say: 'Ford built the cars. The Government built the roads. We built the trailers.'

23

Schoen liberated individual yearnings, but he preached the virtues of the organisation, summing up his business philosophy with the initials IFDOAS: Intelligently Follow the Directions of a Superior. Schoen believed in profit but also national interest, telling workers that 'the United States allows us to exist and it would not long continue to do so if we did not put its interests first'. The 'group-think' of Sam Schoen is as much a part of the American story as the individualism of Steve Wozniak.

The rivalry of the individual and the collective, the clash of hope and doubt, have shaped American history with the same frenzied certainty that we witnessed at that football game. At first, it can be hard to see any logic in the spectacular collision of forces, but look closer and you begin to understand a method in the madness.

There are guiding rules and boundaries to the march of American history and they were put in place during the 19th century as waves of pioneers headed west in search of their 'manifest destiny'. As they began to settle, America's contradictory impulses were subsumed into two rival forces: 'Frontier' and 'Ritual'.

Frontier is the spirit of the steadfast pioneer. It embraces individual freedom, courage, ambition, innovation, dissent, endurance and self-reliance, but also isolation, risk, insecurity and ruthlessness.

Ritual is the spirit of the community. It stresses laws, institutions, values, security, cooperation, patriotism and civic pride, but also boundaries, rules, conformity and self-righteousness.

Think of Frontier and Ritual as two competing 'teams' battling for control of the American personality. A drift towards the worst aspect of one personality tends to provoke a rise in the best aspects of the other, but the effort to strike a balance is an uncertain, messy and often painful journey. This creative tension is the hidden code that unlocks America's past, present and future.

The first person to really capture the permanent dysfunction unleashed by America's westward expansion was Frederick Jackson Turner. In a landmark speech in 1893, he summed up the spirit of the frontier as 'that restless nervous energy, that dominant individualism working for good and evil, withal that buoyancy and exuberance which comes with freedom'. Turner believed the great surge into the vast western wilderness made the US a coherent nation. It was on 'the crucible of the frontier [that] the immigrants were Americanised'.

Turner realised that the frontier was a place of disorder as well as dynamism. 'The frontier is productive of individualism,' Turner wrote. 'The tendency is anti-social. It produces antipathy to control, and particularly to any self-control.'

The spirit of Frontier would have to be contained if it was to survive. As the pioneers of frontier life became settlers, they needed order in their lives. They looked to shared rituals to make the frontier fit for human habitation. The first great ritual was justice; for every outlaw, there had to be a sheriff. As towns became communities, the rituals of faith and family life soon followed. For commerce to thrive, property had to be protected, land had to be divided and the federal government had to set boundaries. As the frontiers expanded, the rituals of patriotism became even more important, providing the glue that held together a nation of almost uncontainable contradictions.

The creative tension of Ritual and Frontier has mattered most during America's periodic bouts of reinvention and trauma. The great transformational leaders of the past fifty years have tried to relieve the fear of change by invoking Ritual. Martin Luther King relied on explicit patriotism in that momentous speech in Washington in 1963: 'Land where my fathers died, land of the Pilgrims' pride. From every mountainside, let freedom ring!' When it suits them, politicians also stoke up fear by invoking images of the frontier. Remember how George W. Bush chose to frame his 'war on terror' in the days after 9/11. 'I want justice,' he said. 'There's an old poster out West, as I recall, that said, "Wanted: Dead or Alive".'

When politicians are looking for a lesson in how to balance Ritual and Frontier, they look to Ronald Reagan, who came to power during the crisis of confidence that followed Watergate, Vietnam and the Iranian hostage crisis. He understood that Americans were looking for more than a mere recognition of their insecurity: they wanted their fears turned into historical parable, and Reagan delivered. He posed as the rugged individual of old, who would clean up the town and face down the outlaws. He walked with a swagger but talked softly about the future with the accent of the past, as his biographer Lou Cannon would later put it.

Reagan had his own fantasy version of the shining city, and its cornerstones were Frontier and Ritual:

> I've spoken of the shining city all my political life,
> but I don't know if I ever quite communicated
> what I saw when I said it. But in my mind it was a
> tall proud city built on rocks stronger than oceans,
> wind-swept, God-blessed, and teeming with people
> of all kinds living in harmony and peace, a city with
> free ports that hummed with commerce and
> creativity, and if there had to be city walls, the walls
> had doors and the doors were open to anyone with
> the will and the heart to get here.

Ronald Reagan realised that at a turning point in history, Americans want clear contrasts to guide them, alternate images of Ritual and Frontier. With the help of the San Francisco advertising guru Hal Riney, Reagan offered that contrast during his successful bid for re-election in 1984. His 'bear in the woods' advert captures the Frontier side of the equation, featuring a lone hero standing firm in the savage wilderness (suggesting President Reagan standing up to the Soviets).

The second commercial, 'Morning in America', is about the revival of Ritual. The music is rich and upbeat and every frame appears to have been filmed at sunrise. 'It's morning again in America,' says Riney. We then see images of a young couple at their new home, a boy saluting the flag and a mother attending her daughter's wedding. 'This afternoon 6,500 young men and women will be married, and with inflation at less than half of what it was just four years ago, they can look forward with confidence to the future.'

To many around the world, Reagan was defined by a dangerous, fearful foreign policy, but to many Americans he brought renewal. He found the combination of Ritual and Frontier which matched his turbulent moment in history. In doing so, he changed the way that politicians talk about the pain that comes with great change. Reagan would have an impact on Democrats as well as Republicans. He taught them that transformational leaders have to connect with history, take account of doubt as well as hope and speak to voters in language they don't expect from politicians.

Reagan's brand of Frontier and Ritual still shapes American politics. It echoed through the rhetoric of the 2008 presidential election. John McCain and Barack Obama drew heavily from the past, from Reagan all the way back to Winthrop, as they searched for language to match the hopes and fears of the new America.

Part One:
The Place

Because we don't belong in this nuthouse of a city!
We should be mixing cement on some open plain …
Biff Loman, Death of a Salesman

1.
Kissimmee – The End of the Real America

Kissimmee is the new America on a budget. The main drag of strip malls and cheapish hotels offers you little charm, but charm is not what brings you to Central Florida. The tourist comes for Disney World. Others come to build their own personal vision of the shining city.

In the old days, if you wanted a job in Kissimmee you went to the sprawling cattle ranches and citrus groves. But by the end of the 20th century tourism and construction had taken over as the biggest employers. Disney World and a fairy-tale housing boom turned this sleepy cousin of nearby Orlando into a booming Sunbelt suburb. Its population grew by more than 50 per cent in the 1990s and, as it expanded, Kissimmee developed its own exceptional identity. People here are much younger than in the rest of Florida and far more diverse. Whites are just another minority group, Latinos make up more than 40 per cent of the population and one in four residents was born in a foreign country.

Kissimmee represents change, but, unlike the 'monied burbs' and 'boomburbs' in the Western deserts and mountains, this is still the blue-collar version of the new America. Income levels are lower than the Florida average and so is the level of educational achievement. So when recession came, the people of Kissimmee found themselves on the fault line of reinvention; change had been particularly good to them, but the economic meltdown was especially savage and sudden.

There is no other word for Kissimmee's transition from boom to bust but ugly. At the beginning of 2007, the median price of a house in Kissimmee was over $250,000. By the end of 2008, the price had fallen by more than $100,000. In a working-class suburb like Kissimmee, property had been the gateway to wealth and income and now that gate was slammed shut. In one of those quirks of history, this economic car crash happened in the midst of a landmark election campaign. Once again, the clash of hope and fear was set to dictate America's course, and that confrontation would be decided on a suburban battlefield, in a place like Kissimmee.

—•—

In the previous presidential election, the Sunbelt suburbs were Bush country. In 2004, George W. won Kissimmee's Osceola County by a margin of 5 per cent. But in the explosive autumn of 2008, Republicans could not take anything for granted. That is why sister Sarah came calling at Kissimmee's Silver Spurs arena, just ten days before the election.

Sarah Palin was not due on stage until 3 p.m., but the women at the top of the queue left home at 5 a.m. to be guaranteed a place. Some had seen both John McCain and Sarah Palin multiple times. You just knew they liked Sarah better.

'Gun-slinging momma, goin' to beat Obama,' one woman sang (to the tune of 'Everywhere We Go'). 'Putting on her lipstick, taking on the dipstick.'

She wandered up and down the queue, nodding approvingly at the slogans on the T-shirts in front of her.

'Respect the lipstick.'

'It's time we had some pink in the White House.'

'The Sara-cuda.'

'Sarah's Pitbulls.'

'My mama beats your Obama.'

'Speak softly and carry a hockey stick.'

'Don't mess with Sarah.'

You could use the word empowerment to describe the core message here, but backlash would also have worked. This was less a broad declaration of feminism than a rebel yell of girl-power.

There were a handful of men in the line outside the Silver Spurs arena. They were more intense and deeply ideological. A few wore shirts with Sarah's smiling face above the words 'arctic fox', but more popular were monosyllabic jabs at the opponent. A particular favourite was a shirt with 'Nobama' on the front and 'Don't tax me, Bro' on the back.

Tom Brandon had brought three generations of his family to see Palin. He was a conservative Christian who had been no more than lukewarm in his support of John McCain until Sarah was added to the ticket: 'You just really get the sense that she stands for the values that make this America.'

Tom was unique at that event in that he smiled broadly and shook hands warmly. Otherwise, there was an overwhelming sense of victimhood in the crowd and seething anger at enemies in their midst. The media contingent had been positioned strategically on bleachers in the middle of the arena; a juicy target for sustained vocal hostility throughout the afternoon.

The atmosphere only changed when Fox News host and conservative commentator Sean Hannity appeared in the press enclosure. He was greeted like a partisan rock star and a chant of 'Sean, Sean, Sean' rang around the arena in a Mexican sound-wave. A flood of autograph hunters surged toward him, knocking barriers to the floor. Hannity seemed elated but also shocked by the fervour as he signed McCain campaign posters and copies of his books.

Lots of good money is made by conservatives and liberals who feed the base with views that tickle their biases, particularly insults directed at the MSM (mainstream media). One of them is Elizabeth Hasselbeck, the lone conservative voice on the daytime talk show *The View*.

She was Sarah Palin's warm-up act in Kissimmee. As the Alaskan governor stood smiling behind her, Hasselbeck said she couldn't help being 'sassy' because the liberal media was being 'deliberately sexist' in reporting the cost of Palin's wardrobe ($150,000).

'I'm most impressed by her accessories,' she said, 'like the flag pin she wears in honour of her son and our military – men and women – fighting abroad.'

When Hasselbeck spat out the word 'they', to describe the media, some in the crowd turned to hurl abuse at the reporters cowering in the middle of the arena. I heard one voice, high up in the stand, shouting, 'Shoot them all.'

The smile never left Sarah Palin's face during the warm-up. When Hasselbeck had finished, and it was her turn, Palin immediately told the crowd what made them special.

'You are such a welcoming and patriotic state, Florida,' she cooed, shaking her head, as if mindful of just how exceptional such national pride had become in this age of relativism. 'That's what I love about you. You have always been proud to be American.'

In that simple introduction was the balance of Ritual and Frontier that Republicans offered American voters in 2008: a folksy populism in which 'they' were coming to get 'us'.

John McCain may have been the presidential candidate but he allowed his running mate to define him with this honey-coated roar of narrow conservative values.

Palin offered herself and John McCain as the frontier heroes, ready to do battle on behalf of their exclusive tribe: the 'real' Americans.

It was a compelling vision that played well to the partisan crowd inside the Silver Spurs arena. It seemed possible its angry tone would appeal to blue-collar Americans in the fearful suburban subdivisions of Kissimmee. But it was such an ideological and outdated vision of national destiny that it had no hope of playing in the sprawling ambiguity of the Sunbelt suburbs. In 2008, the 'real' America was no match for the new America.

—•—

The 2008 election began with an epic contrast between individual optimism and collective gloom. In April 2008, a *New York Times*/CBS News opinion poll found that 81 per cent of people believed that 'things have pretty seriously gotten off on the wrong track', up from 35 per cent in early 2002. Yet, for all that collective pessimism, Americans appeared to be personally optimistic. In a poll taken by the Pew Center in late 2007, 65 per cent of Americans said they were satisfied overall with their lives, one of the highest rates of personal satisfaction in the world.

But that was before the fear of recession gave way to actual economic crisis. By the time the presidential campaign reached its climax, the giants of Wall Street had been laid low, millions of homeowners faced foreclosure and talk of recession had been replaced by speculation about full-blown depression. By the end of 2008, a *Washington Post*/ABC News poll found that personal optimism had vanished, with two out of three Americans worried about maintaining their standard of living. Almost the same number said they had already been hurt by recession, and more than half had suffered because of the stock-market plunge.

35

As public and private gloom coalesced during the course of 2008, the dynamics of the presidential election shifted. Foreign-policy concerns like the war in Iraq slipped off the agenda to be replaced by economic dread. Barack Obama and John McCain struggled to match the evolution of collective and personal gloom and find the right balance of Frontier and Ritual to match it.

To his credit, John McCain had a singular insight into the doubt that shadows the American psyche. McCain talked about it in the language of the 'silent generation', who came of age in the stifling Cold War certainties of the 1950s. While he chose not to dwell on the mental scars of his years of captivity in Vietnam, he gave a revealing speech in March 2008 in which he talked of the stark realities of his childhood.

> When I was five years old, a car pulled up in front of our house in New London, Connecticut, and a Navy officer rolled down the window, and shouted at my father that the Japanese had bombed Pearl Harbor. My father immediately left for the submarine base where he was stationed. I rarely saw him again for four years. My grandfather, who commanded the fast carrier task force under Admiral Halsey, came home from the war exhausted from the burdens he had borne, and died the next day.

By his own admission, John McCain confronted doubt by rebelling. He spoke openly about his tantrums as a child and his reckless behaviour on his return from Vietnam. But he emerged from the darkness with a fierce appreciation of his country and its exalted sense of honour and ritual. At a moment of national soul-searching that was a deeply attractive proposition.

John McCain was a living embodiment of American ritual. If there was anyone who could speak convincingly about security in a time of crisis, it was a man who had survived a POW camp and made a career in the public service. Ritual was something John McCain was born to represent. It was the Frontier part of the equation that he had a problem with. After all, how does a Republican senator who had voted with George Bush's policies 90 per cent of the time persuade Americans that he would be a pioneer of change?

Through the summer of 2008, McCain showed signs that he was gaining traction with his ad-nauseam claim to be a 'maverick', a lone political gunfighter willing to face down the elite in Washington, even if it meant clashing with his own party elders. With each retelling of this Reaganesque parable, John McCain seemed to gain confidence in the redemptive power of the Frontier.

It may have been that existential awakening which led John McCain to look to Alaska for his running mate, to the state that claims to be 'the last frontier', where people refer to the rest of the United States as the 'lower 48'. In picking Alaska Governor Sarah Palin, he undoubtedly boosted his Frontier credentials, but he immediately became a prisoner to her narrow vision of American Ritual.

Sarah Palin's coming-out speech to the Republican convention in St Paul was arguably the most remarkable political debut in US history. It will be remembered for what Palin looked like, how she sounded and that immortal line about lipstick, hockey moms and pitbulls. But the speech itself (written by one of George Bush's wordsmiths, Matthew Scully) deserves to be read closely for its stark, haunting insights into the American conservative notion of Frontier and Ritual.

From the very outset, Palin was the steadfast pioneer, relating her heroic struggle as governor of the last frontier, 'when I stood up to the special interests, and the lobbyists, and the Big Oil companies, and the good-old boys'. She then loyally proceeded to cast John McCain as the ultimate Frontier hero, describing him as an outsider 'who doesn't run with the Washington herd', someone who 'is not looking for a fight, but sure isn't afraid of one either'. She appealed to American voters to take the maverick out of the Senate and put him in the White House:

> There is only one man in this election who has ever really fought for you in places where winning means survival and defeat means death. And that man is John McCain. You know, in our day, politicians have readily shared much lesser tales of adversity than the nightmare world in which this man and others equally brave served and suffered for their country.

There was something pure and admirable in Palin's presentation of McCain as a brave loner facing down evil on some distant frontier. But what followed was Palin's definition of Ritual, which was far more complicated and potentially damaging. In a few short lines, the entire civic character and communal goodness of the United States were vested exclusively in the residents of small towns.

> I grew up with those people. They're the ones who do some of the hardest work in America, who grow our food, and run our factories, and fight our wars. They love their country in good times and bad, and they're always proud of America. I had the privilege of living most of my life in a small town.

Palin borrowed an elegant quotation from a 20th-century journalist called Westbrook Pegler to hammer home her point: 'We grow good people in our small towns, with honesty and sincerity and dignity.' Palin didn't credit Pegler in her speech, which was probably smart. In his later life, Westbrook Pegler was a notorious extremist and anti-Semite who once said of Robert F. Kennedy: 'Some white patriot of the Southern tier will spatter his spoonful of brains in public premises before the snow flies.'

In fairness, the source of Palin's homage to the 'small town' wasn't the problem. The great flaw in her vision of Ritual was that its time had past. The small town no longer decided elections. The Sunbelt suburbs were the new centre of political gravity, and all that Frontier talk of moose-hunting, pitbulls and snow-mobiles just didn't cut it in places like Kissimmee, no matter what the angry, partisan crowd in the Silver Spurs arena might tell you.

The Republican base loved Sarah Palin but failed to see just how limiting her appeal would be on election day. 'They won small towns,' demographer Robert Lang would later comment, 'but the problem is not enough people live in small towns. America's new small towns are called suburbs.'

Sarah Palin would become something of a scapegoat among Republican leaders crawling from the electoral wreckage. But John McCain chose her. He made the potentially fatal decision to wed himself to her vision of Ritual, to abandon his hard-fought reputation as a moderate. He bought into her notion of the frontier as a mythical wilderness, when it exists only in the fables of conservative Americans. Time and time, he ignored the rise of the new America.

Of course, that is not the way it looked in the wake of the Republican convention, as summer turned to autumn. Sarah Palin's debut and McCain's burnished maverick brand changed the dynamic of a presidential race that previously seemed to be moving inexorably in Obama's favour.

By 14 September 2008, McCain had retaken the lead in the polls, crossing the 50 per cent mark in some surveys and enjoying a stunning surge in support from self-declared independent voters.

On 15 September, Lehman Brothers filed for bankruptcy, and the rules of the electoral game changed once again.

John McCain decided nothing had changed. The fundamentals of the economy were sound, he told voters. Instead of playing to his strengths by stressing the need for a safe choice, he continued towards the frontier at breakneck speed. He abandoned preparations for his first debate with Barack Obama and rushed back to Washington to try and broker a bail-out of the financial system. Just as quickly, when his efforts failed, he returned to the debate he had tried to cancel. It was just what a maverick would do. It was also the wrong thing to do.

McCain's erratic, impulsive reaction to the global financial meltdown made Obama look serene, mature and safe by comparison. It was an impression confirmed by McCain's increasingly aggressive attacks on Obama, which turned off the independent voters he had so successfully courted. At a moment when Americans were looking for a strong, silent lawman, McCain came across as the dangerous outlaw. He had thrown away his trump card – Ritual – in a desperate play of the wild card – Frontier.

—•—

History shows that US politics tends to move in cycles, with groundbreaking leaders emerging in response to crises. Abraham Lincoln came to power after the Civil War, FDR at the height of the Great Depression and Reagan after the Iranian hostage crisis. Now, Americans had a multitude of crises to choose from: 9/11, Iraq, Afghanistan, Hurricane Katrina and economic meltdown from Wall Street to Main Street. From the very beginning, Obama had an advantage: Americans were in the mood for a steadfast pioneer.

All this will feed that retrospective certainty that Obama could not have lost. But that ignores the fear of change that shadowed the demand for something new. It also underestimates the historic power of conservative political activists to exploit that fear and the traditional inability of liberal politicians to feel blue-collar pain.

And at first sight, Barack Obama looked like your typical big-city liberal. In front of those early crowds in the snowy heartland of Iowa, he was always one charming, languid gesture away from smug. However, those who knew him well understood that doubt would become part of Obama's appeal. He would eventually turn his battle with insecurity into a parable about his generation, those raised in the shadow of Vietnam, Watergate and racial tension.

Obama talked about his relationship with the American dream as if it was a difficult parent. In his campaign book, *The Audacity of Hope*, he wrote that as a man of mixed heritage, he had 'no choice but to believe in a vision of America'. He spoke of love and affection for his elders but also alienation. In a groundbreaking speech on race in March 2008, he spoke about his grandmother 'who on more than one occasion has uttered racial or ethnic stereotypes that made me cringe'. Most striking is the way he described his grandfather in his first book, *Dreams from My Father*.

> His was an American character, one typical of men
> of his generation, men who embraced the notion

41

of freedom and individualism and the open road without knowing its price, and whose enthusiasms could as easily lead to the cowardice of McCarthyism as to the heroics of World War II. Men who were both dangerous and promising precisely because of a fundamental innocence; men prone, in the end, to disappointment.

These words express the wariness of the generations driving the American reinvention. They still believe in destiny, still feel the thrill of restlessness, but they believe that the American dream will have to change if it is to survive. A new balance will have to be found between hope and doubt, between the individual and the collective, but the bottom line is this: things cannot stay the same.

Obama's balance between Frontier and Ritual was an easy sell to a generation who had come of age during the Bush years. Their demand for change was unequivocal. But what of those who stood to lose from change? What about the working-class Americans who embraced a transformational boom and lost everything? What about those who feared the diversity of this new America, who felt threatened by its youthfulness and by its many different shades?

In his battle with Hillary Clinton for the Democratic nomination, Barack Obama seemed to fall into the bad habits that destroyed many progressive contenders before him. He was portrayed as aloof and elitist by Clinton and played into her hands by speaking about doubt in a way that sounded eminently logical to young, diverse Millennials but insulting and patronising to older blue-collar Americans. Case in point: his comments about the bitterness of small-town Americans who 'cling to guns or religion or antipathy to people who aren't like them'.

In almost every primary contest where working-class white

people or older Americans were a core constituency, Obama lost by large margins. Where the economic crisis was biting hardest, and personal doubt was greatest, Clinton was winning big. Obama eventually prevailed over Clinton, but not before a perceived weakness was exposed. To those who wanted stability at a time of spiralling insecurity, he just didn't seem authentic.

This gave Republicans a real opening. They hammered home the perception that Obama was a phoney. Some of Sarah Palin's best lines in that convention speech returned to the theme of 'God and guns'.

> In small towns, we don't quite know what to make of a candidate who lavishes praise on working people when they're listening and then talks about how bitterly they cling to their religion and guns when those people aren't listening. No, we tend to prefer candidates who don't talk about us one way in Scranton and another way in San Francisco.

Forget Scranton and San Francisco. It would all come down to how Obama talked to the people of Sunbelt suburbs like Kissimmee.

—•—

Barack Obama arrived in Kissimmee four days after Sarah Palin. She had half-filled the 8,000-seat Silver Spurs arena. Obama had to move outdoors, to the nearby Osceola County Heritage Park, because tens of thousands were expected to show up at his event. There was an added attraction in former president Bill Clinton, who was due to appear with Obama at the late-night rally.

Supporters travelling to the event came down Route 192 and turned just by the offices of Watson Realty. A sign outside the building said: 'Stop in for a Free List of Foreclosures'. In those eight words were both the challenge and the opportunity for Obama. It was no longer enough to peddle hope to his young, multi-racial base. He needed to master the kind of easy economic populism which had made Bill Clinton a hero to blue-collar Americans. If he was to win in places like Kissimmee, Obama needed to combine the idealism of 'Yes, we can' with the stark realism of 'It's the economy stupid'.

That night in Kissimmee, he certainly turned out his base. When the perimeter gates opened at sundown, the few hundred early birds who rushed towards the compact, circular stage appeared to be almost exclusively young and affluent and ready for change. But in the great mass of people who followed was the proof that this campaign was now a movement drawn from every strata of American life. Immigrant families with picnic baskets and hard-hatted construction workers, elegant middle-aged ladies and elderly African American couples, red-neck boys with mullets and clean-cut, two-car, two-point-one children suburbanites. This crowd would have looked right at home at the Sarah Palin rally on Sunday. They could have passed for 'real' Americans.

Within spitting distance of Disney World, they were searching for a dream but also some recognition of their reality. Latino actor Jimmy Smits was their warm-up act. He played the dream presidential candidate, Matt Santos, on *The West Wing* and tonight his job was introduce a real and potential president. He roared at the crowd, hurling his voice and passion beyond the floodlights, into the darkness: 'Here we are near Disney World, where dreams come true. Well, my dreams are going to come true next week.'

Just as Smits wrapped up his high-energy cheerleading, a motorcade rolled past the stage with a detachment of at least 50 outriders. Just minutes later, a local politician approached the microphone and said simply: 'The 42nd president and the next president.' Bill Clinton and Barack Obama walked to the podium and turned in a circle to acknowledge the crowd. They briefly got tangled in each other's arms before grasping hands and holding them aloft; the past champion embraces the contender.

Clinton spoke first and offered a well-argued endorsement of Obama's leadership qualities. It was not the warmest speech he had ever made, but Clinton effortlessly combined big ideas with empathy, the very same ability which made him a popular president among the common people; the very same trick that made him a very hard act to follow.

When Obama took over, it became immediately clear how much he had evolved since those first stump speeches in Iowa. Back then, there was a mechanical fluency to his delivery when he talked about real people, as if their stories were being read from cue-cards lodged behind his eyelids. Tonight, he seemed fully invested in every word he uttered. His voice had been liberated from the inner-autocue and the warmth it carried sounded spontaneous and sincere, a trait which only the very best politicians possess.

Obama had channelled the instincts of the man sitting beside him. His speech was full of the predictable centrist arguments Democrats have been making for decades, but they were delivered with the kind of folksy flourish at which Clinton excelled. Obama defended his policies without sounding defensive. The McCain people had accused Obama of being a closet socialist. His response made *them* sound shifty.

'They found evidence that I shared my toys when I was in school,' Obama joked. 'That I split my peanut butter sandwich and gave half to a friend.' Clinton rocked with wild laughter beside him. Obama pivoted skilfully away from socialism to Christianity to hammer home the ultimate point of this riff. 'The Bible tells me that I am my brother's keeper.'

45

Obama had learned to talk to real people, rather than merely speaking about them. And on that chilly night in Kissimmee, there was a striking lack of smugness. His idealism sounded more mature and realistic. Obama had become the steadfast pioneer, comfortable with himself and the road ahead. Just like Reagan, he had learned to mix doubt and hope and turn it into a parable. And as with Reagan, that parable could be understood by all Americans, or at least a solid electoral majority.

'I don't believe for a moment what I see in the polls,' he says. 'Power concedes nothing without a fight.'

Tens of thousands heard those words in that field near Disney World but tens of millions saw the 30-minute campaign Obama aired on national television that very same night. There were more echoes of Reagan in the opening seconds of the advert, in a golden light creeping over gently waving fields of corn. But this wasn't morning in America, it was sunset.

Each vignette in this masterful advert told the story of a nation at the edge of darkness. In the most telling line of all, a worker at a car plant in Kentucky says, 'We are going to lose America as we once known it [*sic*].'

When Obama appeared, he was sitting in an elegant, stately room not unlike the Oval Office. He was at once political and personal, speaking about his father and how he was 'shaped more by his absence than his presence'.

In an instant, you could see yourself in Obama, but you could also see him as your president. On that night in Kissimmee, and in that commercial, Obama had pulled off a trick worthy of John Winthrop and Abraham Lincoln and FDR and, of course, Ronald Reagan: he had persuaded his fellow Americans that the only thing that would keep them safe was change. He convinced them that their only hope of sanctuary was reinvention. He had found the blend of Frontier and Ritual to match the new America.

On election day, John McCain and Sarah Palin were beaten like a gong in Osceola County. Bush's five-point victory there in 2004 became a 20 per cent blowout for Obama in 2008.

He made it look easy. But it wasn't. He won because he learned and evolved to match the uncertain rhythm of the Sunbelt suburbs. And he won because the Republicans lost their way along the frontier of this new America.

2.
Surprise – The Sunbelt Frontier

Some people say the frontier is a state of mind. They are wrong.

The frontier is a real place. It runs along the edge of the Arizona boomtown of Surprise. About a hundred yards beyond a bingo hall called the Riverboat Village, just before West Bell Road becomes Sun Valley Parkway, there is a sign which says: 'Next service 10 miles.' That's it. The frontier. The boundary of the shining city. The spot where the insatiable desires of a 'westering nation' collide with the savage certainty of the wilderness.

If you are not paying attention, the border will be passed by as a peripheral blur. But with your senses primed, you will feel the churning sensation of flight, as if you had just hurled yourself off the edge of the map. If you are lucky enough to realise you have reached the frontier, it is worth pulling over to appreciate the savage certainty of the boundary which bisects Arizona's Sonoran Desert.

Looking back, your eyes are drawn to the hazy outline of the Phoenix cityscape, a good 25 miles away. In the near distance is the pronounced edge of the low-slung city of Surprise, marked by a long line of houses in various stages of completion, their timber ribcages and stucco box frames sitting in mute testament to the thrusting human hand that created this frontier.

If you had continued driving away from the city, the highway would have led you on a meandering journey around the 30,000 acres of Arizona's largest mountain park. On either side of the road, there is nothing but desert stretching across the steepening slopes of the White Tank Mountains. Every couple of miles, a yellow sign repeats the warning 'Watch for animals'. Coyotes, raccoons, squirrels, cactus wrens, roadrunners, rattlesnakes and the occasional wandering mountain lion rule the wilderness side of the frontier. Were it not for the sanctity of the mountain park, that frontier would have already been pushed farther into the desert, making way for the metropolitan beast that churns up an acre of land every hour.

Somewhere in the desert are inanimate reminders of human life in the form of petroglyphs carved into the occasional rock. These are the visual record of the world as seen by ancient Native American tribes such as the Hohokam who first settled the Valley of the Sun, in which Phoenix now sits. The drawings were etched into a substance known as 'desert varnish', a unique geological substance that forms on clay-covered rocks which have been baked and frozen by the wild fluctuations of day and night in the desert. Just a few years ago, a petroglyph etched into desert varnish was discovered in the White Tank Mountains which scientists believe could be the only record in the Western Hemisphere of a supernova that appeared in 1006, the brightest supernova visible from earth for more than 5,000 years.

The desert provided a canvas for the very earliest Americans to create a vision of reality that was both mundane and fantastical at the very same time. In the 21st century, their descendants had their own version of desert varnish in the endless expanse of light-brown stucco and manicured greenery that now creeps across the desert.

—•—

When they were naming towns in Arizona, impulse seems to have played an important role. How else do you explain

Snowflake, Bumble Bee, Friendly Corner, Happy Jack, Two Guns and the deliciously toxic Arsenic Tubs? The names of Arizonan towns can also pose an existential challenge; as in Why, draw attention from an unfortunate past; as in Brilliant (formerly known as Swastika); or may simply describe the first thing early settlers saw in the fields around them (which possibly explains the towns of Cherry, Strawberry and Sunflower).

Occasionally, the name tells a story of old frontier days, which is certainly the case in the eastern Arizona mountain resort of Show Low. Legend has it that two duelling neighbours named Cooley and Clark decided that the town wasn't big enough for both of them. They chose to play cards to decide who could stay. At a crucial moment, Clark told Cooley, 'If you can show low, you win.' Cooley drew a deuce of clubs. 'Show low it is,' he said.

In each of these names, you hear the sound of a restless nation. As Arizona's official state historian, Marshall Trimble, puts it: 'It was almost as if the people didn't expect to be there very long.'

Perhaps Homer C. Ludden had movement on his mind when he founded the city of Surprise in 1937, naming it after his hometown in Nebraska. As a state legislator and property developer, he was an ambitious man, but there was no earthly reason to think his new creation would amount to anything; Surprise was nothing more than a single gas station and a few houses dropped onto a square mile of farmland. That is pretty much the way it would stay for more than half a century.

The turning point came during the 1990s when retirees flooded into the Phoenix area looking for a lease of life in the dry, clear air of the Sonoran Desert. Surprise bordered one of the biggest new retirement communities in the Phoenix area, the Sun City Grand, and it wasn't long before it succumbed to the onward march of manicured country clubs, early bird restaurants and 'age-restricted' housing developments. By 1995, 10,000 people lived in Surprise and during the next five years the population more than tripled.

After the surge of elders came a torrent of young, low-income families fleeing congested urban areas, particularly those in California. They may have had limited means but they brought unlimited potential, and by the end of the 20th century, Surprise was the fastest-growing city in what would soon be the fastest-growing state in the Union.

The 2006 census estimates put the population at 85,000, but in 2007 city officials claimed that more than 100,000 people lived in Surprise. The same officials said that their city had another three decades of growth in it and expected the population to reach 650,000 by 2040, which would be 65 times the number living there just a half century before. To put this in context, the 2000 census found that just 44 people still lived in Homer C. Ludden's hometown in Nebraska.

As you struggle to find words to describe Surprise, you could easily settle on 'exceptional', but that would be misleading. Surprise is an outpost on a new American frontier which winds its way from California's Inland Empire, through the Mojave and Sonoran deserts, across the Colorado River and the Rio Grande, bisecting border towns such as Las Cruces and San Antonio, running through the Hill Country of Texas and skirting around the vast urban black hole that is Dallas before reaching the Gulf of Mexico. On this boundary, the divinely mandated pursuit that has defined America since the Pilgrims stepped off their boats is creating countless boomtowns like Surprise.

These places do not just reflect the unfolding reinvention of America; they are shaping it. New rituals are being forged along this frontier. While the process is familiar, the scale is unprecedented. Millions upon millions of Americans are making a decisive shift away from the overcrowded cities that still dazzle the world in favour of an unprecedented urban experiment in the arid earth of the American Southwest.

The historic scale of this modern gold rush was revealed by the 2000 census, which found that America's population centre is moving south and west at a rate of three feet per hour, five miles per year. In the past 40 years, 84 per cent of the growth in the US population has occurred in the south and west of the country, and the current predictions are that by 2030 two out of three Americans will live in what is commonly known as the Sunbelt. The closest anyone has come to finding a name for all this is the 'Great Dispersal', a phrase coined by author and commentator David Brooks.

This is not just a population shift but a change in the focal point of American life. One hundred years ago, all ten of the biggest cities in the US were within 500 miles of the Canadian border. Today, the Census Bureau reports that seven of the ten most populous cities are within 500 miles of Mexico. Phoenix has replaced the birthplace of American democracy, Philadelphia, as America's fifth-largest metropolitan area. In the words of America's most respected demographer, William Frey: 'It's hard to think of the cradle of liberty being overtaken by a rough-and-tumble Western town, but that tells you something about the nature of our country. We're a country that's always seeking new horizons.'

Phoenix is by no means the only magnetic force at work in this Great Dispersal. While Arizona was the fastest-growing state in the US in 2006, Nevada held that title for the previous 19 years, and its biggest city, Las Vegas, saw its population increase by 250 per cent in a quarter of a century. Parts of Texas have also become a draw for those seeking a new life, with the state capital, Austin, increasing in size by 140 per cent in recent decades.

Not everyone fleeing the big coastal cities makes it as far as the desert; a constant stream of migrants continues to leave Los

Angeles, but many of them get only as far as the boomtowns of Riverside and San Bernardino, which lie just beyond LA County. Cities like Surprise have been cropping up with increasing frequency in what is being called the New Sunbelt, which includes Georgia, Utah, Colorado and North Carolina.

To begin with, I want to keep our focus on the stretch of the 'Sunbelt Frontier' that fits within traditional boundaries of the West and Southwest, not just because that makes it easier to measure, but because the changes there have more clarity and potentially more consequence than others. The Great Dispersal as it affects California, Nevada, Arizona, New Mexico and Texas is an unprecedented collision of all the forces that have shaped the United States, in both recent years and recent centuries. It is as if this vast stretch of desert had become the country's particle accelerator, propelling the American dream towards a chain reaction with a million contradictory fragments of the past and present.

History burrows deeper into the collective psyche here, the birthplace of Wild West fable, and so does geography; the forces of the frontier take on a wild kinetic energy in a region shaped by a territorial boundary with Latin America. Perhaps most intriguing of all is the sweet-and-sour relationship between the citizens of the Southwest and the spacious but unforgiving environment they have chosen to live in; nothing illustrates the clash of dreams and reality that is America better than the search for paradise in a landscape that is as hot as hell.

Above all else, the Southwest seems to have liberated Americans from the accepted limits of city and suburb. Under endless skies, they live inside a vast, overlapping patchwork of sovereign neighbourhoods separated by variations of the same sun-kissed American dream.

—•—

Just as demographers try to gauge the width and breadth of the shift towards the Southwest, they are struggling to find a name for the way Americans choose to live when they have settled there. The word 'suburb' has long been irrelevant in analysing exploding cities like Surprise, but what do you put in its place?

'Exurb' caught on for a while, but it doesn't come close to describing the metropolitan experiment playing out in the American Southwest. Just how, for example, do you categorise the Phoenix suburb of Mesa, which is now bigger than Miami, Minneapolis, Cleveland and Atlanta? How do you label communities of 300,000 or 400,000 people that were unknown desert hamlets 20 years ago? As one demographer put it, the new exurban form of living is 'the dark matter of the universe': it's very hard to see, but somehow it has more mass than all the planets, stars and moons put together.

At one recent count, there were more than 50 words to describe the rise of sprawling new communities in the outer orbits of big American cities, particularly in the South and West. When you see some of the labels on that list – 'galactic city', 'exopolis', 'edge city', 'penturbia' and 'urban galaxy' – you get the impression that Americans in their millions have moved to some futuristic colony on another planet. The analysis of these new metropolitan centres is infected by the same fear of the unknown that gripped ancient map-makers who imagined serpents at the edge of the known world.

The label that seems to fit the reality best is 'boomburb', coined by Professor Robert E. Lang of Virginia Tech. Strictly defined, it describes a city of more than 100,000 people in the shadow of a bigger city which has grown by double digits over a sustained period (the fairly predictable label for a booming exurb of between 50,000 and 100,000 people is 'baby boomburb'). So if you believe the claims of local officials, Surprise is now a boomburb of Phoenix. Again, we need to put that in context: there are seven other boomburbs in the greater Phoenix area and all are bigger than Surprise.

If we broaden our view, we see that the Sunbelt has become a giant petri dish for these evolving urban organisms. As of late 2007, there were 54 boomburbs in the United States and all but nine were located in the Southwest. The fastest-growing among them was Henderson, the runaway offspring of Las Vegas, which had grown by more than 4,700 per cent in the last half of the 20th century. All along the Sunbelt Frontier, boomburbs are becoming forces to be reckoned with. You may not know much about Chandler, Mesquite, Arlington, Plano or Tempe, but you could argue that they reveal more about the inner workings of the 'indispensable nation' than Los Angeles, New York or Washington.

The first important lesson about the boomburbs is that they have largely broken free of the gravitational pull of their once-dominant neighbour. For example, Surprise is no longer a satellite of Phoenix; it is an independent entity which has gone looking for its own balance of Frontier and Ritual in the footsteps of the earliest pioneers and settlers.

Boomburbs are cities in the US sense and don't easily match the European definition. In American parlance, the word 'city' does not necessarily relate to the size of a community; plenty of cities in the US are nothing more than small towns. 'City' is best understood as a declaration of independence.

Boomburbs might look like sprawling extensions of other cities, but they are what is known as 'incorporated cities'. They are fiercely independent entities in their own right, with considerable autonomy over their finances. But to build a tax base, they need to attract people from other places and land from the private sector. So from the moment it is incorporated, the aspiring boomburb has an innate desire to expand, a sort of 'growth gene'.

It works like this: a property developer buys land on which he or she will build a housing development. The developer asks the city to annex the land and provide the basic amenities. In return, the city gets more tax revenue when new residents move in (it will often privatise essential services into the hands of residents, as we'll see later). If the developer also builds a shopping mall, the city can then expect more revenue from sales taxes. The boomburb may get extra land from the federal government and occasionally annex small unincorporated suburbs. The bigger it gets, the wider its tax base. At some point in this process, the satellite city becomes a boomburb.

What makes the Sunbelt Frontier so boomburb friendly is that it is one of the few regions with the land to accommodate these new urban empires. Throughout American history, it was the West that provided the land that fed American expansion. In his timeless essay on the American frontier, Frederick Jackson Turner wrote: 'The Western wilds, from the Alleghenies to the Pacific, constituted the richest free gift that was ever spread out before civilised man.' He was correct, although he had less luck with his next prediction: 'Never again can such an opportunity come to the sons of men.' More than a century later, developers and planners keep building on the gift of free-ish land and – crucially – Americans keep flocking to the frontier to live on it.

—•—

They come in search of their destiny and their dream home, which are one and the same. Throughout American history, homeownership has been the most enduring landmark of success. 'A man is not a whole and complete man,' said Walt Whitman, 'unless he owns a house and the ground it stands on.' The search for completeness led the original pioneers to log cabins and picket fences. Today, it pushes them all the way to that line in the sand in the Arizona desert.

The frontier runs for miles on either side of West Bell Road through a line of boundary housing developments that offer every property in every conceivable colour and material, as long as it is brown stucco. The great observer of the infant United States, Alexis de Tocqueville, said that an American will build a house and sell it before the roof is on, and that is exactly what they are doing in the Carrington section of the Surprise Farms estate.

The perimeter of the development forms the boundary between civilisation and wilderness. There are cars in the driveways and kids cycling around the culs-de-sac, but some of the houses at the edge of the development are still unfinished, their timber frames exposed to the dry, scorching heat.

There are no straight lines in the development. The early suburban planners introduced curved streets in the belief that they discouraged strangers from cruising the pristine new neighbourhoods they were creating. Today, they are still being used to persuade Americans that a suburban street offers sanctuary from the harsh geometry of city life.

The development is built facing inwards, so what you see from the main road are the ugly backsides of the houses, but follow the winding laneways into the development and each property takes a distinct personality. When you purchase a house here, you acquire a little design quirk so that you still feel like an individual. It could be a nuance, like an extra high portico, or more of a statement, like an extra thousand square feet of property.

The top price for a house in Carrington is $229,950 (€147,000). That buys you four bedrooms, a two-car garage and two and a half baths (and no, I don't know what half a bathroom looks like). Carrington sits right on the border between Surprise and the White Tank Mountain Park, which seems to make it marginally less expensive than houses deeper inside this evolving boomburb. From the look of the families in the development, this will be the first step on the property ladder for many of them, the first giant leap toward completeness.

The mania that infected Surprise and boomburbs like it at the very peak of its expansion has eased. Back in 2005, when they were building one new house every six minutes in Arizona, housing developments in Surprise had a lottery system for prospective buyers. Where there was no lottery to whittle down the crowds, people camped out overnight.

If and when the young pioneers decided to move deeper into the heart of Surprise, they had a stunning array of options, even before house prices tumbled. At the high-point of the property boom, in the autumn of 2007, the average price of a house in the Irish capital was €411,000, which worked out at roughly $570,000. If you used that money to buy property in Surprise, your options would have included a five-bedroom house on West Becker Lane in the Rancho Gabriela subdivision with three bathrooms and more than 3,500 square feet of space: all that for $20,000 less than the price of the average house in Dublin.

On North 179th Drive there was a 3,000-square-foot house with four bedrooms and three bathrooms and space for four cars in the garage. The house was built in 2006 and had a private swimming pool. The only drawback is that it had no fireplace, which, frankly, is not the deal-breaker it might have been back in Ireland.

Among the other houses you could have bought for the average price in Dublin, one extended to 4,366 square feet while none offered less than 3,000 square feet of living space. The average size of a house in Dublin in 2005 was 1,064 square feet.

Space to build a new life is what drew millions of Americans to the Sunbelt. Even after more than a decade of rapid development, there were a little over a thousand people living in every square kilometre of Phoenix, which compares favourably to Manhattan where the same space would be occupied by 25 times that number of people.

Surprise offers the completeness of ownership and space to breathe, but the magnetic X-factor is the promise of reinvention. The Sunbelt Frontier offers you the chance to be a pioneer and build your own personal version of the shining city. If you didn't get there in time to help build your neighbourhood, you can still vaguely smell the paint from the lustrous walls of your dream home. In late 2007, on houses.com, only one of the houses advertised for sale in Surprise was built before 1969; 506 were built between 2000 and 2005.

Space, reinvention and ownership. And constant sunshine. What's not to like about life in a boomburb? Well, perhaps the answer is that it is still a 'burb'. No matter how intense, spacious and sunny it may be, this is still the suburban experience, and that means it is the prisoner of decades of derision and cliché.

Look at how awful the American suburb looks to the average Hollywood director. Perhaps the most powerful indictment of the perceived emptiness and alienation of suburban life is *American Beauty*, in which Kevin Spacey plays a doomed suburban father who lives a brief moment of glorious rebellion before he is killed. The movie opens with this damning premonition: 'My name is Lester Burnham. This is my neighborhood; this is my street; this is my life. I am 42 years old; in less than a year I will be dead. Of course I don't know that yet, and, in a way, I am dead already.'

The conventional Hollywood wisdom about suburbanites is that they lack any self-awareness. When a rebellious spirit like Lester Burnham reminds them of their shallowness, they set out to destroy him. One of the chief suspects in his eventual murder is his viciously conformist spouse. 'That's my wife, Carolyn,' says

59

Lester, by way of introduction. 'See the way the handle on her pruning shears matches her gardening clogs? That's not an accident.'

Such classy jabs at suburbia make us feel lucky we do not live there. They remind us why we are better than suburbanites. Suburbia is the ultimate American morality tale; its emptiness makes our life so much fuller and rounded by comparison.

The reason those images feel so credible to us is that there always seemed to be evidence to back them up. To begin with, suburbs in the United States have traditionally lacked diversity. They have been sanctuaries for the white middle class, fleeing the insecurity of multi-ethnic cities. Once there, these bourgeois refugees tend to gravitate towards people exactly like them, live in houses just like theirs and pursue lifestyles just like theirs.

The pressure to conform may be intense but, strangely, it does not seem to forge a genuine sense of community. The conventional wisdom suggests that the level of social engagement in the suburbs is far below what it is in the traditional city neighbourhood. Surveys have shown that this is especially true of young suburbanites, who have tended to participate less in their local government or politics.

An army of sociologists have come forward with credible theories to explain the apparent emptiness of suburban life. There are the obvious sources of alienation, such as the sheer sprawling scale of suburbia and the reliance on driving rather than walking. In the most insightful history of the American suburb, *Crabgrass Frontier*, Kenneth Jackson writes: 'Streets are no longer places to promenade and to meet, but passageways for high-powered machines.'

When neighbours become drivers, they lose any notion of kinship; they become competitors. The consequences are vividly illustrated in the book *Suburban Nation*, written by three reform-minded planners. 'You are competing for asphalt,' the authors say, 'and if you so much as hesitate or make a wrong move, your neighbor punishes you … The social contract is voided.'

The book cites two studies to illustrate the effects of this alienation. First, a survey which showed that the highest percentage of road-rage incidents were recorded in suburban counties (three of them Sunbelt boomburbs). The second was a psychological assessment for driver behaviour in car parks. It found that drivers took 21 per cent longer to leave a parking space if someone else was waiting for it and 33 per cent longer if that person honked their horn.

The emergence of suburbs in the scorching Southwest also fostered the spread of another obstacle to social engagement: air conditioning. It gave you yet another excuse to stay inside your dream home and avoid outside contact. Some blame air conditioning for the death of the front porch, which acted as a kind of social magnet in traditional urban neighbourhoods. Neighbours would gather in the cool of the front porch to talk and to bond.

Kenneth Jackson describes the front porch as the physical expression of community, 'where doors need not be locked, where everyone was like family, and where the iceman would forever make deliveries. With a front porch, one could live in Brigadoon, Shangri-La, and Camelot, all in one.'

Boomburbs have been lumbered with the same old negative preconceptions. You hear the familiar disdain in that long list of alternative labels for surburbia's latest incarnation. Some, like 'anti-city', 'stealth city', 'disurb' and 'slurb', present these new communities as urban vampires sucking the life out of decent old-fashioned cities. You get a similar impression from the term 'exit ramp economy', which describes the extent to which these new centres leech their commercial life off the freeway network.

Somehow, we have become prisoners of our prejudices. In reality, the suburbs were never as empty as they were made out to be. Much of the case against suburbia is based on studies from the 1950s and 1960s and owes a lot more to anecdotal opinion than to established fact. Where there were clearly problems in suburbia, they were caused by racial or economic segregation, which weakened local government and turned groups of citizens into conformist tribes. But times change, and our perspectives need to change with them. It is time to say our final goodbye to Lester Burnham. May he rest in peace.

—•—

Life in the American suburb is being reshaped by a dramatic shift in preferences. There is a backlash against the privatisation of life in old suburbia. In the boomburbs of the Southwest, this rebellion is being expressed as a nostalgia for 'small-town values' and an elemental craving for community. This generation of settlers is desperately searching for a whole new set of civic bonds which have the potential to fundamentally reorder suburban life. This renewal of community spirit will be the cornerstone of a new civic era in American history.

You could see this process in another historic shift from the individual to the collective, but I prefer to view it through the prism of Frontier and Ritual. The rise of the boomburb is yet another rush to the frontier. The Americans now flocking to the South and West are pursuing the same dream that animated the original Wild West pioneers. Now, as then, they discover that the frontier is harsh and unforgiving. The pioneer eventually becomes a settler who seeks to transform a collection of rugged individuals into an ordered community. The construction of that community will require the components of Ritual. They will provide the civic cement to transform the American frontier into the American heartland.

The bland conformism we associate with suburban life is

being replaced by something more unpredictable, more rounded. The boomburb is an innovation in the way communities are built and, like every great innovation, it is going to have consequences far beyond its narrow borders. Frontier has collided with Ritual in the boomburbs of America and we might all feel the resulting tremors in the years to come.

In towns such as Surprise, the brash individualism of the pioneer is clearly giving way to the civic rituals of the settler. Granted, you would be hard-pressed to find evidence of reinvention as you drive into Surprise. Turning from Grand Avenue on to West Bell, there is nothing but all the usual franchises and generic commercial clutter. All that distinguishes Surprise from every other exurban thoroughfare in America is the classy desert foliage along the margins and the occasional citrus tree.

Driving seems to be the only sanctioned form of movement, so the visitor feels like a voyeur. As you cruise past the master-planned communities and private golf clubs along West Bell, you are a gate-crasher who can't find the house with the party. There are some nice new restaurants sprouting up along Bell, but something strange happens when you pull into the car park around the back. There is nothing behind the long line of stores and chain restaurants but an expanse of desert scrub. It feels like you have just wandered out back on a movie set and discovered, as Gertrude Stein once said of her Californian hometown, 'there is no there there'.

But take a second look at your surroundings. What looks to an outsider like the heart of the boomburb is often the periphery of the lives of the people who live there. Home Depot, Subway, Target, Wal-Mart and Taco Bell are landmarks rather than a reflection of the lives people lead.

On your way into Surprise, you probably missed the signposts directing you to a hidden reality. At Greenway and Grand you saw the beautiful young woman speeding across the level-crossing on a Harley, her long blonde hair blowing behind her. But did she register? There was the sprawling U-Haul centre at the corner of Bell and Grand but what did that tell you? You were probably too busy to notice the Sprouts wholefood market. And what about the Latino family with the big SUV that just passed you in the car park? Or the two teenage Goths flying by on skateboards? Or that giant baseball stadium you could see in the distance? Or the pathways around the artificial lake in the gated community you just passed? And what do they mean on those posters in the middle of the road, the ones that read: 'Surprise – Live, Work, Play'?

Let's take that last clue first. From the moment you arrive in Surprise, you feel the messianic spirit of civic reinvention. City officials have set out to transform what was once a rough frontier outpost into a 'perfect' community which satisfies that renewed desire for small-town life. The city's official website says: 'Surprise is a collection of distinctive neighborhoods with a small town feel and big city amenities', and it has done a remarkable job in selling itself as a kind of desert playground.

It successfully courted two of America's biggest baseball teams to set up their training camps in the city, luring them away from their old Florida bases with the help of a $48 million training facility and stadium. That opened right about the same time as a regional library, an aquatic centre, a recreation centre and a 57-acre public park – the centrepiece of a newly created downtown, just like small towns used to have.

Surprise works on several levels, not all of them visible to the outsider. Like almost all boomburbs, it has the money to provide top-notch physical amenities, such as schools, fire stations and hospitals, but to also satisfy the intangible desires for security, exclusivity and innovation. Each boomburb styles itself as a brand, selling potential residents a way of life that will distinguish them ever-so-subtly from the boomburb up the road.

Within the brands, there are sub-brands, like Prasada, a vast new master-planned community in Surprise which will eventually stretch over 3,300 acres. The name comes from the Sanskrit word for 'grace', which captures perfectly the sense of other-worldly contentment which fortifies these master-planned desert communities like fluoride in tap water. Just to make completely sure you know you are not in Kansas any more, the Prasada website greets you with a quotation from Eleanor Roosevelt: 'The future belongs to those who believe in the beauty of their dreams.'

The word you hear over and over again in these boomburbs is 'lifestyle', as in the sales pitch for Prasada, which promises 'a dynamic community designed to stimulate the senses with architecture, activities and lifestyle pursuits'. Words like 'stimulate' and 'pursuit' matter deeply here. All across the Sunbelt Frontier, I imagine planners and developers trawling through the thesaurus to find ways of summoning up an epic journey away from all the suburban clichés. The Prasada pitch speaks of walking and talking and communing with nature:

> Masterfully planned streetscapes, trail systems, family oriented communities and open spaces will provide residents and visitors with a sense of renewal, and the project's unique architectural design will be carried throughout all aspects of the development, reflecting the fluid and refreshing nature of water. Reflecting the community-oriented nature of the development, Prasada's streetscapes and pedestrian facilities will be designed to provide easy navigation and encourage interaction.

Like any one of the mass-luxury brands which emerged from

the last part of the 20th century, the boomburbs trade heavily on a shift in perception, promising intimacy amid the sprawl. Their planners are selling the very opposite of the calcified ethos which had become associated with the suburbs. While their new hyper-suburban experience shuns both the blandness of the old suburbs and the vulgarity of crumbling cities, it worships the notion of community.

Beyond the conformity of the strip mall are pathways, outdoor seating, bike paths, recreational lakes, soccer schools, self-help seminars, organic food stores, mega-churches and ethnic restaurants. Just like the fusion cuisine that has come to dominate American menus, the boomburb offers a blend of lifestyle trends that looks awkward but feels so 'tomorrow'. Boomburbs are, to quote Robert Lang, 'proving grounds for a 21st-century suburban cosmopolitanism'.

You would never describe the last generation of suburbs as 'hot', but that is exactly the label being sought and applied to many of the fastest-growing urban centres on the Sunbelt Frontier. *Money* magazine looked at 271 small to mid-sized cities in the US to determine which were the hottest – in other words, the fast-growing – cities where residents can 'expect big-time benefits from small-town life'. The boomburbs and baby boomburbs dominated the list and most of the hot towns were in the West, including the top three: Plano, Texas; Anaheim, California; and the Phoenix boomburb of Scottsdale.

The core of the Great Dispersal is a generation of young, upwardly mobile families who have given up on the coastal cities but not on their metropolitan ethos. Their shared aspiration is to create lasting, material change on the new frontier.

Generally, what these new pioneers are creating are communities with more depth and more potential than the suburbs that are firmly fixed in our minds. But it would be wrong to create an alternative but equally false generalisation. Not everyone in Surprise is a wine-sipping, world-travelling, bicycle-riding, granola-eating, new-age Liberal. This is still America. It is God's country.

And yet God is working in mysterious ways on the Sunbelt Frontier.

3.
Radiant – The Freestyle Evangelical

They look like the best wedding band you have ever seen. The older of the two female singers bounces on the soles of her feet in a way that makes you want to bounce with her. The woman sharing the melody with her has movie-star blonde locks and a pair of snazzy glasses on her pretty face. The young man beside her is playing acoustic guitar and leans into the microphone to add his voice, closing his eyes briefly and waving his long, curly black hair gently in time with the music. The second male voice belongs to a black singer wearing a fetching orange shirt. The bass player behind him catches the eye of his drummer and smiles. He has a red beard, a big earring and hair stiffened with gel.

Life doesn't get better than this. Playing music, spreading joy and singing the praises of the Lord God Almighty.

> The heavens declare your greatness,
> The oceans cry out to you,
> The mountains they bow down to you.
> So I join with the earth and give my faith to you.

Christian rock is an acquired taste but the band at Surprise's Radiant Church this Sunday morning makes it easy to like. The crowd streaming in the door of the cavernous auditorium wastes no time in showing its appreciation. The band has only been on stage for one song and there is already clapping and singing, with all ages following the lyrics streaming across two giant screens behind the band.

> Open the eyes of my heart – I want to see you.
> High and lifted up, shining in your glory.

This crowd makes no concession to formality. There is not a jacket or tie to be seen. In fact, you could count on one hand the number of people with long trousers and long-sleeved shirts. They have come to praise the Lord Jesus in shorts, T-shirts and assorted items of sporting apparel.

This doesn't mean that the swelling crowd lacks passion. Far from it, there is real devotion here. Some of the women have their hands in front of their faces, palms facing inwards. The young couple among them stand mute, their arms draped around each other, rocking gently but emphatically to the music.

Walking among them is a man in a red-print Hawaiian shirt. He bears himself well and is perhaps a little more subdued than the shirt suggests. His is authoritative but solicitous, like a hard-working hotel manager. Out of nowhere comes an occasional bearhug, arms wrapped around chests, palms pounding on backs (slightly less pounding with the ladies). This is Pastor Lee McFarland, founder of Radiant Church. Fisher of souls. God's brand manager in Surprise.

The band is now on its third song and Pastor McFarland is now heading for the stage to join them.

> You are high and exalted, worthy of praise,
> With my heart I will love and adore.

Members of the congregation sense that the service is about to begin and they hurry into the soft red, comfortable chairs arranged in gentle semicircular rows facing the stage. There is not a pew, statue or collection box or vestment in sight. This feels more like a Cineplex just before the lights go down and the show begins.

'Praise the Lord. God is amazing.'

Pastor Lee is merely thinking out loud on the stage. The official welcome is left to a very good-looking woman called Victoria, who appears in a taped message on the screens behind the stage.

'Please turn off your cellphones and put your pagers to vibrate.'

Then the main feature begins. Pastor Lee is sitting on a high stool behind a lectern and the first thing he is going to do is sell you a ticket to a water park. There will be baptism in the warm waters of the wave pool at 9 a.m. this coming Saturday followed by a day of food, fun and friendship.

'Now I know what you're thinking: "There is no way I want anyone to see me in a bathing suit from this church." You would be amazed when we go to Waterworld, God strikes us with a special kind of blindness. We can't see cellulite, we can't see wrinkles, we can't even see flesh.'

There is a drawl in the pastor's voice: a slow, affected Southern touch. It makes him less preachy and gives his comedy shtick an authenticity it might not otherwise have.

'It looks like it's probably going to be hot.'

Irony from the preacher man. The faithful laugh.

'It's a great way to spend a day as a family. It doesn't dawn on you until you are there about an hour and you start going: "This is cool."'

He draws the last three words out with the knowing tone of a hip teenager.

'You are saying, "Na, I don't want to get baptised; I'm going to get wet." Well, you are already wearing your swimsuit.'

After his sales pitch for the wave-pool baptism, Pastor Lee has a little more house-keeping to do (changing the date of the father–son camping trip) before he moves on. Then you think he is about to get serious. But the band strikes up again.

> God is bringing a brand new day.
> No more fear, it's a new day, no more worry, it's a new day.

And a couple of minutes later, the pastor is back in his chair. This is it. Now he's going to rain some righteousness down upon us.

'Innit hot out there?'

Excuse me?

'It's so hot that chickens are laying hard-boiled eggs. It's so hot, the trees are whistling for the dog to come over.'

That hot, huh.

'It's so hot that if the temperature drops below 95 at night, you call it … ' – here the Pastor pauses and raises the middle two fingers of his hands in 'air-quotes' – 'chilly.'

Just one more time: how hot did you say it was?

'It's so hot, you get condensation on your butt from the hot water in the toilet bowl. That's really weird.'

Yes. He did say it. In a church. In front of a congregation of American evangelical Christians, an assembly not known for their love of anatomical gags or irony.

The pastor went on too long for this to be simply a badly judged warm-up. The jokes got appreciative laughs in all the right places. Clearly, the faithful come to Radiant in the full expectation of an irreverent tone. The humour may be slightly off-colour, but it is gentle and inclusive. Pastor Lee knows his audience likes

71

to be challenged but never judged, to be drawn out of themselves without ever leaving their comfort zones. Rather than lecture to them, his sermon is a running dialogue in which he plays their role and his own simultaneously. He is one of them, only better.

'Turn to Second Chronicles in your bibles,' he tells the worshippers, signalling the approach of the sermon.

'The eyes of the Lord strengthen those who are fully committed to Him. If you are discouraged and a little tired and a little burnt out, this verse will become one of your life verses.'

The pastor can't seem to resist another joke.

'It's a bit like a breakfast of bacon and eggs. The chicken is involved but the pig is totally committed.'

Now comes the challenging part. The pastor asks his audience what they are committed to during the various stages of their lives, from cradle to grave. What follows is less a spiritual pep-talk than a lesson in life, delivered in a mesmorising 30-second sound bite.

'Human nature does not want to serve other people. Human nature says let's talk about me. Who is going to meet my needs? People will leave a marriage saying: my needs are not being met. People will have an affair: my needs are not being met. Who is going to help me? Who is going to take care of me? Who is going to give to me what's due to me? Me, me, me, me, me.'

All the lost souls in their T-shirts and shorts are bonded at that moment. They are no longer alone with their human weakness; it has been shared and diluted and ultimately will be erased, as long as they heed Pastor Lee and his gentle call for collective redemption.

'And Jesus says you gotta lose that. You gotta lose that. Give up that type of focus in order to find true life. God says stop worrying about your own welfare and start helping out.'

And Radiant is where you start helping out. The very act of

turning up today is the first step to salvation. Pastor Lee is waiting to make you feel special, loved, appreciated.

'Do you know what's made Radiant Church such an amazing church? *You* are amazing. You are the secret of Radiant Church. Hundreds of you volunteer here each weekend. We still need you. You are amazing. When you come forward and say, "I want to be involved," we say, "We've been waiting for you."'

If the medium is the message, then Radiant speaks volumes. It tells you more about the evolution of suburban life in America now than any mocking Hollywood movie or dry, academic treatise. In Radiant, we see the move from Frontier to Ritual unfolding before us in technicolour. In Pastor Lee McFarland, we are presented with an American classic: the pioneer-turned-settler around whom history turns.

—•—

Back in 1996, he was simply Lee McFarland: a well-paid executive with Microsoft. He was an unsettled 36-year-old in search of a mission. He loved God and had enrolled in a correspondence course to learn how to be an evangelical pastor. But what happened next was far beyond the call of religious duty.

McFarland quit his job, sold his house, packed up his SUV and drove with his wife and two kids from Washington state to Surprise, then a lonely desert hamlet (and, as McFarland would later recall, 'a radically unchurched area'). He set out to recruit members for a new church, but the initial response was disappointing. He soon tried a more informal approach, going from door to door in the new housing developments in T-shirt and jeans asking questions about what these new, young families wanted from religion. He took the answers, came up with the sales pitch for Radiant Church and put it in a leaflet, which he posted through the letterboxes of thousands of those light-brown stucco houses: 'At Radiant you'll hear a rockin' band and a positive, relevant message. Come as you are. We won't beg for your money. Your kids will love it!'

Pastor Lee held his first service in the hall of a local elementary school in September 1997 and 150 people turned up. Within two years, the attendance was 350, which the new preacher thought was a perfect size for an informal and intimate church. But he had not reckoned on the wild expansion of Surprise or the lure of Radiant's laid-back Christianity. By 2002, Pastor Lee was preaching to a weekly congregation of 2,000 people, which made Radiant officially a 'mega-church'. The congregation would eventually swell to 5,000 and force Radiant to build a new campus to accommodate the crowds and the stunning array of innovations which define the church.

Pastor Lee's formal 'sermon' is just one part of the Radiant experience. When it is over, the real business begins. You leave the main auditorium through a set of wide double doors into a lobby filled with desert sun, streaming through the high glass ceilings. To your left is a long trestle-table laden with a mound of Dunkin' Donuts and an orderly queue forming in front of it.

Since every Sunday is a perfect Sunday at Radiant, there is good coffee to go with your doughnut. The Radiant Café dominates the far corner of the lobby with its brown marble counter and giant chalk-board menu hanging over the heads of its young volunteer staff. Before you order, a young woman behind the counter asks you for your first name.

'Hi, Mark, what can I get you?'

When the drink is served ('Triple-skinny-grande-latte for Mark') it comes in a Starbucks cup, which answers the question: what would Jesus drink? If he didn't have time to queue, he could always swing his car around to the Drive-Thru Latte Stand in the car park.

The Radiant gift shop is just a few feet from the café and it is jam-packed with polite people in casual clothes. The shop sells any product that can carry an inspirational slogan or the word of God, from CDs to jewellery. The head sales assistant flits between racks of sweatshirts and T-shirts, answering questions and gauging sizes. She has jet-black hair interrupted by pronounced blonde streaks and is set apart from the shoppers by the stylishness of her clothes. She hardly has the time to tell you just how busy the shop has become. 'It's insane,' she says. 'We are begging for more room.'

The doughnuts and Starbucks and religious fashion arranged around that lobby form a first impression designed to tell the new arrival that they are being offered a brand with hidden depths. When Pastor Lee talks about the marketing strategy at work in that lobby, he sounds every bit the former Microsoft salesman.

'We get them in the door by talking about things that are relevant to their lives. We might mail out a flyer that says: "How to have a great marriage. Come join us this summer and we'll talk about improving your marriage." Well, every married couple that reads that will think, "Maybe my marriage isn't the greatest." Then they'll go, "It's free, I'll get a doughnut. Wow, they have a Starbucks and they say it only lasts an hour. That's good. It doesn't encroach on my life." And then we say, "They are in the door. Now we can say more to them than just the marriage part."'

The trick works just as well on kids as it does on adults. Down the corridors which lead away from the lobby are a series of rooms devoted to Radiant's children's ministry. Mikki Garland used to be the children's pastor before she got promoted and is perfect for the role. She is bright, beautiful and down with the kids, but not so much that she couldn't pull off the occasional stern lecture. She's happy to provide a guided tour, knowing she will meet some familiar young faces, and when the first door is opened, a surge of noise and light floods out.

This is the 'Elevate' room, catering to children between the age of 10 and 12. The energy in the room could light up a small city. There is a little stage where the host is gamely trying to keep the kids focused on a competition that is actually a cover for what Pastor Mikki describes as an 'age-appropriate' bible lesson. Radiant's kids band, Corn Dog Blue, is standing by, waiting for a chance to grab some attention in a room that is almost unbearably hyperactive.

There are games systems and televisions hanging down from the ceiling, pool tables and basketball hoops in the corner and a set of round couches they call 'the conversation pit', although it is hard to see how anybody, let alone a prepubescent child, could concentrate on the spoken word when everywhere they look is another stimulus. The kids rush backwards and forwards in front of the stage like crashing waves on a sunny shore. One or two stop briefly to high-five Mikki. A young girl gives her a hug. As she untangles herself, Mikki describes the method to this madness.

'We asked these kids: what do you want to see when you walk in the church? What's your dream? They said we want basketball and games systems and live music. So we made it happen. We gotta keep them coming back week after week.'

'And they come back with their parents?'

'Right.'

'And that's the idea?'

'That's right.'

Mikki is smiling now, happy to see that the broader game plan is appreciated.

'We are winning. We are succeeding.'

Nobody here feels the slightest bit embarrassed that they have turned God into a mega-brand. Another church might resent the observation that its main building looks like a shopping mall. At Radiant, that is a selling point. Another preacher might object when a magazine writer describes Radiant as 'the blue jeans church'. Pastor Lee posts the comment on his website.

'Marketing the church is sometimes felt to be a bad thing,' the pastor says. 'But Jesus was the ultimate marketer. He said, "I will make you fishers of men." These days he might have said, "I will make you a great marketing manager."'

It would be easy to equate the hard sell at Radiant with the money-grabbing TV evangelists of the 1980s, the kind who sold hellfire and damnation and lived in mansions. But that would be a mistake. There is no evidence that Pastor Lee does this to enrich himself. Apart from his prized Harley-Davidson, he shows no outward sign of wealth. In fact, I detect a wistfulness in his daughter's voice when she describes the life of luxury her family left behind when the pastor left Microsoft.

The monied televangelists of the 1980s are what American Christianity used to be. Radiant is what it has become: a fierce free market in which churches must become distinct brands to preserve market share. The mega-church has the same economies of scale as a corporation, giving it the ability to provide a far more comprehensive 'lifestyle experience' than the local branch of the big religious franchises, whether they are Catholic or Protestant. A church like Radiant is always looking for an unseen niche, and that requires careful, almost obsessive, attention to the detail of daily life. That makes a church like Radiant an unerringly accurate barometer of the tastes of its catchment area, in this case the boomburb of Surprise.

Competition has always defined the American religious experience. Many countries have an established religion linked directly to the institutions of the state. In the United States, church and state are officially separated. You would think that would weaken religion by removing it from the public sphere, but the opposite is the case. Religion has had the freedom to develop independently of government into a great marketplace of ideas and beliefs. Each church competes for congregations and each Christian is encouraged to act like a consumer, testing out variations of their favourite brand. The latest survey shows that 40 per cent of Americans have changed their religious affiliation since childhood, making the market for God a particularly volatile one.

It is becoming ever more volatile thanks to the Great Dispersal. As millions of Americans move to the Sunbelt, they leave behind their old churches and go looking for new ones. Increasingly, they search for a new form of religious experience, one that reflects the contours of their new lifestyle. Religion must change to suit their lives and not the other way around. The new generation of pioneers are looking for their own personal Jesus.

The United States is still among the most religious societies in the Western world, with 70 per cent of Americans saying religion is important to their lives. But a growing number (14 per cent) declare that it is not, reflecting a small but significant secular shift in US society. There is also an increasing proportion of Americans who describe themselves as 'spiritual' or 'religious' but are disenchanted with the established religious denominations. One in six Americans now say they have no fixed affiliation to any church and that rises to one in four among 18 to 29 year olds.

These trends pose a challenge for the mega-churches, but they also create an opportunity. Houses of worship like Radiant must compete harder in a more individualised marketplace, but they are also better equipped to do so than smaller conventional churches. That advantage is reflected in their explosive growth; it is now thought that there are more than 1,000 evangelical churches in the United States, each with congregations of more than 2,000. Mega-churches have grown fastest on the shifting sands of the Sunbelt Frontier and, while they each proclaim themselves to be unique, they are cut from exactly the same cloth. Pastor Lee likes to describe Radiant as 'the red-haired step-child' of the mainstream evangelical movement, but in truth there is a rapidly expanding brood of red-haired step-children that looks set to inherit the family silver.

America's most successful churches follow the same corporate strategy as Radiant. Over at the Carson Valley Christian Centre in Nevada, Pastor John Jackson describes himself as 'PastorPreneur' and has written a book with the same title. Other Boomburb mega-churches trade on a stunning array of services, from banking to tax advice. In Phoenix, the First Assembly of God has a store of medical equipment it lends to worshippers. In Houston, the Lakewood Church offers martial arts to what it calls 'Christian warriors', while, across town, the Second Baptist Church has a full-sized football field.

Far and away the biggest influence on the mega-church movement is Rick Warren, the founder of the Saddleback Church in California's Orange County. He is the original of the species. He sports a goatee beard and Hawaiian shirt and wears no socks. He fills his services with self-help advice and Christian rock, and he is the most successful religious entrepreneur on the planet. His book, *The Purpose-Driven Life*, has sold more than 25 million copies, putting it in the same league as *The Da Vinci Code*. Warren came to international attention when he was chosen by Barack Obama to deliver the benediction at his presidential inauguration. It was a controversial choice, given Warren's opposition to gay rights, but, once again, it showed Obama's understanding of the hidden currents of change at work in this new America.

Warren has built up a model mega-church ministry at Saddleback, which attracts more than 20,000 people to its 120-acre campus every week. Such is the success of Warren's 'purpose-driven' formula that it has been adopted by tens of thousands of like-minded pastors. He compares his method to an Intel operating chip that can be inserted into the hard drive of any church.

Among Rick Warren's devoted followers is Pastor Lee McFarland, who learned much of what he knows about running a church during training conferences at Saddleback. When asked which person he admires most, Pastor Lee says Rick Warren.

We can see how the rise of the 'purpose-driven' movement is transforming the style of American religion, but is it changing the political outlook of the 40 per cent of Americans who describe themselves as evangelical? Churches like Radiant reflect the evolving preferences of the Sunbelt Frontier, but to what extent are they agents of transformation in American society? In short, is there any chance that the casual shirts and risqué humour represent a shift away from the fundamentalism we have come to associate with American Christianity?

The truth is that it is too early to tell.

Pastors like Lee Mc Farland and Rick Warren still deliver an uncompromising version of biblical reality amid all the talk of self-help and personal empowerment. Warren makes no secret of his belief that 'heaven and hell are real places' and that 'Jesus is coming again'.

The traditional theology of the mega-church is matched by a strong bias towards the Republican Party. Back in 2004, the demographic group that played the biggest role in George Bush's re-election was white evangelicals. Exit polls showed that Bush captured 78 per cent of their votes, a 10 per cent improvement on his performance in 2000.

There was no great tectonic shift in the political loyalties of Christians in the 2008 election. Obama won just 24 per cent of the evangelical vote, a modest improvement on the Democrats' showing in 2004 (when their candidate John Kerry won 21 per cent of evangelicals). But something significant happens when you look at the voting patterns among the young evangelicals:

one in three evangelicals between the ages of 18 and 29 voted for Obama. Exit polls also showed these young Christians held more liberal views than their parents; just 9 per cent of evangelicals overall support gay marriage but support rises to 26 per cent among the Millennial evangelicals.

There is no hard evidence yet that the 'purpose-driven' movement has created substantial distance between American Christians and the Republican Party. But cracks have appeared in the evangelical monolith which will only widen as a new generation asserts its influence. Perhaps more significant is the growing maturity of the relationship between religion and politics, a trend fostered by the evolving sensibilities of the Sunbelt boomburbs.

The movement, moderation and optimism which define a city like Surprise is giving rise to the 'Freestyle Evangelical'. The phrase is used to describe the new generation of Christian pastors who are moving beyond the narrow grounds of sex and morality to define their world view. These leaders are generally much younger than the traditionalists who have guided the evangelical movement, and they express a subtle disdain for the 'culture war' that has raged around wedge issues such as homo-sexuality and abortion. The Freestyle Evangelical looks beyond the traditional boundaries of evangelical culture for new alliances, new issues and new influences. That's what makes the rising generation of boomburb pastors agents for change.

There are overt liberals within the 'purpose-driven' movement, such as Joel Hunter, who runs a successful church outside the Florida resort city of Orlando. He is the author of *Right Wing, Wrong Bird: Why the Tactics of the Religious Right Won't Fly with Most Conservative Christians*, a title that pretty much sells itself. He is to the left of most traditional Christians but he was chosen by the evangelical movement to be the voice of Creation Care, their campaign against global warming. Environmentalism is increasingly a high priority for a younger generation of church leaders, who agree with Joel Hunter when he says, 'As Christians, our faith in Jesus Christ compels us to love our neighbours and to be stewards of God's creation.'

Evangelicals have not abandoned old certainties, but they have broadened the agenda of Christian activism to include issues where they have common ground with old liberal enemies. So in the mega-churches, you hear plenty of talk about Darfur, climate change, social justice and volunteerism. You will also see Freestyle Evangelicals building broader coalitions across partisan and ideological lines.

Once again, Rick Warren has pointed the way forward, creating alliances with the likes of Bono and Bill Gates in his campaign for global justice and courting controversy with his campaign against HIV/AIDS. His decision to invite Barack Obama to Saddleback Church for a conference on that issue in 2006 incensed traditional evangelicals. Warren was unrepentant as he stood on the stage with Obama and conservative Senator Sam Brownback. 'I've got two friends here, a Republican and a Democrat,' Warren said. 'Why? Because you've got to have two wings to fly.'

The leadership of pastors like Joel Hunter and Rick Warren represents a gradual trend among Christians, not a radical break. The Pew Foundation on Religion and Public Life has broken down the evangelical community into traditionalists and centrists. Its surveys suggest that the two camps are of about equal size now but experts agree that the centrist camp is growing. It may be a long-term process, but those Sunbelt mega-churches are already having a moderating influence on the relationship between religion and politics.

It is easy to misread the political sympathies of American Christians, particularly in light of George Bush's strong showing among evangelicals in 2004. Historically, American Christians have actually had divided political loyalties. A little over half of all evangelicals voted for Jimmy Carter back in 1976, and as many as one in three white evangelicals voted for Bill Clinton in 1996.

Successive Democratic candidates, including Barack Obama, have made great play of their faith. Back in 2000, George Bush was asked for his favourite philosopher. He famously said Jesus Christ. What few people remember is that his opponent, Al Gore, said that his guiding principle was 'What Would Jesus Do?'

The Freestyle Evangelicals have broader horizons, and while that does not necessarily mean they will turn Democrat overnight, it does mean they are part of the broader reinvention of American life. The boomburb mega-churches are mediators between Christianity and popular culture. Traditionalists sought to define their faith by what it was against. Pastors like Rick Warren and Lee McFarland judge success by their ability to prosper in the mainstream of American life. In this sense, they are agents of change. They know their markets. They understand that their Sunbelt congregations are chasing a version of the American dream that is both optimistic and personal. They know this latest generation of pioneers is looking for a form of religion that is confident, non-judgemental and adaptable.

Young Americans are still chasing individual dreams, but the mega-churches deliver the collective purpose they so clearly crave. The Freestyle Evangelical has come of age in a chaotic, bitter and harsh era. What they want most is sanctuary. They have had their fill of Frontier. Now it is time for Ritual.

—•—

Back in Surprise, the adult service is over, but the teenagers are still pumping with sweat and adrenaline on the south side of the Radiant campus. They are part of a weekly event called Octane, which is a tailored version of the Radiant formula: rock music, T-shirts and shorts – and a sense of purpose.

The music is self-consciously edgy and the volume just short of deafening. The star of the church's youth band is an Asian American bass-guitar player with a long dyed-blond mop of hair cascading over his eyes. He plays with one foot resting on top of a speaker and his head rocking back and forth, inciting the teenager worshippers to move. A line of boys at various stages of adolescence responds by wrapping arms around each other and headbanging in time with the bass tones bouncing off the walls.

The student pastor, Travis Hearn, takes the stage during a break in the music to offer the teenagers a mission.

'Everyone stay standing. We are going to look for an offering to help our missions in the eastern Horn of Africa. Give generously. If you can spare your last $100 bill, it will all go to a water project.'

The pastor knows there's not too many $100 bills in this crowd; he is being ironic. He speaks with Radiant's trademark irreverence, leading these young people to a cause greater than themselves but never pushing them beyond their comfort zones. You also see something you were only partly aware of: a desperate attempt to reach a rising generation.

In everything we have seen in Radiant, the common denominator is youth. Those Hawaiian shirts and shorts and risqué jokes are not just part of a sales pitch; they are a visible challenge to the mistakes of an older generation of Christian leaders.

'We are going to do an offering song. This song rocks. This is hot. This is your chance to go crazy. But first let's bow your heads. You guys can rock out after I offer a prayer.'

In another church, the prayer might come from a written text, but here it comes in the loose, shifting syntax of a Freestyle Evangelical.

'God accept our offering. Use it for your kingdom. Use it for our friends in Africa, to offer them clean water and not just clean water, but living water and that is you, Jesus.'

In the space of just two hours on the Radiant campus, you will be offered self-help, redemption, a crèche for the kids, a doughnut and coffee and now a chance to save the world. If you decide to linger there is the promise of so much more. Come back on Friday night for 'Celebrate Recovery', a forum for the drug-addled, sex-addicted, chemically dependent or generally messed up individual in need of a psychological group hug. 'We all got stuff' is the group's motto. 'Join us as we work on it together.'

Mikki Garland's recent promotion put her in charge of Radiant's counselling programmes. She seems a bit young to be shouldering such an intense burden, but under that layer of innocent warmth and good humour, there is a steely, dispassionate core. As we walk back to the church's main building, she talks about some of the tragic cases she has taken on in recent months. She is counselling a young woman who is four months pregnant and recently widowed. Her husband was killed when he wrapped his car around a tree. The first place she turned was Radiant Church.

'I sometimes pinch myself,' she says, 'and ask why God has chosen me for such important work.'

Pastor Mikki started out at Radiant as an intern for Pastor Lee and then went to a Christian university in Texas where she met the man she describes as her 'soul mate'. Surprise drew her back, and now she and her husband both work at Radiant. As we walk through the lobby one last time, it becomes clear that Mikki is working through her own personal demons.

'When I was about five years old, my parents got a divorce and I just grew up thinking, "I want to help people who are going through the same thing."'

Radiant is that kind of place. It invites you to reveal your hopes and your doubts and promises no judgement. All it asks of the people who walk through its doors is that they commit on some level to talking, sharing and taking part. It offers sanctuary but also reinvention – that perfect balance between Frontier and Ritual.

The stragglers are still nursing their coffees and polishing off the doughnuts and Pastor Lee is walking among them, connecting.

'I've come maybe six or seven times,' says a plump young man who has brought his wife and two young sons. 'It's awesome.'

Pastor Lee nods and smiles, but instead of responding to the man, he turns to face the children.

'These are the boys, right?' he says, and points to one of the kids' T-shirts which carries the logo of a football team from Pittsburgh.

'Steelers? Oh my God. I'm a Broncos fan.'

Now it's clear why it is hard to accept Lee McFarland as a preacher. Radiant is a self-contained town and Pastor Lee is the mayor. In his presence, in his church, with all these people around, you never have to worry about the troubles of the world. Here in the lobby of Radiant Church, between the doughnuts and the iced coffee, we have found the heart of a boomburb, the urban core we couldn't find as we drove up and down West Bell Road.

Radiant is an imperfect and partial example of transformation. After all, this particular town centre has its own restrictions. Just as those gated communities exclude the 'other', the mega-church excludes the unbeliever. There will even be some faithful Christians who will see dangerous delusion and self-centredness in its rituals. Yet for all that, few places can guide us through the transition from Frontier to Ritual quite like Radiant. Not many people can explain the process of reinvention quite like Lee McFarland.

'Americans love to reinvent themselves. They always want to start over and make it better. Our church is an example. You can drive five miles from here and you are in the middle of the desert. There is just something about creating a new community in the wilderness, one that is better than what we have left in the cities.'

Reinvention cannot happen without rebellion, but in the United States it is often hard to distinguish between the old order and the new. Sometimes, all you have to go on are the coffee and doughnuts and the words of a computer salesman turned preacher.

'We challenged everything about church. We left no stone unturned. We just kept saying to ourselves, "Let's do it all different."'

4.

Gilbert – Conservative with a Small 'C'

Dave Rodriguez is a fire fighter the same way other people are short or tall, blond or red-headed: it's in his genes. His father was a volunteer member of the fire department and, as a kid, Dave would follow him out on calls, cycling his bike in hot pursuit of the fire truck.

Dave grew up to become a battalion chief in the fire department in his hometown of Gilbert, Arizona, the fastest-growing city in the United States. A constant smile lights up his dark complexion, telling you that he can't quite believe he is being paid to do the very thing that makes him happiest.

Dave is the boss at the city's newest firehouse, which he also helped to design. He walks out of the gleaming, open-plan kitchen and dining area into a weight room that would do a big-city gym proud. Upstairs, there are individual bedrooms for his fire fighters which look cleaner and more comfortable than you would expect from a mid-range hotel. But Dave is most proud of the two brass poles at either end of the firehouse.

'I made sure the poles were mounted in front of a full-length window,' he explains, 'so that the kids going by might see a real fire fighter in action.'

This is the fourth new firehouse built by the Gilbert Fire Department in just four years. Two more are under construction.

On this windy stretch of East Williams Field Road, the firehouse is one of the few buildings that is actually finished or not for sale. It is the anchor that will eventually secure the half-built community growing up around it.

Dave Rodriguez remembers what Gilbert looked like when it was just another hard-scrabble farming community. His grandfather settled here in the 1920s, when it was known as 'the hay capital of the world'. In 1970, 1,900 people lived in Gilbert. By 2007, the population was 191,000 and 1,000 new residents were coming every month. That's the equivalent of one new person arriving every hour of every day.

Gilbert certainly has that boomburb 'growth gene' but it also has a piece of civic DNA, an innate desire to renew community life. You hear it when you listen to the city's mayor, Steve Berman, who says that Gilbert's eventual goal is 'to be the only 300,000-person small town in America'.

At a Labor Day barbecue, Dave Rodriguez gathers his newly assembled team and their families. Many are new arrivals who have come from out-of-state. Some traded workaday careers for one of the most venerated jobs in America. Almost every man in that firehouse repeats a variation of the same line to describe the complete fulfilment their jobs delivered: 'The only other job that could possibly be better than this is being a golfer on the PGA tour.'

Dave Green is perhaps the most striking of all. He talks of public service with the kind of unthinking innocence that confounds foreigners. He beat every other new recruit on the entrance exam for the Gilbert Fire Department, even though he is in his fifties. His wife is a police officer in a tough part of Phoenix. His son just left on his first deployment with the US Air Force to Iraq. 'Saying goodbye was the most difficult thing I have ever done in my life,' he says, his voice catching in his throat. Dave moved to the Sunbelt to work a little, play golf a lot and

89

prepare for a comfortable retirement, but I suspect he will not give up this job lightly. It sets him apart in a society where distinction is so hard to come by.

For others, a fire fighter's job offers sanctuary from the dysfunction and disorder of life on the frontier. Jeff is the sunny, shaven-head driver of the newest truck in the firehouse, a job he loves almost as much as his hobby. 'Bro,' he says, with endearing intimacy, 'the only reason I'd give this up is if I had a shot at music.' Jeff then begins to talk in unsettling detail about his childhood travels with his father, who once played with the heavy-metal band Stallion. The band had a measure of success in the 1970s when it toured with some of the rock legends of the day, including The Eagles and Kiss. As a boy, Jeff spent a lot of time on the road with his father and the band. The vice, addiction and excess around him taught Jeff all he needed to know about human frailty.

The boy became a man who loves three things above all: the shiny fire truck with the Stars and Stripes sprayed on the grille, his wife (whom he calls 'stud') and God (the word 'Yahweh' is tattooed on his arm in Hebrew lettering). Short of headlining a rock festival, life doesn't get better than this. Especially when you know how empty life can actually be.

Self-esteem gushes forth in conversation with Dave Green and Jeff, drawn from a bottomless well of community pride. Up there with faith and family, fighting fires is about the purest expression of the American ideal. It was that way before 9/11, but the sacrifices the New York Fire Department made that day have cemented the status of the fire fighter as the last remaining icon of the American frontier. In a desert boomburb like Gilbert, the fire fighter is the modern Marlboro Man, an über-masculine symbol of safety, standing rock solid in the midst of a deluge that threatens to wash away everything.

That firehouse in Gilbert brings Frontier and Ritual into

perfect alignment. It stands as a sentinel amid the frenzied construction work continuing for miles along either side of East Williams Field Road. It adds material and spiritual value to the community that is growing up around it. The boomburb brand promises small-town values and that firehouse delivers them.

The new building has enough staff and equipment to cope with the Apocalypse, even though there will never be enough fires to justify the expense. It's best to think of this as a downpayment on the mental health of a frontier community. It is an expensive but effective way of telling a fresh generation of pioneers parking their U-Haul trucks and over-loaded SUVs in the driveways of their new Mission-style McMansions: the journey is over, you are home.

There is something touching about the huge investment of humanity and decency that has gone into these fire stations. To see the fastest-growing city in the United States guided by such genuine civic purpose gives you hope for the new America that goes beyond one historic election or one president. In fact, it is tempting to see those fire fighters as symbols of a new era, in which community replaces confrontation as the driving force in US politics.

Gilbert offers us that hope. But it also shows us how much would have to change.

—•—

It would be nice to leave Gilbert with one single image: a passing kid staring in awe at the heroic fire fighter rushing to save a life. Unfortunately, that is not going to happen.

A few miles from the firehouse, we have just pulled up at a sandwich shop at the edge of a shopping complex on Val Vista Drive. Two police cars have crept into the car park and pulled up short of a dark blue SUV, just a hundred yards from where we are standing. Police officers emerge from their cars with pistols drawn chest-high pointing in the direction of a black man climbing out of the passenger door of the vehicle. They wait for him to clamber face down onto the scorched asphalt and put his hands behind his head before they approach, still with pistols drawn.

As more police cars arrive, there is the whiff of someone else's mortality mixed up in the stink of danger. The urge to turn away is strong but not half as powerful as the compulsion to watch. The officers begin a slow, methodical search of the man's jeep, keeping at least one weapon trained on him at all times. This scene plays itself out like a movie: a bad slasher flick that repels you more than scares you. But at least the drama ends with a whimper, not a bang.

If you come from a country where firearms don't have a place in polite company, you are much more sensitised to a telling show of power like this one. It taunts you into all kinds of generalisations about race, guns and policing in America. But past mistakes tell me that the easy judgement is not always the right one.

The police seemed professional. There was no brutality. Perhaps there was just cause for the drawn guns. If so, is there really a moral to the story? Perhaps it is simply this: the Sunbelt is still the frontier. For all the comforting rituals of the firehouse, people here still look to a sheriff with a gun.

The only guarantee of peace of mind on the frontier is the strict observance of the rituals that bind neighbours to the harsh enforcement of the rules that protect citizens against strangers. Safety in a town like Gilbert requires that bad things happen to bad people.

It has always been this way on the frontier, in fact as well as in fiction. In one of the first popular novels of American literature, *The Pioneers*, Judge Marmaduke Temple explains the impatient strain of Western justice: 'Living as we do, gentlemen, on the skirts of society, it becomes doubly necessary to protect the ministers of the law.'

The same exacting standards govern relationships between individuals. In the movie *The Shootist*, John Wayne plays a lone gunfighter reflecting on the philosophy of a hard, frontier life: 'I won't be wronged. I won't be insulted. I won't be laid-a-hand on. I don't do these things to other people, and I require the same from them.'

The frontier offers a personal space over which you are promised absolute control, but to guard that fiercely prized independence, pioneers need an extreme level of security. In the wrong circumstances, that combination turns the tension between Frontier and Ritual into a self-destructive spiral. Instead of the good balancing the bad, the worst aspects of the two personalities began to reinforce themselves.

The civic pride of the fire fighters told us that we were in the most forward-looking and optimistic place in the United States, but politics here is still flavoured by the sour taste of history. Even as the Sunbelt is being transformed, it still battles the savage, self-destructive instincts of the earliest American frontier.

—•—

The southwestern stretch of the Sunbelt *is* the Wild West, give or take a century or two. From the Mojave Desert to the Gulf of Mexico, the legends of the original frontier are never far from people's minds. But you don't hear much about the grubby, brutish and harsh place the Wild West was before Hollywood got its hands on it.

The first great Westering wave of movement in the 19th century was a chance for the little man to escape from the ruling elite, whether that was feudal landlords in the old country or

Yankee nabobs back East. It is easy to eulogise these early pioneers but the freedom many of them sought was shallow and savage.

In their book *Frontiers*, Robert Hine and John Mack Faragher say: 'If freedom is defined by the absence of external restraint, then they were a supreme example of free men ... but if freedom is a state of mind, it is arguable that men like this were maladjusted, and their aversion to society was based on a restless pursuit of something they could neither find nor define.'

The frontier also spawned a type of rough and ready politician who would shape the political culture of the Wild West – 'men with the bark on', as the artist Frederic Remington put it. Some came from the Southern states laden down with prejudice and rebellion. The legendary Davy Crockett made the move from Tennessee to Texas in 1836 only after his political career had stalled. 'I told the people of my district that if they saw fit to elect me, I would serve them faithfully,' he told a crowd. 'But if not, they might go to hell and I would go to Texas. I was beaten, gentlemen, and here I am.'

The rough frontier ethic was shaped in large measure by Ulster Protestant immigrants (who would become known as the Scots-Irish). They initially made landfall in the South, but their influence would spread as America expanded West. Perhaps the most famous Scots-Irish politician was Andrew Jackson. 'Old Hickory', as he was known, first gained prominence battling Indian tribes in Tennessee at the turn of the 19th century. In 1828, he was elected the seventh president of the United States.

Nobody messes with the descendants of Andrew Jackson. You are with them or you are against them. If you believe one of Jackson's early biographers, that certainty was forged in Ireland: 'It appears to be more difficult for a North-of-Irelander than for other men to allow an honest difference of opinion in an opponent.'

'Jacksonian' is a term that American political scientists apply to the aggressively nationalistic strand in American life. In his book *America Right or Wrong*, Anatol Lieven offers a particularly harsh (and perhaps simplistic) assessment of the link between Jacksonian tradition and Ulster Protestants, 'who after settling Ulster and largely exterminating its Gaelic Irish Catholic population, later brought their fundamentalist Protestantism and their ruthless warfare with them to the Americas'.

The Jacksonian tradition was carried along the advancing frontier by leaders like John C. Calhoun and Sam Houston. The nationalism of these Scots-Irish pioneers was writ especially large in Texas, which provided fertile ground for values of 'toughness, maleness and whiteness in defence of family, race and nation'.

The unforgiving quality of Texas life finds expression in a uniquely sharp sense of humour. In his exceptional book *People of Paradox*, Michael Kammens offers us this example, taken from the sign over a hotel in an old Texas frontier town:

> Come to Van Horn to live.
> The climate is so healthy,
> We had to shoot a man
> To start our graveyard.

In case you think the dubious frontier psyche was fashioned solely by Ulster Protestants, think again. Immigrants from all parts of Ireland played a part. In his evocative book *How the Irish Won the West*, Myles Dungan captures the spectrum of instincts which drove these Irish frontier-men – and women: from the humanity of public servants such as Thomas Fitzpatrick, the drive and courage of businesswoman Nellie Cashman, all the way to the savagery of Indian-killer Jim Kirker, who collected $200 for the scalps of every one of the 500 Apache warriors he hunted down in Mexico and New Mexico.

Some believe that these Irish Americans were brutalised by their own desire for respect and belonging. The Irish had arrived in America to find that they were looked down on by the Yankee establishment of the East coast. It would take generations for the Irish to prove that they were real Americans. Anatol Lieven says that 'Irish-Americans sought to overcome their exclusion not only through militant nationalism but specifically through being "First in War".'

Whether they created it or not, the Irish and Scots-Irish were in the vanguard of a fiercely traditional and rebellious conservatism that would shape the American Southwest. 'Frontier days in Texas are not so far in the past,' wrote author Warren Leslie in the 1960s. 'The man who fights, who resists trespass, who takes no orders from groups or from other men and who will not compromise – this is the frontier man, and he is still around in Dallas, and in Texas.'

Above all else, the politics of the frontier celebrates mavericks such as Senator Barry Goldwater of Arizona, the man credited with the renaissance of American conservatism. He became a national figure in the early 1960s but extolled the virtues of the Sunbelt, where he said 'individual initiative made the desert bloom'. His manifesto, *The Conscience of a Conservative*, popularised a distinctly Western brand of conservatism with an emphasis on self-reliance, hostility to government and devout anti-communism.

Goldwater lost the 1964 presidential election to Lyndon Johnson, but his ideas guided a movement which carried another Sunbelt conservative, Ronald Reagan, to the White House and inspired the conservative revolution that redrew the American political map. That realignment has given the Republican Party victory in seven out of ten presidential elections since 1968.

In their portrait of America's conservative movement, *The Right Nation*, John Micklethwaite and Adrian Wooldridge describe how the early Sunbelt suburbs influenced American political culture: 'These Westerners were natural individualists: people who lived in bungalows, not apartment blocks, and who relied on cars rather than public transport … and they judged people usually by what they achieved rather than where they came from.'

The last great realignment of American politics began in the Sunbelt four decades ago. In 2008, the American West backed Obama. So, does that mean the Sunbelt has embraced a new progressive realignment? Has its prevailing political climate changed for good? Or do the bitter, hard-edged traditions of the frontier still drive the most dynamic part of America?

—•—

To answer to this question, we have to revisit our Frontier and Ritual formula. As pioneers on a Frontier begin to settle, they tend to move toward the moderating influence of Ritual. That gradual journey is exactly what is happening on the Sunbelt Frontier right now. The evidence suggests that as the boomburbs settle, and civic rituals take root, citizens begin to move away from the hard edge of frontier conservatism towards the political centre. The political loyalties of the boomburbs are increasingly up for grabs, with voters evenly balanced between the Republican and Democratic parties, particularly at local level.

This change in political culture is at least partly explained by the rise of a highly participatory form of self-rule in boomburbs. More and more Sunbelt neighbourhoods are controlled by 'homeowners' associations', which act like private governments. They raise their own revenue and contract in essential services such as refuse collection and maintenance. They also set the rules which govern public life in their neighbourhood.

If boomburb residents have to look for help outside their master-planned communities, they look only as far as City Hall. Municipal government is run by part-time elected officials with the same fierce commitment to self-reliance and participation. If they need another school or firehouse, they hold a referendum and vote to float a bond.

There are broader risks with this kind of privatised democracy (which we will come back to later), but, clearly, it has positive elements. Most importantly, it helps to revive the civic engagement which many believed the suburbs had killed off. It also takes the hard edge off of political culture.

Linda Talbott is an elected member of the Gilbert town council and a mirror to the city's soul. Vivacious and tactile, you could not have a better advertisement for the social charm of boomburb living. She came to Gilbert from Georgia 20 years ago and is a zealous advocate for the evolving traditions shaping America's fastest-growing city. To Linda, tradition does not necessarily mean the narrow, religious morality we have come to associate with American conservatism. 'I would describe myself as socially liberal and fiscally conservative,' she says. 'I am a capitalist.'

Gilbert is barren ground for extreme ideas of any kind. People here are well read and well off; the average resident of Gilbert is significantly more educated and richer than the Arizona average. They work in a variety of premium business positions, either located inside the city or in nearby boomburbs. For many, the primary business in Gilbert is having and raising kids. Linda tells me with inordinate pride that Gilbert has a younger population than the American average and has higher fertility and marriage rates than anywhere in Arizona. 'An average of four children per woman,' she claims.

Gilbert and Surprise were good to George W. Bush. Initially, these boomburbs were attracted to him less for his classic Frontier sensibility than his promise of Ritual, expressed in that slogan 'compassionate conservatism'. He could not have won in places like Gilbert unless he came across as moderate and optimistic. In 2004, Gilbert and its surrounding county backed Bush for a second time, after he stirred up the kind of frontier fears which resonated with communities still 'on the skirts of society'.

However, by 2008 a backlash was developing along the Sunbelt Frontier. Bush's second term had managed to disillusion committed Republicans like Linda Talbott. Even in the rapidly growing suburbs like Gilbert, the prevailing wind was blowing against the Republicans.

Gilbert, and most of the other Phoenix boomburbs, is located in one of the most solidly conservative counties in the United States, Maricopa County. It also happens to be Senator John McCain's home turf. Yet, even against the home-town candidate, Barack Obama still managed to take a bigger share of the vote in Maricopa County than John Kerry did back in 2004, cutting McCain's margin of victory to just 8 per cent (Kerry had lost to Bush by a 15-point margin).

Across the Sunbelt in 2008, the trend in those fastest-growing suburbs was away from the Republicans. The Metropolitan Institute at Virginia Tech examined the voting patterns in what it called the 'Metropolitan Fringe' and found that Obama increased the Democratic vote from 40 to 45 per cent in the 'emerging suburbs' and from 38 to 42 per cent in the farthest flung 'exurbs'. The same study looked at the Obama vote in 'mature suburbs' and found that he had increased the Democratic vote to an emphatic 57 per cent majority.

What these results suggest is that the suburbs of the new America have a political life-cycle in which they emerge as conservative bastions and mature into something more moderate and potentially more progressive. The 2008 election suggests the speed of movement of that life-cycle has quickened, with all stages of suburban evolution tending towards the Democrats.

In part, the trends are a response to the Bush era (and

perhaps Obama's unique appeal). But there is evidence that the move toward Democratic candidates in the last two election cycles reflects an underlying decline in frontier conservatism. Take a look at the 2006 mid-term elections in Arizona when a proposal to ban gay marriage was on the ballot paper. Despite its conservative heritage, Maricopa County rejected the proposal, and Arizona became the first state to reject a ban on gay marriage that year.

Priorities change as suburbs settle down and forge new civic bonds. At some invisible tipping point, God and guns and all the other hot-button issue of the 'culture war' become so much less important than the quality of public transport, water quality or local schooling.

Rising petrol prices and falling property values have also speeded the trend away from the 'wedge' issues such as gay marriage and abortion. As suburban voters question the value of long commutes and extravagant development, they start to question their traditional frontier conservatism. Studies by the Brookings Institution have found a correlation between the rise in the Democratic vote in the 2006 elections and the early fall in house values and rise in fuel prices.

Once again, this is a suburban evolution but not a revolution. Suburbanites are looking for pragmatism and competence in their political leadership. Their move into the Democratic camp is partly a backlash against the mismanagement of the Bush years, according to Robert Lang: 'The suburban dweller is saying, "I've had it, enough is enough, and I'm going to vote for a change of parties that changes everything."' But Lang has a warning for complacent liberals: 'The Democrats don't own these people – it's about the state of the Republican Party.'

Democrats have become the safer choice on the new American frontier at a time of crisis. But in that, the yearning for security must be treated with respect. Obama learned to talk to the Sunbelt suburbs during the 2008 campaign. His party would do well to remember one thing above all, says conservative commentator David Brooks: 'They, or any party, will run astray if they threaten the mood of chastened sobriety that has swept over the subdivisions.'

Sober and chastened certainly describes the mood on that 'metropolitan fringe'. Now it's time to move on to what we might call the 'cosmopolitan fringe' of the Sunbelt suburbs.

—•—

Driving into Ladera Ranch is like slipping into a warm bath. The 4,000-acre master-planned suburb doesn't quite sprawl, it seeps inexorably across the foothills of the Saddleback Mountains near Mission Viejo like a rising tide of goodness and warmth.

There are differences you notice about Ladera Ranch the moment you drive through the first traffic barrier (open by day, closed by night). The first is the roundabout. It is traditionally an alien concept in Orange County and all across America because it requires drivers to have faith in the good judgement of an approaching stranger. Perhaps in such an ostentatiously close community, the stranger will turn out to be a neighbour, but driving through that roundabout is like falling backwards into someone else's arms; it requires a level of civic trust you would not have found in suburban America a generation ago.

As you go deeper into the community, the streets seem to get narrower. Everything feels more intimate. Ladera Ranch is divided into villages and neighbourhoods, all either respectably affluent or modestly rich. A group of ten or more villages is called a neighbourhood. At the heart of each village is a clubhouse, which is designed to reflect the different architectural theme of its village. All around the clubhouse are parks, pools, playgrounds and open areas. The phrase 'housing development' doesn't even come close to capturing its essence. Ladera Ranch did not develop. It was conceived.

Back in 1999, before a single house was built, the promoters of Ladera Ranch sent out surveys to 20,000 people who had responded to a billboard campaign along the freeways of Orange County. Some of the questions were eminently predictable, asking people to choose between playing fields and nature trails. There were slightly more intrusive questions which asked respondents to rate the importance of life goals such as 'making it big' or 'finding your purpose in life'. But when prospective buyers reached the section entitled 'values', it was clear they weren't being sold just any old suburb.

The questions asked people to rate how strongly they agreed with various statements. 'We need to treat the planet as a living system,' read one. 'Abortions should not be legal unless there's a threat to life,' read another. It also asked people to agree or disagree with the declaration: 'I have been born again in Jesus Christ.' There were questions about corporate greed, divorce, foreign travel and the pros and cons of 'experiencing exotic people or places'.

As Ladera Ranch took shape, the survey enabled the marketers to divide potential buyers into 'values subcultures' and to socially engineer the villages and neighbourhoods that made up the new community. The more conservative-minded buyers (labelled the 'traditionalists') were directed towards the Covenant Hills neighbourhood where homes had classic architecture and big family rooms and cost anything up to $5 million. The more liberal, socially aware 'Cultural Creatives' were led in the direction of Terramor, where houses are fitted with photovoltaic cells and bamboo flooring. Other categories of new homeowners included status-conscious 'winners' and 'winners with heart'.

The designers of Ladera Ranch could not care less whether the people who live in their community are muesli-eating lefties or bible-bashing conservatives, but they correctly understood that on the Sunbelt Frontier, the selling point of any master-planned community is how it 'feels'.

The people who move to these developments have far bigger expectations of the suburbs than their parents once had. They are looking for more than a way of life which simply supplies job, house, money and class. They want to surround themselves with a style of life shaped by their own personal preferences in architecture and colour, sport and music, faith and politics.

To meet that desire, developers have to rely on a branch of social research called psychographics. Where demographic research tells you about people on the basis of their age, race and sex, psychographics tells you about their attitudes, personalities and values.

'We were trying to characterise the lens through which people see the world,' said Brooke Warrick, who heads the marketing firm that sold Ladera Ranch. 'A community is a collection of symbols and images. And we wanted our symbols and images to be better than the other guy's.'

As a marketing exercise, Ladera Ranch was a big success and is now home to more than 20,000 people, but, as an experiment in social engineering, it was less accomplished. One resident of the 'culturally creative' and environmentally sensitive enclave of Terramor told a journalist from the *Washington Post* that a neighbour had turned his so-called 'culture room' into a TV room with a 50-inch screen. Another had installed a big swimming pool and $100,000 worth of landscaping. 'The truth is, I got a neighbour with a Hummer. I doubt he's very soul-searching.'

Still, almost ten years after it was built, Ladera Ranch speaks eloquently of the lives of the people who live on the Sunbelt Frontier. The various neighbourhoods still look like miniature versions of the shining city, radiating contentment and well being, despite the unspoken reality of economic crisis.

Ladera Ranch speaks of a revival of civic life and a more optimistic conservatism. It reflects the political sensibilities of Orange County, with 'traditionalists' outnumbering 'cultural creatives' (the local records show political donations in this area heavily favour the Republican Party). But it is even younger, richer and better educated than its Arizona counterpart. Unlike Gilbert, it reflects America's growing diversity: more than one in four people who live there are either Asian or Latino, and more than one in three is drawn from some ethnic minority.

Ladera Ranch offers a peek inside the emerging political consciousness of the cosmopolitan suburb. The citizens of these communities do not want to be segregated into ghettos based on either ethnic background or 'values subcultures'. They want to make a statement about their lives, but they do not want to be defined by race or politics. When they come to a place like Ladera Ranch, they trade a narrow, static definition of suburban values for the optimistic, interactive and diverse culture of the cities they left behind. They do take their traditions with them as they head down the freeway towards the new frontier, but their definition of conservative has an increasingly small 'c'.

—•—

Noah McMahon stands beside the sleek silver Land Rover in the driveway of his elegant Tuscan-style house and guides us in. He appreciates how easy it is for visitors to get lost in the warren of culs-de-sac that make up Covenant Hills. Noah makes it clear on the phone that people in Ladera Ranch no longer take all that talk of social engineering seriously. But, for the record, he is a 'traditionalist'.

Noah once worked for Richard Nixon. In the 2008 election cycle, he donated the maximum individual contribution of $2,300 to Mitt Romney, the solid social conservative in the race for the Republican nomination. When I bring up a famous local preacher with a liberal reputation, Noah uses the phrase 'fundamentalist Christian' to describe himself. But at the very same time, there's something worldly about him, despite his beard, saggy jeans, olive green shirt and fundamentalist Christianity.

In the open stone kitchen of his house, he introduces his wife, Debbie, and their two young daughters, Sydney and Shawna. The conversation turns to travel, and Debbie tells me the kids travelled the world with their parents. Shawna recounts the story of her most recent trip to Majorca with the trademark politeness and confidence of a well-bred American pre-teen.

When Noah starts to talk about his business interests, it's hard to keep up. First, there is his marketing and events management company with a celebrity client list ranging from the Beach Boys to skateboard legend Tony Hawk. Noah's primary contract is for the relaunch of one of the biggest casinos in Las Vegas. Then there is his other company, Zero-G, specialising in 'space entertainment and tourism'. It is the only commercial operation offering the experience of weightlessness. It has flown its customers (including Tom Hanks and Stephen Hawking) into lunar, Martian and zero-gravity on board a specially designed jet called *G-Force One*.

Noah had invited me to his home to talk politics with a small, intimate gathering of Gen-Next, a network of young professionals based in Orange County. The group has no explicitly partisan agenda, but it is mainstream conservative and solidly Republican.

Noah's fellow members arrive a few minutes late. Michael Davidson works full-time for Gen-Next and has a certain youthful star quality. He cut his teeth as a conservative activist on the fiercely liberal campus of Berkeley University and was a national leader of America's college Republican movement. He

105

seems destined for great things and is already heavily involved in Arnold Schwarzenegger's campaign to win another term as Governor of California.

Dave Luzuriaga is a successful engineer with no clear Republican pedigree. He proves to be the most ideologically thoughtful of the group. He talks with passion about his father coming from Ecuador to embrace the American dream. 'I'm here because I am a big believer in capitalism,' he says.

Within minutes, all three men have staked out their priorities for the Super Tuesday primary, which is just days away. Dave begins by saying, 'I am a firm believer that the Republican Party needs to be moderate.' When it's time for Noah to speak, I expect him to disagree and opt for that frontier tradition of conservatism. But what comes out of his mouth is criticism of President Bush and his mishandling of the nation's finances. 'When it comes to spending money,' he says, 'Bush wasn't very conservative.'

All three agree that the big issue facing Orange County in the approaching general election is the economic insecurity people here feel in their bones. 'February has just been the worst month,' Noah says with a chilling emphasis.

But the harsh realities of the economy are quickly dispensed with as the three young conservatives list their priorities. Again, it is Noah who surprises the most. 'You know, I take the long view and that's why ecological issues matter to me,' he says, unprovoked. 'People say that conservatives don't care about environmental issues, but we do.'

Dave talks of his frustration at the rapid disintegration of his country's standing in the world, saying it 'deeply saddens me what has happened under Bush and Cheney'.

'Candidates like Mitt Romney and John McCain got the message in this election,' Michael says. 'We didn't appreciate the way leaders squandered a conservative opportunity. We need to change.'

Noah, Michael and David show no sign of deserting the Republican Party. But they speak for that vast swathe of young traditionalists who have come to hate the demagogues of the political right who speak in the name of Goldwater and Reagan. They are looking for a more civic-minded conservatism that is less tribal and more open to the world. 'Moderate' is not the best word. 'Pragmatic' is better. They are looking for Republicans who can move with the changing lifestyles of younger Americans. What they want is a leader who can speak with authenticity on issues which defy existing political difference, issues like the environment.

Make no mistake: these three men have nothing but disdain for the Democrats (their hatred of Hillary Clinton borders on mania). But more than any other group, the young conservatives of Orange County reflect the transformation unfolding around them. Their lifestyles and businesses are built around innovation. They may express gloom about the way the country is going but they are sincerely optimistic about their own lives. And that is why they are looking for a new type of conservative, someone ready to shift the balance slowly, carefully away from old notions of Frontier, towards the safety of Ritual.

The three men all have commitments after our meeting. They need to leave as soon as our conversation is over. Dave is rushing back to see his kid's softball game. Noah is off to view two properties deeper into Covenant Hills that he is interested in buying as an investment. Michael is on the prowl for property and even though the million-plus asking price is out of his league, he asks Noah if he can come. When I ask if it really is a good time to be buying houses, they both look at me in surprise, as if I hadn't been listening properly.

'I am very optimistic,' says Noah with patience. 'It's just going to take a conservative to sort this out.'

I wonder if Noah and the guys, in their heart of hearts, ever really expected a conservative to win the race for the White House in 2008. As it turned out, their party was lucky to hold on to Orange County. Back in 2004, Bush's margin of victory here was greater (in terms of raw votes) than any other county in the nation, leading local conservatives to anoint it 'America's most Republican County'. But in 2008, Obama narrowly missed out on an historic upset, coming closer to winning in Orange County than any Democratic presidential nominee since Franklin Delano Roosevelt in 1936.

The trend in places like Ladera Ranch is repeated in 'monied burbs' across the Sunbelt and beyond. The wealthier and better educated the burbs get, the more cosmopolitan they become and the greater their appetite for a change. It is not the demand for simple pragmatism that you hear in that 'metropolitan fringe' but a search for a political consciousness deep enough to accommodate big ideas such as climate change and global leadership. Sometimes the yearning for change is not enough to change partisan attachments as deep as Noah's, but increasingly the wealthy, educated suburbanite is drifting farther and farther away from the frontier conservatism of yesteryear.

In the past, it was a safe bet that wealth brought you closer to the Republicans but the situation seemed to reverse itself in 2008, when nine out of ten of the states with the highest income went for Obama (the only exception was Sarah Palin's oil-rich Alaska). Back in 2004, just 37 per cent of those earning over $200,000 voted for the Democrat. In 2008, a majority of the same wealthy few voted for Obama.

Some believe the cosmopolitan trend we see in the 'monied burbs' reflects the broader rise of a 'creative class', operating within an environment of ideas and activism rather than consumption and production. More and more, the best educated are following high-tech industries to a new suburban frontier, changing the way those suburbs feel and how they vote. As their numbers grow, the relative importance of less-educated Americans declines (Back in 1940, 80 per cent of adults over 25 were non-college-educated whites. Today, it is less than half.) And as the influence of this creative and well-educated cohort grows, it seems their preferences become more pronounced; in 2008, 58 per cent of those with a post-graduate degree voted for Obama.

Of all the trends at work in 'monied burbs', the growing importance of young people is the most exciting. In Orange County in 2008, Democrats increased their support among 18 to 25 year olds by 55 per cent, accounting for the historic closeness of the election there. Orange County represents more than a trend. It points us to a generational shift. If you are young in the new America, Obama was right, 'this is your moment'.

Part Two:
The Generation

The more we get together, together, together,
The more we get together, the happier we'll be.
Cause your friends are my friends and
my friends are your friends.
The more we get together, the happier we'll be.

Popular modern American nursery rhyme

5.
Brownsville – The Joshua Generation

Everybody loves a parade, but this one is beyond beautiful. Even the man employed to shovel the horse shit off Elizabeth Street seems a little misty-eyed as he contemplates the spectacular grace of it all. The women on horseback in front of him are dressed in colours so vivid they may leave a permanent imprint on his retinas. The lead rider is a blaze of glossy tangerine ruffles, running from her chin all the way to her tiptoes. She is wearing an inscrutable smirk like the young woman who follows her. On her head is a wide-brimmed sombrero turned up at the back. It is hard to make out the detail of her face, but, when she turns her head, the shadow disappears and the colours of her dress are reflected onto her skin. Amber and lime. Sublime.

The horses keep walking and the women are soon gone. They are heading for the bridge that spans the Rio Grande. It connects Brownsville on the US side with its twin city of Matamoros in Mexico. Locals tell you that this is the only parade that starts in one country and ends in another. It happens once a year during a festival called Charro Days and celebrates the collision of Mexican and American culture which shapes life here in southern Texas. In other parts of the West, you use the word Latino to describe those with Latin and South American roots. Here the term is Mexican American or Hispanic.

The crowd along the parade route is five and six deep in places. The early birds sit out in front on folding chairs munching Frito Pies, a sloppily delicious concoction of chilli and tortilla chips. Happy gangs of people are perched on the upstairs balconies of the weather-beaten wooden houses along Elizabeth Street. Each passing display is greeted by the same generous roar of approval: the boys in a Mariachi band; more horses and riders; an enormous inflatable bottle of Tecate beer; another Mariachi band; portly old men from the local Shriner chapter riding miniature motorcycles; a high-school marching band; a local radio host surrounded by dancing girls in short pants; the next marching band; Mexican cowboys on horseback; the man with the shovel.

The even-handed cheer turns into a collective roar when a long red convertible appears with police officers running by its side. It carries the parade's guest of honour, Angelica Vale, the star of the hit Mexican telenovela *La Fea Más Bella*. The finale of her show was one of the most-watched Spanish-language broadcasts in US history. She may be unknown to a wider world, but she is a celebrity of the very highest order in this town.

The frenzied roar dies down as the convertible passes. The crowd seems a little exhausted by the outpouring of worship and politely applauds a series of cars carrying local dignitaries. But as a vintage jeep comes into view, the applause gets warmer and louder. Sitting together on the back seat of the vehicle are State Senator Eddie Lucio Jr and his son, State Representative Eddie Lucio III, stalwarts of the Democratic Party in South Texas.

The word 'dynasty' does not do justice to the Lucio family. The cheers that you hear from the crowd tell you that these men have a connection with their electorate that most politicians can only dream of. They don't just represent people here; they reflect their aspirations. Like the firehouses of Gilbert, they anchor a

114

community which has been on the wrong side of the frontier, even if it is on the American side of the border.

The older Eddie has been a public representative for almost 40 years, yet doesn't look old enough. He has had some health problems and is hard of hearing in one ear but any fair-minded stranger would put him in his early fifties. He is neat, almost dapper. His thick black hair is parted with precision. He speaks with a rich baritone and the hint of an accent.

Eddie Lucio grew up in a small house in Brownsville with his five brothers and four sisters. His father fought in the Second World War and was injured twice during the Americans' gruelling advance through Italy. A powerful, uncomplicated strand of patriotism has been handed down from father to son. 'My dad was a disabled veteran,' Eddie says, 'and he preached citizenship and American-ness to us. He told us even though we were Mexican-American, we should never hyphenate who we were.'

But Eddie learned another lesson from his elders about the brutality of life in the early frontier days. Mexican Americans were often victims of those 'Jacksonian' settlers who came to tame the new border territory, including members of the Texas Rangers, the now celebrated citizen militia. Eddie's grandfather was forced to flee into Mexico after witnessing the killing of a local farmer by a ranger who wanted his land.

Life in Brownsville still has a hard edge to it, but clearly the Lucios have come a very long way since the bad old days. To get to the Senator's home, you travel ten miles out of Brownsville into the flat, tropical scrub on either side of San Marcos Road. At the appointed turn, you follow a street full of trailer homes and small, boxy bungalows. It leads you to a set of electronic gates with the distinctive Texas star in the middle. In the circle around the star are the words 'Senator Lucio'. Behind the gates is a causeway which leads across a lake to the Senator's six-acre retreat.

Besides politics, Eddie Lucio's big passion is golf. One of his brothers is a professional at a local course and between them they run a company that builds golf carts. Sitting behind the wheel of one of those carts, Eddie's early reticence slips away and he leads you on a captivating journey through his faith and his family. He is deeply religious and has the Stations of the Cross posted on timber frames along the five-mile stretch of pathway that winds around his land. He talks about idyllic warm summer evenings out on that lake with his wife. They will take a glass of wine on to a pontoon boat and sit and listen to the sound of the birds in the thick canopy of trees and bushes.

Eddie Lucio's is a success story. He is a symbol of power, influence and public service. He says that local schoolchildren were asked to name their public representatives and when each position was called out – Congressman, Senator, Governor – they kept repeating the name 'Eddie Lucio'. But with all the pride, I detect in him a hint of ambivalence or perhaps a touch of weariness.

Eddie tells me a strange story. At a civic reception, a man approached him. 'I could see the way he was sizing me up that he was trouble,' he says. 'He came up and said, "I don't like you." After a pause he told me, "But I will vote for you because you helped my father."' It turns out that Eddie had stopped and helped an old man who had a flat tyre and no jack. It was the man's father. 'That is politics in South Texas,' he says with a not-all-that-comfortable smile.

Eddie Lucio pulls the golf cart up in front of the house and leads me into the kitchen where we meet his son. The younger Eddie comes across as the kind of man who is permanently in transit. This morning, he left his house without having breakfast. Even as he is introducing himself, he is opening the door to the pantry and helping himself to a cereal bar and a diet soda. But he has a rare knack that you see only in the very best politicians:

116

the ability to make a genuine, human connection in spite of a short attention span. He asks questions and considers the answers, never breaks eye contact when he is speaking and is respectfully silent when his father talks, yet he is not afraid to pick him up on something when he disagrees.

Eddie Lucio III was elected to the State legislature at the age of twenty-seven. He has the looks and attitude of a star athlete, which is not surprising since he almost made it as a professional golfer. 'It just didn't work out,' he says with finality. He went back to law school in the state capital, Austin, and thought long and hard about his future. Explaining why he finally chose politics, he says, 'I saw the way people would look at my father. I heard the things he had done for them.'

Eddie's father admits that the Lucio name played a role in his eventual election but says his son deserves most of the credit. 'He beat two really experienced attorneys. Anyway, the family name might help you get in the first time, but it takes hard work the second time.' As we walk into the garden, the father leans in close and says, 'He will be Governor of Texas. I have no doubt.'

Down at the water's edge, the two men begin to talk about the presidential election campaign, which is still at the primary stage. Voters across Texas will choose between Barack Obama and Hillary Clinton in a few days' time, and both the Lucios are prized gatekeepers to the Hispanic community. Close as they are, these two men are on opposite sides of this defining political battle. The older man is backing Hillary Clinton, while the son is supporting Barack Obama.

'My son and I have a difference of opinion on the presidency,' says the father. 'My judgement is based on the fact that I have known Hillary Clinton since her husband ran for president. I know them and they know our struggles. Eddie can speak for himself.'

The younger man doesn't need an invitation. His rhetoric has a slightly more packaged feel than his father's, but there is no less passion.

'If I was basing my support on who I was loyal to I would go with the Clintons. I had my Bill Clinton T-shirt when he was running back in 1992. But right now, with so much at stake, we really need to look at who is best for America.'

Policy has nothing to do with the disagreement between father and son. It is all about the personality of the politics they embody. Life has taught the father that you don't get anywhere without paying your dues, showing respect to your elders and never flinching in the face of your enemies.

'I want to look at experience and when someone comes to me and says, "I want the most important job in the country," I want to make sure that someone is seasoned, that it is someone who has never walked away from a fight. I am describing Hillary Clinton.'

The son has learned a different lesson. Times have changed in South Texas. A new generation is on the rise in America. Move with the times or move over.

'We have had 20 years of the same and we need someone who will show the world that America is changing its course. It's important that we have that once-in-a-generation candidate. That's who I believe Obama is.'

If the father is irritated by the presumptuousness of his son's choice, he doesn't show it. Instead, there's something almost unbearably poignant about what he says next.

'My once-in-a-lifetime candidate was gunned down. It was Bobby Kennedy. I cried and cried for a long time when he was no longer around. I felt like Eddie did, that he was the rising star that America needed, but you know …'

Then the father is back to his riff about Hillary Clinton's experience and strength. But it is hard to concentrate on what he is saying. The image of this hard-grafting veteran politician as a young man, closing the door of his room and crying after the assassination of his generation's shining hope is too raw.

It is not the first time I have heard this searing sense of loss from a man of Senator Eddie Lucio's age and political inclination. Just weeks before, a liberal small-town mayor in Iowa called Jerry Kelley had told me how more than a few townsmen had phoned him to say the same thing. 'They told me they were in Vietnam when Bobby Kennedy was killed. They were denied their chance to vote for a transformational leader back then. They never got it again. Not until now, with Obama.'

But Senator Lucio reveals the flip-side of the same coin. He is a pragmatic man who believes that there is no second coming in American politics. His generation's chance has passed. It is foolish to pretend otherwise. Beware false prophets from another generation, he seems to say, and stick with what you know.

You hear a similar expression of wounded frustration from women of Eddie's age who had to fight the same battles that hardened Hillary Clinton. As the Pulitzer Prize-winning columnist Ellen Goodman has put it: 'Sexism, slurs and struggles wore grooves down their memory lanes.' For these veterans of struggle, the comparison of Obama to Bobby Kennedy is an insult. Hell no, they seem to say, if Bobby was alive today, he'd be voting for Hillary.

If any such bitterness has crept into the Lucio family, both father and son are anxious to defuse it. They reach across to grab each other's shoulders or arms and begin as many sentences as possible with the phrases, 'I agree with Eddie …' or 'My father is right.'

'We are colleagues and we are family,' the son assures me. 'We mind those relationships and, if we don't, my mom will come and bang us over the head.'

The father swiftly joins in.

'At the beginning of the day and in the middle of the day and at the end of the day, we are family. Nothing will divide us. That's our culture.'

There truly is sunshine at the heart of this relationship, but something sharp is hiding in the shadows. It is a clash of generations. You see it most clearly in the son; he guards his impatience closely, but it is there. When he was 12, he joined the other members of his political dynasty to help get Bill Clinton elected. Now he has no time for the Clinton dynasty. The torch must be passed from one generation to another.

The bond between father and son is strong enough to survive their differences, but the differences are there nonetheless. Where the father insists that he is no hyphenated American, the son talks of discovering the hidden lesson of his ethnic identity while at college in Austin. 'I became more Hispanic than I had ever been because you rely on that culture to remind you who you are, to give you a voice.'

The son means no disrespect to the father, but he is clearly trying to find an identity outside his father's shadow. He entered politics because he wanted to emulate his father's achievements, but he speaks with impatience about the need for new leadership, for a new politics. And as if to underline the point, he is the first to leave his chair by the water's edge.

His father is late for another interview and still has to dress for the parade later in the day. His aide, Louie, is now pointing at his watch, but the older man has one last thing to show his visitors. 'This area is famous for its citrus fruits,' he says, as he walks towards the grapefruit trees, alive with green and yellowy pink. He asks Louie to go and get some plastic bags. He wants his visitors to take some fruit with them on their journey to Austin.

This veteran politician is happier now than he has been all morning. All broad smiles and talk of how much he loves South

Texas. He insists we fill the bags with grapefruit. Each fruit is the size of a small football. (The next morning, one of the grapefruit will be taken from the bag, the skin peeled back and the rose-coloured fruit torn in half. The juice will cascade like water all over the carpet of an Austin hotel room.)

Eddie Lucio Senior has lived a life of achievement. At the centre of his six acres, we stand by that grapefruit tree, basking in his happiness. He has reached his destination. It is time for another generation to shoulder the burden.

—•—

On 4 March 2007, Barack Obama was still considered to be a long shot in the race for the White House, but he made a speech that day in Brown chapel in Selma, Alabama, which deserves a place in history. It marks the moment when the Joshua generation officially showed its hand.

Obama travelled to city of Selma to mark the 42nd anniversary of Martin Luther King's march on Montgomery. In his speech, he described the leaders of the civil rights movement to as leaders of the 'Moses generation':

> We are in the presence today of a lot of Moseses. We're in the presence today of giants whose shoulders we stand on, people who battled, not just on behalf of African Americans but on behalf of all of America; that battled for America's soul, that shed blood, that endured taunts and torment and in some cases gave the full measure of their devotion.

Obama said that the Moses generation had left a lasting legacy to those who followed, particularly himself. But as the

121

speech continued, it became clear that Obama had come to announce the arrival of a new generation as much as applaud another. He pointed out that Moses never crossed the River Jordan. God stopped him short of the Promised Land. The Moses generation would wander in the desert until a new generation was born and a new leader called Joshua took over.

> The previous generation, the Moses generation, pointed the way. They took us 90 per cent of the way there. We still got that 10 per cent in order to cross over to the other side. So the question, I guess, that I have today is, what's called of us in this Joshua generation? What do we do in order to fulfill that legacy; to fulfill the obligations and the debt that we owe to those who allowed us to be here today?

In that speech, Barack Obama was offering a genuine insight into the seeds of the next American reinvention. The Joshua generation does exist and it fits neatly into the cycle of generational conflict that shapes American history. It is a process that historians Neil Howe and William Strauss describe as the 'the intersections of the seasons of life with the seasons of time'.

Strauss and Howe are pioneers of the study of generational struggle. To try to understand the United States, they say, without paying attention to the rivalry of generations 'is like trying to understand the movement of the oceans by looking at the breaking waves while ignoring the tide'. They believe that every 80 years or so, a Joshua generation appears in America. It is a 'civic' generation which sets out to rebuild after the excesses of an 'idealist' generation. Its purpose is to restore balance to a society that has lost its way, to defuse the fervour and conflict the 'idealists' had provoked.

At key moments in American history, the rise of this generation coincides with a political realignment, which comes roughly every 40 years. Just as history moves between 'civic' and 'idealist' generations, political power tends to switch every four decades between liberals (pushing the public dimension of politics) and conservatives (emphasising the freedom of the individual). To put that in a context with which we are already familiar, American politics is a pendulum swinging between Frontier and Ritual. The last great realignment began with Richard Nixon's victory in 1968; Republicans went on to win the next seven out of the ten presidential elections and made Sunbelt conservatism the dominant philosophy of an era.

You don't have to be a genius to work out that if you add 40 years to 1968 you get 2008. Obama's victory is consistent with the prophecy, but what about a broader generational transformation? Have we reached that once-in-a-lifetime junction of history? There are certainly signs of a civic revival in the most dynamic parts of America, but before we go jumping to any conclusions, let us take a closer look at the Joshua generation.

The first important thing to know about the Joshua generation is that its biggest component is the Millennial generation (a name chosen by the Millennials themselves in a national survey). There is some disagreement about when they were born: some say as early as 1978; others say 1982. Either way, they are the largest generation in American history, with anything between 80 and 100 million members. This is the generation Eddie Lucio III speaks for.

To understand what makes the Millennials tick, you have to understand the generations that preceded them. There is Generation X, a neglected group, full of alienation and ironic detachment, now slouching towards middle age. They live in the shadow of the generation that sets the pace of American life:

the rapidly ageing Baby Boomers, born in the years after the Second World War. This is Senator Eddie Lucio's generation.

If you accept the Strauss and Howe definition, the Boomers are the 'idealist' generation who were 'reared in an indulgent manner and are driven throughout their lives by their deeply held values'. They are prepared to fight for their ideals, even if that means permanent conflict. They are in touch with their inner selves and place a high premium on self-awareness and individual achievement. The Boomers were the Moses generation who struggled to change the world but eventually were sucked into three decades of 'culture war' in which liberal notions of personal freedom were pitted against the (often more dominant) conservative version.

By contrast, the civic generation are 'reared in a highly protected manner so that an orientation to societal challenges, problem-solving, and institution-building marks their adult lives'. They are team orientated, focused on results and have little desire to contemplate their 'inner life'. If they are going to rebel against anything, it is the Boomer notion of rebellion. As Strauss and Howe put it: 'It's more correct to call Millennials anti-Boomers, history's correctives for the mistakes they perceive that their parents are making.'

Plenty of American writers are falling in love with the Millennial generation, comparing them to the last 'civic' generation in American politics: the GI generation or 'Greatest generation', which elected Franklin Delano Roosevelt, backed the liberal vision of his 'New Deal', won the Second World War and then came back to build the suburbs.

Their biggest fans see in the Millennials 'a remoralising of American society', to quote Francis Fukuyama. I get the sense that many of these Millennial enthusiasts are actually parents of Millennial kids who believe their model offspring reflect well on their parenting skills. The Millennials are certainly the most looked-after kids in American history. One 2005 study showed that 9,000 books on self-esteem in children were written during the 1980s and 1990s, just as Millennials were being raised. By comparison, just 500 books on these topics were written in the 1970s when the poor GenXers wandered about aimlessly in search of adult supervision. Some have suggested that the Millennial era can really be traced to the moment when the first 'Baby on Board' sticker was placed on a minivan or the first bicycle helmet was placed on a reluctant kid's head.

The principal by-product of all that care and attention is a remarkable confidence. As they come of age, Millennials do share the public doubts of other generations. In a poll taken in June 2007, 70 per cent said that their nation was on the wrong track. But other surveys show that the Millennials are hugely optimistic about their own lives, about their potential to move ahead in life, about the likelihood of doing better than previous generations. They also have an enormous faith in their own ability to create change. In that 2007 survey, 77 per cent said that their votes would have a great bearing on who became the next president.

As well as having faith in themselves, the Millennials have faith in technology; it is their first language. All they know about communication, they have learned from MySpace, iPod, Napster, Wii, Ti-Vo, Facebook and YouTube. Nobody understands the tools of the American reinvention better than they do. Surveys shows that 90 per cent of 18–30-year-old Americans use email and the Internet. One poll in 2006 found that 18–25-year-olds spend an average of 21.3 hours a week online. Another survey in 2007 found that 80 per cent of Millennials over the age of 14 had created a personal profile on at least one of the social-networking sites and three-quarters said that they updated their page every week.

Once again, what is important here is the group. The technology the Millennials favour connects them with a wider world rather than consigning them to an empty room. Their group orientation points them to socially productive behaviour such as joining and volunteering. A survey of American college campuses in 2005 showed that 83 per cent of those entering their first year had volunteered at least once in the previous year and 71 per cent said they volunteered on a weekly basis.

All the evidence suggests that the Millennials have faith in rules. They use fewer drugs, have less pre-marital sex and break the law less than previous generations. There were three million acts of teenage crime in America in 1993 just as Generation X was slipping into its slow, self-destructive spiral. In 2003, there were just 300,000 (and remember, there are far more Millennials than GenXers so the figures underestimate the relative fall in criminality).

What is remarkable about all this social goodness is that it emerges out of the suburban sprawl which some analysts predicted would bring America to its knees. The Millennials have bucked almost every trend established by the GenXers and the Boomers except one: their drift to the boomburbs. We know that by 2000, 50 per cent of Americans lived in suburbs, and there is every sign that their Millennial kids will continue to circulate within the boomburb universe, even if they move to a different part of it.

If you need further proof of this trend, just talk to the jewellers. In 2007, the International Diamond Exchange (IDEX) urged the jewellery industry to follow the Millennials as they migrated ever deeper into the Sunbelt (market research shows they share the Baby Boomers' love of bling). IDEX cited statistics from the US Department of Commerce which showed that nine of the top-ten growth markets for Millennials are in Sunbelt states; they are expected to increase their consumption by 40 per cent in Arizona and 35 per cent in Nevada. All this should be compared with an average national growth in consumer markets of 5 per cent.

These trends will be hard to believe if you still see migrants to the Sunbelt suburbs as older, white working-class refugees fleeing the noisy, multicolour reality of modern America. That perception is no longer valid. The Sunbelt is getting younger, more diverse and more industrious. It is also more educated. Between 1995 and 2000, the increase in the number of people with college degrees in Phoenix was greater than in any other city in the United States bar Atlanta. Las Vegas, too, saw its graduate population rise by over 20 per cent in the late 1990s. Demographers are now talking of 'Bright Flight', with booming job markets on the Sunbelt Frontier drawing in a flood of well-educated professionals.

At some point in the last 20 years, the dynamo of American capitalism moved out of the big cities. In the 1990s, three-quarters of all new office space was created in the suburbs, and job growth there was three times higher than in the downtowns. Again, the most intense growth was felt along the Sunbelt Frontier, from northern California to the 'Silicon Hills' in Austin, Texas, the headquarters for computer giant Dell and an increasingly important centre for high-tech research.

As industry migrates, so too do the Millennials, and what comes with them are the trappings of a cosmopolitan community. As they put down roots, the Millennials are demanding the perks of big-city living in sprawling suburbs or old frontier towns. As the writer Joel Kotkin puts it: 'Espresso and art follow good jobs, not the other way around.'

In certain parts of the Sunbelt, you certainly have to look for the cosmopolitan presence amid the generic clutter, and that makes the discovery all the more fulfilling. One of the genuine pleasures of a journey through the Southwest is stumbling across well-adjusted Millennials in cool little pockets of Sunbelt bohemia. Some Southwestern towns have the added attraction of being college towns. That's where you meet the Joshua generation at its grittiest, hairiest best (my personal recommendations are week-night music in the open-air courtyard of Emos in Austin or drinks and dinner at John Dillinger's last hide-out, the Congress Hotel in Tucson).

Drive out into the desert and you will eventually run into one of a growing number of 'New West' communities, transformed from hardy frontier outposts into hotbeds of cool. Many were established by old hippies and Boomers searching for themselves but they have swollen with the flow of incoming Millennials. Take the town of Bisbee in southern Arizona: once a violent frontier copper camp, it is now a hip artists' colony with a distinctly liberal feel about it (the stickers on the wall at St Elmo's Bar say: 'Pray for a secular state' and 'Impeach Bush').

Even in the sprawling boomburb constellation that surrounds Phoenix, you can find superficial reflections of the range of Millennial tastes: dive bars in Mesa, Sushi in Gilbert, Thai in Chandler, Goth music downtown. In Scottsdale on any given Friday you can watch the beautiful Millennials parade into the bar at the über-chic Mondrian Hotel or watch them play high-school football just up the road.

H.G. Wells predicted that the city of the future would be transformed from places of business into 'a great gallery of shops and places of concourse and rendezvous'. Boomburbs are not necessarily what he had in mind, but there is an awful lot of rendezvous-ing going among the Sunbelt Millennials. Perhaps the best guide to the soul of a modern American city or suburb is the listings on Meetup.com, which connects people with like-minded clubs and groups in their areas.

If you look up listings for Gilbert, for example, you see plenty of self-realised Boomers at play in groups such as East Valley Psychics (63 members), the Wild Outdoors Christian Fellowship (102 members) and the Adults 'Swingers Lifestyle' Group (it has only three members, which seems to defeat the purpose). But there is a distinct Millennial presence among the hundreds of people signed up to groups for single friends, Childfree Friends, Shooting Pool, Ultimate Frisbee and Dungeons and Dragons.

Extend the search to the wider Valley of the Sun, which includes Phoenix and its boomburbs, and things get even more interesting. You might well detect a Millennial backlash against Boomer spirituality in the 300-member strong Phoenix Witches Meetup Group, the Phoenix Werewolf Meetup Group (21 members) and the Atheist Anti-Church Fellowship (33 members). It is hard to decide what to think about the Phoenix Procrastinators Meetup (10 members). And as for the 19 members of Wonderbreath, your guess is as good as mine. But there is just no doubt about which generation is being served by the Arizona Karaoke Community, Phoenix New in Town Girls Night Out, 20s and 30s Social Meetup, and In Our 20s & New to Phoenix. When you add them together, these groups have more than 1,000 members.

Now we have met the Millennials in their natural habitat. We know they like each other's company and don't like conflict. They sound like nice, polite young people, but nothing yet suggests they hold a candle to the GI generation; the invention of Facebook hardly ranks up there with the defeat of Nazi Germany.

Really.

How much faith can you have in a generation that would rather socialise than start a revolution?

6.
Orangewood – No Me without Us

'Happiness,' says the girl with the blonde hair and a cute button nose.

'Very good,' says her teacher, Randy Tucker.

His class is discussing the Declaration of Independence and its promise of life, liberty and the pursuit of … what, class?

Happiness.

Very good.

'Did the Declaration of Independence tell us we are guaranteed to be happy?'

The answer comes in a hesitant chorus.

'No.'

'If it doesn't guarantee us the right to be happy, it guarantees us the right to … what?'

Randy points to another girl, this time with long brown hair and eyes that speak of wisdom beyond her years.

'We have the right to be happy, but it doesn't always mean we are going to be happy. It means we have the right to pru … pursue our dreams.'

Randy expresses particular satisfaction with this answer, rolling his r's in appreciation. 'Verrrry good.'

Randy Tucker is a tall well-built man with a shaven head. When he was younger, he served in the US Marines. There is a photograph of him in uniform at the back of the classroom. He is ruggedly handsome and young behind the glass frame, square-jawed and emotionless. It is the kind of picture you have seen before, a thousand times, next to a headline about American casualties in Iraq. But this portrait is surrounded by life and energy.

Randy teaches the older children at Orangewood Elementary School, which nestles in one of the older, inner suburbs of Phoenix. Their classroom is plastered with images drawn from America's civic fables and unifying struggles. On the wall at the back is a vivid painted rendition of the iconic image of the Marines raising the flag on Iwo Jima. The slogan on the poster reads: 'Now all together.' At the front of the classroom, to the left of the whiteboard, the Stars and Stripes hangs at a 45-degree angle.

Randy's students should be comfortable with the explicit patriotism on display in this classroom; after all, this is the tail end of the Millennial generation. The burden of history sits comfortably on these young shoulders. They see nothing to fear in values, traditions and conventional wisdom.

Which is fine, up to a point. But there is a niggling doubt in the minds of some American elders about what the Millennials bring to the table. They worry about an apparent absence of scepticism and critical thinking. They know that this is a civic generation, but they worry that it is also a cipher generation which will embrace the American ideal without necessarily adding to it.

In a previous class, Randy Tucker had set his class a challenge. He had asked them to cast ballots for their favourite freedom, sort of like America's Greatest Hits. As you might expect from a generation that thrives on communication, the number one freedom was freedom of speech.

'Number two,' Randy announces, 'is freedom to choose how you dress.'

Randy doesn't judge, but from his words you can tell he is a little perplexed.

'Is that what the founding fathers had in mind?' He asks this rhetorically, but then makes a genuine enquiry, 'Why is it important to you?'

'I don't want to wear something ugly,' says one girl confidently.

'It's important to give me personality,' says one of the boys.

With the number three freedom, we are back on safer ground; the children have voted for 'the ability to choose our own leaders'. Then we return to the unexpected. At number four in the freedom hit parade is the 'ability to choose who we will marry'. Randy is gently sceptical.

'I can guarantee George Washington and Thomas Jefferson didn't have that in mind.'

As well as freedom to marry at will, freedom of religion makes it in to the top five, reminding us of the uncommon morality of American youngsters. Freedom to travel without documents is at number six, speaking of their growing wanderlust.

'How many have travelled outside of Arizona?' Randy asks and the hands shoot up.

'All of us, good. Now, what freedom would you sacrifice for?'

It's a tough question which you would never ask of a group of pre-teen children back in Ireland. Of course, there is a completely different context for sacrifice in the United States.

'Remember some of our men and women are sacrificing for our freedom in what two countries?'

'Baghdad,' says a young male voice.

'Yes, but what country?'

'Iraq,' replies the chorus.

'And what other country?'

'Iran,' a boy offers.

'No, hopefully not Iran,' says Randy, and you can hear the little chuckle in his voice. 'Begins with an "A".'

'Afghanistan,' comes a near-unanimous response.

'So, what freedom would you sacrifice for?'

In quick succession, equal rights and religion are mentioned.

'Any other freedoms you'd be willing to sacrifice for?'

Freedom of speech.

Again, with the talking …

You can't help but be charmed by those kids, with their determination to speak and dress and marry as they like. But it is Randy Tucker's empathy and commitment which really leave an imprint. His gentle encouragement is such a contrast to the aggressive coaching you often see directed at American kids. There is positive energy in that class but no over-inflated praise. And there is talk of obligations as well as rights, duty as much as entitlement.

This is the American way, but not always the Millennial way.

—•—

The Millenials are the offspring of 'the era of the worthy child', which was a wider backlash against the moral panic, pessimism and alienation which took a firm grip of America in the late 1970s. Parents set out to raise an 'antidote generation', by banishing bad habits and filling their kids' lives with purpose and positive energy. Studies show that the amount of time kids under the age of 12 spent watching television declined in the 1980s and 1990s by almost a quarter, and the amount of sport they played went up by roughly the same margin.

The Millennials certainly never wanted for active encouragement and affirmation, but some question the impact of that constant praise. Psychology professor Jean Twenge has big concerns about how the Millennials were raised, as you will

133

probably glean from the title of her 2007 book *Generation Me: Why Today's Young Americans Are More Confident, Assertive, Entitled – and More Miserable than Ever Before.*

'They were raised by "helicopter" parents,' says Twenge, 'who constantly hovered over them – providing unending praise, support and, perhaps, unrealistic expectations that the world was their oyster.'

There is a growing body of evidence to support that view. One financial-services company surveyed American high-school kids in 2006 and found that 61 per cent expect to become millionaires in their 40s or younger.

Professor Twenge carried out a survey of more than 16,000 college students that applied a 'standardized narcissistic personality inventory', asking for responses to such statements as 'I think I am a special person'. The survey found that students in 2006 were 30 per cent more narcissistic than the average student in 1982.

As the Millennials enter the workplace, employers feel pressure to keep up with 'praise inflation'. Some top corporations bring in consultants to teach managers how to compliment employees with emails, prizes, 'Celebration Voice Mailboxes' and a range of public displays of appreciation. One Texas company called Scooter Store Inc. has a staff 'celebrations assistant' who throws 25 pounds of confetti at employees each week and passes out 100 to 500 celebratory helium balloons.

If employers do need to chastise their Millennial workers, they have to be very careful. 'You do have to speak to them a little bit like a therapist on television might speak to a patient,' says trend-watcher Marian Salzman of advertising agency J. Walter Thompson. 'You can't be harsh. You can't really ask them to live and breathe the company, because they're living and breathing themselves – and that keeps them very busy.'

Another increasingly common complaint about young

Americans is that they have become intellectually lazy, turning their back on knowledge which is not absolutely vital to material success. Consider a 2006 *National Geographic* poll that found nearly half of 18- to 24-year-olds don't think it is necessary or important to know where countries in the news are located.

Author Jeff Gordiner is particularly tough on the Millennials in his book *X Saves the World*, which is a spirited defence of his own Gen-X cohort. He cites the classic movie version of *Willie Wonka and the Chocolate Factory* as an allegory for our times. The hero is Charlie Bucket, the grounded kid who doesn't sell out (representing Generation X), and the villain, Veruca Salt. Years later, her cry of 'I want it now' will become, according to Gordiner, 'nothing less than a mission statement for the Millennials'.

Gordiner says that this generation of Veruca Salts are so fixated on brands, celebrities and stuff that they won't read anything longer than a caption on a photograph. 'Because literacy leads to self-reflection and critical thinking, and self-reflection and critical thinking open the door to doubt and scepticism, and stuff like that just gets in the way when you're trying to get ahead, and *OMG did you see how fat Britney looks these days?!?!?*'

By now, we have a pretty long list of indictments against young Americans: they are narcissistic, naïve, shallow, ignorant and easily manipulated. There is one last complaint on the charge sheet: apathy.

Just look at their attitude to the Iraq war. Young Americans opposed the war by a big majority but did not follow through with the kind of mass action which characterised the Vietnam era. Their popular culture didn't reflect the sound of protest the same way the music of the 1960s did. 'Let's face it,' said *Rolling Stone* senior editor David Fricke, 'people are distracted ... they spend more time watching *American Idol* than they do voting in the last couple of elections.'

So much of what the sceptics say sounds credible. But something is not quite right. The dark portrait of the Millennials bears an uncanny resemblance to the shallow view of America held by many outsiders. It is the narrow perspective of a green-eyed voyeur peering through the keyhole with a mixture of revulsion and fascination.

—•—

The common thread linking the harshest criticism of the Millennials is a failure of imagination. As the critics prod and poke young Americans, they are mesmerised by the surface details and remain oblivious to the altered consciousness that lurks inside. The Millennials don't just play by different rules; they play a different game, and the greatest game-changing force is technology.

Every aspect of youth culture is different in the digital age. This is sometimes portrayed as a man-made revolution but it makes more sense to see it as an organic process, a cascading mutation which improves with each quickening stage of evolution. You only have to consider the impact of this evolutionary leap on music to see what impact it is having on the Joshua generation.

The advent of MP3 and the iPod, and the online music stores which supply them, has shattered old certainties. Writer Chris Anderson argues in his book *The Long Tail* that the era of the blockbuster is over. People have moved away from the top of the supply chain, where a small number of big hits are sold, towards a 'long tail' where they will find niche music that best reflects their personalities. In the past, 20 per cent of the music has made 80 per cent of the money, but now every piece of music has a market. Anderson reported that every one of the one million musical tracks on iTunes has sold at least once (and the number of tracks has at least doubled since he wrote his book).

In the past, people listened to the same music on the same radio stations and bought their music from a chain of record shops. 'Back in the pre-digital era,' says Professor Robert Thompson of Syracuse University, 'we all fed from the same culture trough, whether you liked it or not.' (That is part of the reason that 1960s protest music had such power; it was the soundtrack to everyone's lives.)

Musical tastes were often limited by where you lived because it took real effort to physically acquire music outside the mainstream. Think of that inquisitive suburban teenager making a weekly pilgrimage to the nearest town in the hope that the dingy basement record shop might have some rarity in stock.

In contrast, in the digital era, you are never more than a couple of keystrokes away from the obscure and exotic sound. The dingy basement record shop in Seattle or SoHo is now open for business in Surprise or Gilbert. The physical barriers between suburbia and bohemia are removed, at least in the online music library.

Digital music not only encourages curiosity, it rewards it, thanks to those unknowable algorithms at the heart of digital technology. With each step you take inside the online music store, a hidden high-tech hand leads you closer to your very own musical nirvana. The ghost in the machine is actually your own inner voice saying, Try it, you might like it. Those who have followed this journey find that their comfort zones are expanded to an extent not easily described. 'As they wander farther from the beaten path,' observes Chris Anderson, 'they discover their tastes are not as mainstream as they thought.'

Hidden depths are exposed as soon as the individual is liberated from the dictatorship of other people's choices. Sophistication is no longer rationed out in hip neighbourhoods of big cities. Quality is no longer determined by an elite band of cultural gate-keepers. Popularity is no longer dictated by faceless brand managers. It doesn't take a computer scientist to see how this might alter a generation's expectations of the society they live in.

Even 'old media' moguls such as Rupert Murdoch see the writing on the wall. 'Young people don't want to rely on a God-like figure from above to tell them what's important,' Murdoch said in 2005. 'They want control over their media, instead of being controlled by it.'

Of course, change brings risks. Like the inflated praise heaped on the Millennials, the hyper-autonomy of the digital age threatens objective standards of quality. Critics make the valid point that much of what is offered along that 'long tail' offers no cultural nutrition. This view is best expressed in an aphorism known as Sturgeon's Revelation: '90 per cent of everything is crap.'

If you are near a laptop, put the book down for a moment and call up the YouTube home page. At the time of writing, the top featured video showed a fast-talking puppet performing a fairytale called the 'Frog Princess'. Below that was a two-minute clip illustrating the visual effects of sound waves on a loud-speaker. Other videos included the continuing adventures of Gregory Shitcock ('the smartest private detective in the world'), something titled 'Robo-Jew Versus the Giant Nazi Woman' and snippets from a new TV series called *The 'Bu* about 'young, sexy people that live in Malibu'.

If you stop right there, at that opening page of YouTube (as many critics seem to do), you will find plenty of reasons to mourn the passing of civilisation, but type a few key words into the YouTube search engine that reflect your definition of high culture, say 'classical music'. If you did that the day these words were written, you would have been transported in seconds to a performance of Prokofiev's Quartet No. 2 Opus 92 for strings, played by the Minneapolis-based Artarian String Quartet. Admittedly, the second-most-popular video in this category featured talk-show host Craig Anderson telling a joke about demented squirrels at a classical music concert, but you get the point.

New media platforms like YouTube give us the tools to bypass the great wall of crud and white noise in the blink of an eye. Forget the 90 per cent of crap; the 10 per cent of quality has never been so accessible. Because there has been an exponential growth in the volume of online material to choose from, that 10 per cent offers so much more than the critics give it credit for.

The digital age hasn't just expanded choice; it has turned consumers into producers. Ordinary people now have access to technology that used to be reserved for the media professionals. They are using it to create a 'mash-up' culture in which images of life are recorded and downloaded and then broken up into bits and pieces, edited, re-mixed, infused with personality and put back on a website like YouTube for all to see.

The great attraction of the mash-up culture is that each individual is guaranteed a corner of cyber-space in which they will excel. Since there is a market for every product, you will never fail to draw an audience. In a virtual world, the Millennial generation will never fall short.

It is also much easier to be an innovator in this environment because when you share your new idea, others make it work. You don't seem to need the same level of intense, exhausting focus to create change. The founder of Meetup, Scott Heiferman, was inspired to make a difference after reading Robert Putnam's *Bowling Alone*, which revealed the decline of community in the United States. 'Although the big joke,' he later admitted, 'is that I never actually read the whole thing. I didn't have the attention span.'

The word 'viral' has come to be associated with the process of online creation and that perfectly captures the social element of the process. The work of any one individual becomes valuable when it contaminates an audience, when it finds a host crowd in which to mutate and spread. On social-networking sites like MySpace and Facebook, each individual life gathers meaning and significance as it is shared with friends and exposed to strangers. This central assumption of the digital age is now the philosophy of a generation: there is no 'me' without 'us'.

The most remarkable meeting point of individual and community is the online encyclopaedia Wikipedia, which, as of February 2009, offered 12 million articles in 262 languages. All articles are collaboratively written by a worldwide team of volunteers and edited by anyone with access to the Internet. Wikipedia works on the basis of consensus and civic trust; people believe it or else they wouldn't visit it in such huge numbers.

There is a strong argument that Wikipedia is open to bias, manipulation and vandalism. But an undoubted advantage is that it is 'a living community rather than a static reference work'. Mistakes tend to get corrected quickly and new information gets added as it becomes available.

Wikipedia also acts as a vital clearing house for information. An important example came in April 2007 when a young gunman went on a killing spree on the campus of Virginia Tech. More than 2,000 Wikipedia editors, some working as far away as Finland, began filtering information as it became available. Their constantly evolving article eventually had more than 140 footnotes, as well as profiles of the killer, Seung-Hui Cho, and a timeline of the attacks. More than 750,000 visited the article in its first two days, an average of four visits a second, and it was highly rated as a reference tool, even by local newspapers.

Natalie Erin Martin is a 23-year-old student from Ohio and

one of the editors who worked on the Virginia Tech article. She gave a remarkable insight into the workings of Wikipedia to the *New York Times*. 'People seem to self-assign,' she said. 'A lot of people went, "Oh, my God! This happened. It's going to be historic. I better make sure this isn't a problem." It has all been out of a sense of personal responsibility.'

It is often said that the problem with Wikipedia is that it only works in practice; it is impossible to understand in theory. The same can be said of the Joshua generation. Forget about Veruca Salt and her screams of 'I want it now'. Keep in mind Natalie Erin Martin and her eternal Millennial truth: 'People seem to self-assign.'

It's also worth remembering that Wikipedia is a living organism and so is this American reinvention. That is not simply a metaphor. The image exists in a physical form on YouTube, where you can find an extraordinary video clip showing a time-lapse recording of that Virginia Tech article in its first 12 hours. The article practically becomes a biological entity, growing and contracting in rhythmic spurts, gaining definition and detail and substance and clarity, mimicking the earliest stages of life.

The Millennials are the first generation of Americans to be raised inside the biosphere of the digital age and to grow in time with the captivating rhythms of social technology. This doesn't mean that we should excuse their faults or ignore their narcissistic streak. But this generation has been endowed with a talent for reinvention and our perspective needs to be broad enough to accommodate that.

Here are a few positive generalisations: young Americans have wider horizons and broader tastes; they embrace change but strive for consensus; they are self-reliant but also social; they are individuals within a collective. They have balanced Frontier and Ritual.

These broad truths hint at a brighter future for America. But

141

there are questions yet to be answered. Will the Millennials live up to their potential as a transformational generation? Will they change America as much as they have altered its culture?

—•—

9/11 defines the Millennials more than it does any other segment of society. It is the event which, according to William Strauss and Neil Howe, has set them on their way to becoming a 'hero' generation.

In the beginning, the Millennials reacted to the attack on the Twin Towers with an outburst of hawkishness. They overwhelmingly backed military action in Afghanistan and Iraq. Some surveys of young people showed they were actually more supportive of the use of force than other segments of society.

But there was a deeper impulse at work. The deepening partisan divisions of the 1990s (which climaxed with the Clinton impeachment saga) made them sensitive to the 'ongoing fragmentation of American life', as Strauss and Howe put it. Even before 9/11, young Americans were drawn to institutions which brought unity and stability.

Perhaps the best way to understand the impact of 9/11 was as a hammer which embedded the 'civic' instinct in the Millennial psyche. It made them appreciate the federal government as a source of cohesion. In 2000, 36 per cent of college students said that they had faith in the government to do the right thing. In the wake of 9/11, 60 per cent gave the same answer. The Millennials are the most pro-government of all generations alive today.

Of course, this will upset the sceptics, who believe that the Millennials are far too respectful of authority. Worse still, these young Americans seem to shy away from a good political fight; three out of four of them say politics has become too partisan. Then there is their apathy; they are too busy messing with their

Facebook profile or watching Britney's expanding waistline to care about who the next president will be.

In truth, young Americans have been apathetic for decades. The number of 18- to 24-year-olds who voted fell from 52 per cent in 1972 to just 36 per cent in 2000. In a poll taken just before 9/11, only 28 per cent of college freshman said that keeping up with politics was important. America was, in the words of the National Commission on Civic Renewal, 'in danger of becoming a nation of spectators'.

And then along came the Joshua generation ready to perform their first great act of political reinvention. Forget the sceptics; they have misjudged young Americans. Millennials are well on their way to becoming the most politically engaged generation in modern American history.

9/11 sent a surge of civic patriotism through all segments of American society. But the heightened engagement faded relatively quickly, except among the Millennials. The survey of college students found interest in politics kept rising, year on year, to the extent that the researchers say that 'for today's freshmen, discussing politics is more prevalent than at any point in the past 41 years'.

In *Bowling Alone*, Robert Putnam was worried about declining civic engagement. Now he is talking about a '9/11 generation', which embodies the civic spirit of the GI generation. 'As we approached the presidential season of 2008, young Americans were, in effect, coiled for civic action, not because of their stage of life, but because of the lingering effects of the unifying national crisis they had experienced in their formative years.'

The stage was set for something big in the 2008 presidential election season. It would turn into what Putnam calls 'the coming-out party' of a new 'Greatest generation'.

But not before one more ingredient was added to the mix: the marriage of social technology and politics. The Millennials needed revolutionary tools if they were to create a revolution. 'If broadcast media brought us broadcast politics,' says Jimbo Wales, the man who launched Wikipedia, 'then participatory media will bring us participatory politics.'

The candidate who best understood this revolutionary force was Barack Obama. His campaign had the benefit of insider information; among its early recruits was Chris Hughes, one of the developers of Facebook. From the beginning, the website my.barackobama.com was the backbone of the Obama campaign. It was more than a point of contact; it was a social-networking hub from which you could download the makings of your own private Obama campaign.

MyBo (as it became known) operated by an adage Hughes brought from Facebook: keep it real and keep it local. It existed to promote meaningful campaign activity in the daily lives of its supporters, encouraging neighbourhood meetings and autonomous campaign activities. It was a platform for virtual phone banks, enabling volunteers to download lists of phone numbers which they could use to canvass from the comfort of their own homes.

Obama's campaign understood that the Internet was more than just a campaign tool. In the digital age, politics also has a 'long tail'. A winning campaign must look beyond big-budget advertising and a generic message. It can afford to devolve power to grass-roots activists because it has the technology to harvest the fruits of their labour.

The revolution reached all the way into the murky world of campaign fundraising. The Obama campaign offered volunteers the tools to set up private fund-raising operations, exploiting the great self-starting instinct of the digital age. All told, 94 per cent of donations to Obama's campaign were $200 or less. By election-day in November, Obama had raised almost $750 million dollars, $100 million more than the combined total for George Bush and John Kerry in 2004.

In much the same way as 1960 was the first election of the television age, 2008 brought the first campaign of the YouTube era. By spring of that year, more than one in three Americans had watched online videos related to the election, according to the Pew Research Center. Most were tuning in to Obama. By summer 2008, his campaign had posted 1,500 videos on its You Tube channel, attracting a combined total of 80 million views.

The videos included campaign training manuals and finely tuned appeals to specific groups of viewers, such as absentee voters in Michigan or Republicans in Ohio. The most popular were Obama in his own words. His ground-breaking speech on race in spring 2008 – all 37 minutes of it – received six million views. Clearly, there was an appetite for the kind of detail that the sound-bite culture of conventional TV coverage would not provide.

The rise of the blogger, the citizen journalist and the 'viral' video-maker was feeding that increasingly ravenous appetite. Obama saw it as an opportunity to bypass the traditional media filter which stands between a candidate and the people. 'Instead of a handful of smart people in Washington telling you what to think, everyone is a journalist,' Gary Hart told me in summer 2008. 'Obama is the first politician to figure out how to use that, just as John Kennedy was the first to use television.'

Of course, the Internet is a double-edged sword. Everything turns up online, including the politician's past indiscretions, verbal gaffes and embarrassing associations. Hillary Clinton said she came under sniper fire in Bosnia; news footage showed otherwise. That footage became a big YouTube hit. So too did the video of Obama's former pastor screaming, 'God-damn America.'

The lesson is that politicians need to approach the revolutionary technology of the digital age with humility and respect. They need to embrace the ethos which shapes this revolutionary technology, the ethos of the Millennial generation: collective, autonomous and viral. One of the smartest observers of Millennial politics is Michael Connery, author of *Youth to Power*. This is how he described the spirit that animates the digital era in an interview with me in the closing months of the 2008 campaign:

> This is a generation which has grown up on remix culture. They have grown up having Facebook and MySpace pages, or blogs and Flickr accounts. They're used to being cultural producers, so when it comes to politics, they don't want to be passive consumers. They don't want to just watch the nightly news, and then go pull a lever. They want to be involved. They believe they have the power to create change because they've grown up having this power.

Politicians need to realise the centralised, top-down political machine no longer works in the YouTube era. Hillary Clinton paid the price for her failure to cope with the generational shift in the politics of the new America. At the outset of the campaign, her chief strategist, Mark Penn, said derisively that Obama's supporters 'look like Facebook'. The Hillary people failed to understand this was a compliment of the highest order and were, in the words of *New York Times* columnist Roger Cohen, 'left like deer blinded by the Webcam lights of the Obama juggernaut'.

In retrospect, you could say the same about John McCain. His decidedly low-tech campaign had no hope of matching the technological agility of the rival operation. And yet, McCain had more affinity with the Millennials than you might think. He shared their distaste of the Baby Boomers and the bitter, partisan bickering that emerged from the 1960s. 'I wasn't there,' he said, referring to his own captivity in Vietnam, 'I was tied up at the time.' He was also a living symbol of the value of public service and personal responsibility, which were Millennial bedrocks, and spoke of patriotic themes which resonated with young Americans.

Not for the first time, John McCain faced overwhelming odds, but he had a fighting chance. Or at least that is how it seemed at the time. But when the votes were counted, it wasn't even close. McCain was hammered by the Millennials. Young voters broke for Barack Obama by a margin of two to one, which was an unprecedented gap. Since 1976, young voters had split between Democrat and Republican by a margin of no more than 2 per cent. In 2008, Obama beat McCain by 34 per cent.

All in all, 23 million young people cast a ballot on election day, which was an increase of more than three million. CIRCLE, an organisation studying civic affairs, estimates that young people accounted for 60 per cent of the overall increase in turnout in the 2008 election. In percentage terms, the overall youth turnout ended up just shy of the all-time record in 1972.

In truth, some had expected youth turnout to be even greater, given the nature of the campaign, but that shouldn't obscure the truly remarkable shift in preferences among the Millennials. The Pew Research Center said their study of voting patterns 'suggests that a significant generational shift in political allegiance is occurring'. Exit polls also revealed a dramatic evolution in the political consciousness of the Millennials, according to the Pew Center:

> Young voters are more diverse racially and ethnically than older voters and more secular in their religious orientation. These characteristics, as well as the climate in which they have come of age politically, incline them not only toward Democratic Party

147

affiliation but also toward greater support of activist government, greater opposition to the war in Iraq, less social conservatism, and a greater willingness to describe themselves as liberal politically.

All this suggests a fundamental realignment in American politics is underway, but the word 'liberal' cannot adequately describe it. The Millennials leading this shift are far more complex than this label suggests. They are less Frontier: showing no interest in the philosophy of individual rebellion which animated past generations of liberals. They are more Ritual: having greater attachment to so-called traditional institutions such as family and country.

Make no mistake, the Millennials are all about change. But they loathe the narrow tribalism that soured their political culture for so long. They are comfortable in the company of people not like them. They are a product of the digital age in which an individual's identity is mediated through a circle of friends; the wider it is, the more virtue accrues. Once the group was something to be rebelled against, now it promises liberation.

All this lends itself to political activism from the ground up, because the only change which Millennials believe in is the kind of change they have a part it in. This was reflected in stunning levels of mobilisation throughout the campaign. According to Pew's post-election survey, 28 per cent of young voters in battleground states said they had attended a campaign event, far more than among other age groups.

One of the small details which made history is the high concentration of Millennials in states that Barack Obama needed to wrestle from Republican control, primarily in that vast swathe of Sunbelt suburbia. That's where his campaign focused its unprecedented fundraising and organisational prowess. It's also where we see the true potential of a generational ethos at work.

Nevada was one of the must-win Sunbelt states. Obama visited the state 20 times during the campaign. By election day, half of all voters in Nevada reported they had been directly contacted by the Obama campaign. That figure rose to 61 per cent among young people.

This was a mind-blowing level of political engagement in a state which had previously plumbed the depths of apathy. Patrick Coolican and Michael Mishak covered the election for the *Las Vegas Sun* and were still coming to terms with the sea-change in Nevada when I met them in December 2008.

'The whole idea of being politically engaged was foreign to the population here,' Patrick explained. 'Vegas tended to attract a certain type of person. People wouldn't bother you. There were plenty of jobs and lots of entertainment, but not until the Obama campaign did we have real engagement.'

That engagement revolved around a now familiar cascade of autonomous action, beginning with the unprecedented registration of new voters. By election day, Nevada had 100,000 more Democrats than Republicans. The enthusiasm started in Las Vegas but it soon spread into conservative heartlands such as Washoe County, which surrounds Reno. Patrick remembers the horror of a Republican consultant who discovered the scale of the Obama movement weeks out from election day.

'He brought his kids to soccer practice in Reno on a Saturday morning and the soccer fields were a staging area for Obama volunteers. It was so depressing for him as a Republican to drop his kid off for soccer and there they all were, hundreds of them with their clip-boards.'

Many of these volunteers organised outside the apparatus of the Democratic Party or the Obama campaign. Mike Misak discovered the backbone of its operation were young, suburban families with no experience of politics: 'They had kids and full-time jobs and were using vacation time to go out and knock on doors; for most of them it was the first time they had ever been in politics.'

A critical factor in Obama's victory in Nevada was the mobilisation of early voters. Among them was an army of Millennials. Nearly 40 per cent of registered 18- to 24-year-olds voted early and opted for Obama by a margin of more than two to one. As Coolican and Misak would write in a post-election article in the *Sun*: 'The Obama tsunami was coming, and the McCain campaign was throwing sandbags on the beach.'

In 2004, Nevada went narrowly for George Bush. In 2008, Obama won here by a margin of more than 12 per cent. And he owed the scale of his victory to Clark County, which includes Las Vegas and the boomburb of Henderson. In 2004, John Kerry won the county with a respectable surplus of 26,000 votes. This time around, Obama had 123,000 votes to spare.

But with such unprecedented mobilisation comes enormous responsibilities. The people who turned out for Obama, particularly the Millennials, expect ownership of the change they helped create. They fully expect this revolution to last beyond one election. As Patrick Coolican puts it: 'There is a small army of activists who we now expect to be part of the political fabric. In terms of citizen action, there's never been anything like it here.'

Barack Obama led a movement not a campaign. By election day, he had 13 million names on various email lists he controlled; two million people had created profiles on My.Barackobama.com; three million people had given him money; and more than 1.2 million had worked as volunteers for his campaign.

This movement was not about to give up, even though their man was in the White House. A month after the election, Obama volunteers met together in 4,500 house parties across the United States to discuss the various issues that would need to be addressed by the new administration, *their* new administration. More than half a million people responded to an online survey asking them how they would like to contribute to the work ahead. It was a daunting example of what politics has become in the new America. As a scholar of online politics, Micah Sifry, put it in *Time* magazine: 'I think Obama is sitting on a volcano.'

That explosive reality seemed to be on Obama's mind in Grant Park on the night of his election. 'What began 21 months ago in the depths of winter must not end on this autumn night,' he told his supporters. 'This victory alone is not the change we seek – it is only the chance for us to make that change. And that cannot happen if we go back to the way things were. It cannot happen without you.' Obama may not be a Millennial himself. But he understands the organising principle of the generation who are sculpting the new America; there really is no me without us.

That philosophy inspired the movement that won the election, but now Obama has to turn that philosophy into a governing doctrine. This is not as easy as it seems. Once inside the White House, Obama was immediately cut off from the collective power of a cutting-edge movement and confronted by a primitive bureaucracy. During the campaign, he had 90 people working just on his social-technology projects. As president, he could bring only 200 people into the White House to run a vast national apparatus, controlling everything from national security to health care.

The former New York governor Mario Cuomo once said, 'You campaign in poetry. You govern in prose.' That may not be good enough for a generation raised with sky-high expectations. They wanted change. They created that change. They think they own that change. And they still want that poetry – and they want it now.

7.
Avalon – We Shall Overwhelm

Hollywood is unsentimental about its own history, but luckily the owners of the Avalon nightclub realised the commercial value of its past when they bought the property a few years ago. Instead of knocking down this old landmark a block from Hollywood and Vine, they revived old memories. Today, the history of the Avalon is one of the building's distinct selling points.

Before it was the Avalon, it was the Hollywood Palace and before that it was the Jerry Lewis Theatre and, before that, the El Capitan, and way back in the beginning it was the Hollywood Playhouse. For over three-quarters of a century, the venue has hosted everyone who ever mattered in the world of music and television, from Lucille Ball to the Beastie Boys. It has staged plays by Henrik Ibsen and a live TV performance of *The Muppet Show*. The Beatles played here in the 1960s, The Clash in the 1980s and Nirvana in the 1990s. Through all its incarnations, the Avalon has been a mirror to the evolution of the American soul.

It has even played a part in the evolution of American politics. In 1952, Richard Nixon delivered his famous 'Checkers' speech from the building. He spoke to millions of television viewers from a set designed to look like the front room in his home. Bill Clinton also came here in 1992 to announce one of the classic fudges of his political career, the 'Don't ask, don't tell' policy towards gays in the military. It was fitting, then, that the

Barack Obama campaign in California chose the Avalon as the venue for its election-night rally on Super Tuesday in February 2008.

From the outside, the Avalon looks like an old Spanish mansion, with ornate carved columns rising alongside the imposing arched window which dominates the sandstone façade. But you are in Hollywood. A young man called Yosi is guarding the velvet rope with a clipboard in his hand and a fuzzy red beard keeping his face warm on this chilly February night. His body is a patchwork of perforations and tattoos all the way from his army-surplus cap to his cycling shoes. 'Media?' he asks. 'Right this way.' The rope is uncoupled and Yosi motions to the club's vaulted, brightly lit entrance.

It's still a full hour before the polls are set to close on the West Coast, but results are already pouring out of the other 22 states holding primaries and caucuses that day. A line has formed outside the Avalon. The assembled faces look like one of those slick multiracial advertisements for designer clothes or deodorant. White and brown, dreadlocked and blonde. The two women at the head of queue are wearing Mardi Gras beads and hats. An African American man with a shaved head is wearing a T-shirt with Obama's image on the front under the words: 'He's black and I'm proud.'

The main hall inside holds 1,500 people and takes forever to fill up. The bulk of the crowd hangs to the back, as if intimidated by the three giant TV screens broadcasting live coverage of the unfolding results. Bad news from New Jersey and Massachusetts. Good news in Missouri and Connecticut. But the crowd seems strangely detached from the wave of results that is surging forth. From the media enclosure up in the stalls, it appears that the people below seem more interested in themselves. And for good reason.

This crowd is a swelling constellation of race, ethnicity and fashion. Nobody seems to be older than 35. There isn't an ugly person in the room (except up here among the hacks). The drink is flowing liberally. There seems to be an edgy, flirtatious vibe in certain parts of the room. Somebody is going to do something quick.

'Yes we can. Yes we can.'

The chant starts somewhere in the back and takes a few moments to get traction. Then it fizzles out again.

The campaign officials decide it's time for a little pep-talk while the crowd waits for their candidate to speak in Chicago. A senior organiser comes to the microphone in front of the screens and speaks a few words in Spanish. He switches to English and recalls the night of the California primary in 1968. It was the night Bobby Kennedy was shot as he made his way through the kitchen of the Ambassador Hotel on his way to claim victory.

'Forty years ago was the last time California mattered in a presidential campaign and 40 years ago people saw hope extinguished in Los Angeles when Bobby Kennedy was killed,' the official tells the crowd. 'That hope has been reignited again with Barack Obama.'

Before he can finish his speech, the crowd lets out a roar. Obama has just appeared on those giant screens. It is as if we are all in that crowded ballroom in Chicago. The candidate is waving to his supporters, and almost 3,000 kilometres away in Hollywood they wave back and chant: 'Yes we can.' The chanting makes it impossible to make out what Obama is saying on that podium. But, eventually, a room that was once filled with the sound of Judy Garland, Louis Armstrong, Joe Strummer and Richard Nixon is now full of the sound of Barack Obama in mid-sentence: '… a campaign that has united Americans of all parties, from all backgrounds, from all races, from all religions, around a common purpose'.

With every pause and punchline there are increasingly ecstatic cheers from all the races and religions here in the Avalon.

154

'We are the hope of the future, the answer to the cynics who tell us our house must stand divided, that we cannot come together, that we cannot remake this world as it should be.'

By and large, the people who walked into the Avalon that night were strangers to each other, swallowed up by a city of enclaves and ghettoes and its history of unresolved tension. But tonight, together, they will feel a moment of clarity and unity. Together, they get to press the reset button. Surrounded by each other, they can honestly believe the world just might begin again.

Yosi guides some of the camera-crews down to the dance floor to watch the climax of the speech. The faces all around us are strained by unchecked joy. A blonde woman close to the bar is hopping on both feet, looking a little too thin, a little too excited and perhaps a little too drunk. A group of black professionals in the centre of the crowd wearing sharp grey-and-black suits are punching the air as if they were cheering on a racehorse. The camera finally settles on one slight young man with a thin goatee beard and red sweatshirt, who is waving an Obama sign with such abandon that he seems to be willing people to look at him, to validate his uncontrolled enthusiasm.

When the speech is over, the chanting begins again. Obama is shaking hands in Chicago and the crowd in the Avalon makes you feel that you are right there with him. Eventually, the screens go mute and the nightclub's sound system kicks in. The song they play is 'I Am Everyday People' by Arrested Development.

The young man with the goatee tells his story with such force that you can almost hear his teeth grind. He says his name is Taj and he has never worked on a campaign before. 'When he is our president, this world is going to change and that is why we are here tonight. This is something that has truly inspired me and I will take it with me for the rest of my life.'

Taj has taken his inspiration and passed it on to the rest of his family including his 92-year-old great-aunt. Just the other day, he sent her a letter telling her how excited he was to be working for Obama: 'She read that letter. She has voted in the last 20 elections as a Republican and she says she can't wait until November to go out and vote for Barack Obama.'

Taj's parents have come to the Avalon tonight. They are former radical activists basking in the reflected glory of their son's happiness. Together they are Moses and he is Joshua: 'I am here with my parents who were hippies in the 1960s marching for civil rights and equal rights and everything and they have gotten involved in this campaign in the last two weeks because they have seen what it means to me and how inspirational it has been – not just Barack Obama, everyone who is working on his campaign because it is about us and that is different than anything we have seen in America ever.'

It is about us. We are the ones we have been waiting for. Yes we can.

These are the slogans that keep Obama's multiracial Millennial army warm at night. Even as they sought to take over from the Moses generation, they had stolen its rhetoric of struggle and inclusion. To be fair to the Millennials, they have every right to embrace this language. They are, after all, the most diverse generation in American history.

When we use that word 'diverse', we are not talking about some progressive state of mind; we are referring to an astonishing fact of American life.

Two out of every five Americans born since 1982 is African American, Latino, Asian or of mixed race. In other words, 40 per cent of Millennials are part of an ethnic minority, compared to just 25 per cent of the previous two generations.

The word 'minority' is now increasingly inaccurate; large parts of the Sunbelt already have a Latino majority. By 2010, 77 per cent of children in New Mexico will have a distinctly ethnic identity, as will 53 per cent of kids in California. Between now and 2025, the number of states with an ethnic majority will increase from six to eighteen. By 2050, if current trends continue, white people will be the minority in the United States. More accurately, they will be just one of many minorities. Among Americans under 18, the shift to a non-white majority is due to happen by 2023.

The changing face of America is partly explained by fertility patterns; in other words, who is having more kids. Since 2000, America's Latino and Asian populations have both increased by nearly a third and the African American population has risen by 10 per cent. By contrast, there was just a 1 per cent increase in the number of white Americans. The ethnic transformation is also driven by historically high levels of immigration which look set to be maintained or increased; by the middle of the century, almost 20 per cent of Americans will be foreign born.

There are some signs of inter-ethnic conflict, which we'll return to a little later, but there is also hard evidence of a multiracial breakthrough in American life. The 2000 census found there were 3.1 million interracial couples in the United States, which is about 6 per cent of married couples.

What is more significant than the hard numbers is the trend: the number of interracial marriages increased by 65 per cent between 1990 and 2000. Racial boundaries are collapsing fastest in the Sunbelt, where most of those mixed marriages are taking place. California is home to one in ten of America's married couples but one in five of its interracial couples. More than one in ten marriages is interracial in Arizona, New Mexico and Nevada.

What we are witnessing, to use a phrase coined by writer Michael Lind, is the 'beiging' of America, and the first beige generation is the Millennials. The process is far more than a demographic trend. It involves a radically different attitude to

157

racial interaction. The rise in the number of multiracial Americans is a direct consequence of growing approval of mixed marriages. As recently as 1995, just a bare majority of Americans approved of interracial partnerships. By 2008, the percentage had risen to 80 per cent.

It is not merely a question of changing attitudes, but real-life experience. The percentage of Americans who know a mixed-race couple has risen from 58 per cent in 1995 to 79 per cent in 2008, and more than a third say they or a close family member have married or live with some one of a different ethnic or racial or religious background

The surge of interracial romance is helping to blur ethnic and racial boundaries. For the first time, the 2000 census allowed Americans to identify themselves as being of two or more races. That category that now includes 7.3 million Americans, or about 3 per cent of the population. It's expected that by the year 2050, one in five Americans will be multiracial.

That trend is even greater among the Millennials. The 2000 census found that 41 per cent of the mixed-race population was under 18. Even the language young people use to categorise themselves is starting to evolve, partly in response to public figures such as Tiger Woods, who describes himself as 'Cablinasian' (or a little bit Caucasian, African American, Native American and Asian).

The Millennials are the most tolerant generation in American history, with 90 per cent reporting that they have a friend of a different race. 60 per cent of 18- to 29-year-olds said that they had actually dated outside their racial group and 95 per cent said that they approved of relationships between blacks and whites. That may not sound like a huge breakthrough until you realise that as recently as 1987, less than half of all Americans took that view. And as recently as four years ago, a biracial politician called Barack Hussein Obama was still the lowliest member of the US Senate.

In his landmark speech on race in March 2008, Obama examined his own remarkable interracial DNA and put it in the context of the American Joshua generation.

> I am the son of a black man from Kenya and a white woman from Kansas. I was raised with the help of a white grandfather who survived a Depression to serve in Patton's Army during World War II, and a white grandmother who worked on a bomber assembly line at Fort Leavenworth while he was overseas. I've gone to some of the best schools in America and lived in one of the world's poorest nations. I am married to a black American who carries within her the blood of slaves and slave owners – an inheritance we pass on to our two precious daughters. I have brothers, sisters, nieces, nephews, uncles and cousins, of every race and every hue, scattered across three continents, and for as long as I live, I will never forget that in no other country on Earth is my story even possible.

You get the clear sense that Obama is most comfortable talking about a post-racial America. Coming into the 2008 election cycle, he was criticised by some prominent African Americans for not speaking in the same charged language as black leaders of the Moses generation. He made no real effort to offer himself as a spokesperson for a coalition of black and brown Americans. But eventually he would be tripped up by the cracks in the shiny veneer of America's interracial trans-formation.

Like any historic shift, this ethnic makeover is not without its tensions and contradictions. But the tantalising possibility in all of this is that decades of 'identity politics', in which insecurity and conflict forced Americans to cling to their tribe, is coming to an end. Perhaps age will trump race, as demographer Bill Frey suggests when he says: 'People under 40 are dating interracially. They are marrying interracially. Their identity with racial groups will not be nearly as strong as their tie to their generation.'

One of the driving forces in America's interracial transition is that historic shift to the suburbs, and particularly the Sunbelt boomburbs. Frederick Jackson Turner said it was 'the crucible of the frontier' that Americanised the first waves of immigrants. Today, the Sunbelt Frontier is the crucible of a new American identity.

Not only are boomburbs the most dynamic parts of America, they are also becoming the most diverse. Forty-five of the 54 boomburbs have Latino populations that are bigger than the national average, and three-quarters have Asian populations that are above the average. One in ten Americans is foreign born, but in the boomburbs it is one in five.

There are boomburbs with little or no racial integration, but times are changing. There were just 41 African Americans living in Gilbert back in 1980; 20 years later, there were 2,000. The golden rule of life on the Sunbelt Frontier is that everything evolves and moderates. The boomburb no longer represents a flight from the melting pot: it is the melting pot.

The growing diversity of suburban life is the next logical chapter in the classic American traditions of mobility and ambition. Just as the Irish in America moved out of their big urban ghettos in pursuit of 'lace-curtain-living' in the suburbs, African Americans are doing the same. The black population of the suburbs increased by more than 26 per cent between 2000 and 2006.

Such is the lure of the new frontier that increasing numbers of new immigrants are following the pioneer trail and bypassing the cities altogether. About four in ten new immigrants are moving directly to the suburbs, according to the latest census figures, and the destinations of choice are predominantly in the South and West. This is a striking break with the patterns of the past where immigrants usually bedded down in ethnic quarters of the big cities for at least a generation before moving out and up.

In 2008, the beiging of the American suburbs helped produce a political transformation. The battleground states which flipped for Obama are also the states with increasingly diverse and suburban populations, like Nevada, Colorado, New Mexico and North Carolina. Once again, change looks inevitable through the rear-view mirror. And, once again, it certainly did not feel that way at the time.

—•—

The crowd in the Avalon nightclub were more interested in themselves than in the big screens on the stage but, in retrospect, they may have been distracted by collective self-regard. The sad truth for that rainbow of Obama supporters was that California slipped out of their grasp. As they doused themselves with alcohol, the screens were telling them that Hillary Clinton was going to win their state by a handy margin.

Latinos had streamed to the polls in California to vote for Hillary Clinton. Even Latinos aged between 18 and 29 backed Clinton by huge margins (65 per cent), just as white Californians of the same age backed Obama by almost the same margin (63 per cent).

All this posed a real problem for Obama. After all, he was the first post-racial politician and California was a state perfectly attuned to his message of generational change. It was a constant theme at his rallies in the days before Super Tuesday. At a giant

161

gathering of UCLA students, the iconic figures of Caroline Kennedy and Oprah Winfrey were among thousands who turned out to anoint Obama. California's First Lady, Maria Shriver, was also there. She might be married to a Republican governor, but she is a member of the Kennedy clan, a Democrat at heart. She declared, 'If Barack Obama were a state, he'd be California.' Writing about the event, a *New York Times* journalist declared that Obama's campaign 'seemed to have a monopoly on what is hip, young and glamorous in California'.

But hip and glamorous didn't cut it in California, or in every other state with a big Latino population. Obama lost primaries and caucuses in the key Sunbelt states of Nevada, Texas, New Mexico, Arizona and California, and in each of these contests, Latino voters plumped for Hillary Clinton by margins of between 60 and 70 per cent. Even the young opted to stick with their own community rather than follow a broader youthful surge towards Obama.

The margins suggested that progress towards a post-racial future would be more complicated than it first appeared. An often unacknowledged source of racial tension is the territorial or economic rivalry between African Americans and Latinos, particularly in huge cities such as Los Angeles. That may well have played a part in Obama's poor showing in the Sunbelt, even if it was not a popular thing for politicians or their advisers to say.

Hillary Clinton's Hispanic pollster, Sergio Bendixen, sparked controversy when he said that 'the Hispanic voter … has not shown a lot of willingness or affinity to support black candidates'. It may have been a crude generalisation, but some credible observers believe there is a nugget of truth to it. It is not necessarily racism at work; it has more to do with the rivalry of two groups in American society who have struggled harder than most for their share of the American dream.

In many ways, what mattered for Latinos in the 2008 election was class, rather than race or generation. They had much in common with working-class whites who shared their economic insecurities, and that showed in their voting preferences in states like California. Away from the rich, hip and glamorous California we all know so well, Obama faltered. He won a big majority among Californians who earn more than $100,000, but Hillary Clinton had overwhelming backing from those who earned less than $50,000.

Take the highway inland from Los Angeles and you come to another California. San Bernardino and Riverside are where many of those suburban immigrants have fled to. Their house prices are lower but so, too, are their incomes. In a property-based recession, 'the inland areas are full of people struggling to hold onto middle-class status,' says Dowell Myers, a demographer at the University of Southern California, 'they are not risk-takers'. In Riverside county, 59 per cent of voters backed Hillary Clinton which was almost exactly the same proportion as in San Bernardino.

The young people we met in the Avalon represent an exciting new force for progress in the United States. But dreams are often sacrificed at the altar of necessity. The Latino families of San Bernardino, Riverside and East Los Angeles proved again that the course of the American reinvention was being shaped by doubt as much as by hope.

In recent US elections, many Latino and Asian Americans opted for conservative politicians above liberal reformers. George Bush won two elections with a great deal of help from Latinos; 44 per cent of them backed him in 2004. Some have suggested that they played a bigger factor in his re-election than evangelical voters. Bush's political guru, Karl Rove, had a long-standing dream of giving Republicans a permanent majority among Latinos by appealing to their conservatism on social issues, their religious devotion and their patriotism.

But the hubris and excess of the Bush years undermined John McCain's appeal to Latinos in 2008. Many of his fellow Republicans had played to anti-immigrant sentiment and were driving Latinos into the Democrat camp. John McCain could see the writing on the wall, publicly concluding that 'the Hispanic vote is turning against us in very large numbers'.

No state better illustrated the ethnic cross-currents swirling through the 2008 election than New Mexico: 42 per cent of its population is Latino, the highest proportion in the US, and there are other significant minorities, including a large Native American community. Among the tens of thousands of newcomers to the state are Asian immigrants, bringing a 'Little Saigon' to New Mexico's biggest city, Albuquerque.

New Mexico has been transformed by all of the forces at work on the Sunbelt Frontier. Cattle ranches still sprawl across the hills outside Albuquerque, but smart, young graduates are increasingly drawn here by the area's thriving nuclear laboratories. Intel also has a major facility in the booming suburb of Rio Rancho. All in all, New Mexico claims to have more doctorate-degree holders per capita than any other US state.

New Mexico is very much an outpost of that new, beige America and yet it harbours conservative instincts when it comes to change. The state went for George Bush back in 2004 and opted for Hillary Clinton in the primaries. New Mexico would be a critical test of Obama's ability to overcome the remaining tensions rippling through an increasingly post-racial nation.

Among Democrats in New Mexico, there were deep-seated worries as late as September 2008. In her neat suburban home outside Albuquerque, I met Evangeline Donkersely, as proud of her Spanish heritage as she was of the 40 years she has given to the Democratic Party in New Mexico. She was still smarting from Hillary Clinton's defeat to Barack Obama, but with lingering sadness in her eyes, she claimed she had moved on and would campaign for Obama. 'You can't sit around and cry,' she told me. 'You have to pick yourself up and move this country into what it should be in the 21st century.'

But Evangeline had a warning to Obama's Millennial supporters. 'You know 18 million votes for Hillary tells you that a lot of women were rooting for her,' she said, 'and some of them are not going to vote in November, especially older people.' Her voice was raised now and carried a touch of anger. 'The youth better come out and vote if they want to see Mr Obama win the presidency.'

The youth heard the warning. Just across the city from Evangeline's house, they were gathering at a community hall – christened 'Camp Obama'. Young volunteers from all over New Mexico had been brought together to focus on one clear task: get the Latinos out for Obama. Ganesha Martin was not exactly typical of the crowd in that training camp. She was an African American lawyer, originally from Texas.

She couldn't have been more honest when she talked about the challenges ahead. 'The older Hispanic generation may have a problem voting for a black man no matter what his message,' she told me, repeating what sounded like an off-the-record briefing from more senior officials. 'But I think because of the grass-roots efforts, and the way we're reaching out to the community, we are overcoming these obstacles in leaps and bounds.'

Those closing sentiments sounded scripted, but the intensity of the focus at Camp Obama made me think there was something to it. Once again, where the Obama campaign found a problem or an opportunity, they had an army of young, self-starting volunteers ready to solve it or exploit it.

In the diverse suburbs of New Mexico, just as in Kissimmee, the ground began to shift in Obama's favour in early autumn 2008. The economic insecurity of working-class Latinos had worked against him in his battle with Hillary Clinton, but against John McCain, it would be an advantage. In any normal election cycle, McCain could have played on 'values' in a bid to attract ethnic votes, just like George Bush before him. But traditional moral issues were off the agenda. Nothing mattered but economics.

Blogger Joe Monahan is one of the cleverest observers of New Mexico politics and as far back as August 2008 he detected a shift in consciousness in those sprawling, beige suburbs. 'People there may have been more concerned with social issues when they voted previously,' he told me. 'But now it's a fight on the economy and Senator McCain is not going to be able to hide from it.'

Throw in the lingering resentment over the wars in Afghanistan and Iraq and this had the making of a breakthrough election for Democrats in New Mexico. 'These are the big issues we don't get in every election,' said Joe. 'War and peace, economic strength and security; right in your face, big decisions that have to be made. That's a big election.'

In a choice between Hillary Clinton and Barack Obama, Latinos had picked Hillary as a safer port in a worsening storm, even the younger members of that community. But they did so primarily on economic grounds, not because of irreconcilable differences between ethnic groups. By the time it came to a choice between John McCain and Barack Obama, Obama had become the safe choice. Change had become the only hope of sanctuary from hard times.

Across the United States, 67 per cent of Latinos voted for Obama (John Kerry got 53 per cent in 2004) and in New Mexico, it rose to 69 per cent of the vote. The state also recorded a dramatic increase in the Latino share of the overall vote from 32 per cent to 41 per cent, which may explain how a Republican state became a Democrat state by a stunning 14-point margin.

'The Latino vote came back to the Democratic Party after a brief flirtation with the Republicans,' said New Mexico's Democratic governor, Bill Richardson, who is Hispanic. 'They turned out, erasing the fame of Latino voters as a sleeping giant and making them an actual giant.'

The Latino giant might now bestride politics like a colossus, but it's unlikely any one single group will have unrivalled dominance over the affairs of the new America. The Millennials would never allow it. They have already passed the post-racial tipping point, in part because of the social technology they have embraced.

The digital age has eroded racial certainties and created what sociologist Dalton Conley of New York University calls the 'network nation'. He believes that as platforms such as Facebook and YouTube elevate the virtue of shared experiences, they create 'crosscutting social groups' which elevate a generation above the tribal loyalties of the past. Mainstream popular culture is also building the foundations of a post-racial America. In the music, film and television coming out of the United States, there is clear currency in ethnic diversity (just ask the creators of that blockbuster Latina franchise *Dora the Explorer*).

There is one potential problem here: the decline of white America is happening at a breakneck pace. As recently as 2000, 74 per cent of voters between the ages of 18 and 29 were white. In 2008, it was just 62 per cent of voters. White Americans are aware that their influence is on a steep decline, which may help explain the potency of the language you hear from conservative politicians. When they talk about the 'real' America they are also talking about a whiter America; plain-spoken, rural and folksy, but mainly white.

In the wake of the 2008 election, the *Atlantic Monthly* published a compelling article entitled 'The end of white America'. Its author Hua Hsu noted the rise of a cultural solidarity among blue-collar and lower-middle-class whites expressed in 'redneck' comedy tours, NASCAR and the renaissance of country music. It is a solidarity defined, in Hsu's view, by 'a yearning for American "authenticity," a folksy realness that rejects the global, the urban, the effete in favour of "the way things used to be"'.

In an otherwise optimistic article, Hsu argued that it is possible to imagine 'white identity politics growing more potent and more forthright in its racial identifications in the future, as "the real America" becomes an ever-smaller portion of, well, the real America'.

I read that article shortly after seeing a post-election map published in the *New York Times*. It showed the United States coloured on the basis of the rise and fall of the vote for the Democratic candidate. A great band of blue across the South and West showed where the vote had increased by more than 5 per cent, where Obama had done best. An angry rash of red showed where the Democratic vote had fallen by more than 5 per cent, where Obama had been solidly rejected. That angry rash ran clearest along the Appalachians, through Scots-Irish strongholds from Arkansas to West Virginia. It was the 'real' America and it wasn't happy.

The 2008 election proved beyond any shade of doubt that the 'real' America – as defined by Sarah Palin and that angry red rash – is over. The future is multi-racial, even if it never quite becomes post-racial. The United States is crossing a new frontier, but the ghosts of frontiers past will continue to haunt it. The genius of America is change. The curse of America is the fear that comes with it.

Part Three:
The Problems

'The past is never dead. It's not even past.'

William Faulkner, *Requiem for a Nun*

8.
Fullerton – The Economics of Fear

The fire in the hearth is roaring and crackling and pouring forth warmth and welcome. John Coffman collected the wood himself, just yesterday. His speech carries a trace of his native Arkansas, and his thick snow-white beard and weathered baseball cap speak to you of foraging and fixing amid mountains and country streams. But John lives in a different sort of wilderness – a rambling forest of low-slung ranch houses hemmed in by the torrential flow of the Orange and Santa Ana freeways.

By contrast, John's wife Grayce appears to be in her natural California habitat. She is a child of the post-war boom which sent millions of city folks into the suburbs of Orange County. She has no pretence, no sharp edges. There is a simple, almost dreamy elegance about Grayce, and she has kind eyes, full of hope for a temperate autumn among neighbours and family.

Grayce and John moved into this house in the suburb of Fullerton 31 years ago. It was built in an age when families still gathered around a dining table out of sight of the television. There is an air of formality in the front room, which is a museum to three decades of family life, full of knick-knacks, souvenirs, holiday snaps and heirlooms. But the farther you get from the front door, the more casual and unadorned the house becomes. Out back, the pool catches the decaying glow of the evening sun which casts lengthening shadows over the heavy plastic sheet that covers the pool furniture. Aside from the buzz of the light planes on their final approach to the nearby airport, there is calm here, comfort.

Grayce's hands offer up the first sign of trouble. Ribbons of skin have come away from her palms, parting company with the angry, livid flesh beneath. She is suffering from eczema, which her doctor says has been triggered by stress. It is the same stress that forced John onto anti-depressants, on top of the medicine he takes to regulate his heart. John is mightily fed up with the fatigue and occasional hallucinations all this medication has brought on.

The Coffmans live with their six grandchildren, two sausage-shaped dachshunds and a seven-year-old goldfish called Jaws. The oldest grandchild, Brittany, is 22 and studies art history at a nearby college. The only boy, Jay, is an 11-year-old sports fan with Attention Deficit Disorder. In between are Lindsay, Sarah, Katie and Megan. The children should be with their mother, John and Grayce's daughter, but she and her husband developed a serious drug problem. One day, things got so bad that John called the cops and took custody of his grandchildren.

Grayce and John tell the story with the minimum of detail, suggesting unresolved pain, but they seem entirely comfortable with the enormous responsibility they are shouldering in what should be their retirement years. They raised four kids of their own and now offer warmth and sanctuary to the next generation.

'I don't hunt and I don't fish. We do this. We take care of kids,' says John. Before he can get out another word, Grayce says, 'We have never had an empty nest.'

Raising six kids did not cause the eczema or the depression. What's haunting John and Grayce Coffman is the nightmare of foreclosure. Since the letter arrived from the mortgage company two months ago, they have lived every waking moment with the prospect of losing their home.

The maths is brutally simple. They are unemployed and receive social-welfare payments of $5,200 per month to care for their grandchildren. Their mortgage payments now stand at $4,500 per month. The couple have about $1,400 saved for a rainy day. They never thought it would rain quite this hard.

'If they want to take my house, they will have to take me, the goldfish, the dogs and the kids,' says Grayce.

It is a rare and rehearsed statement of defiance. As she and John talk through their problems by the side of their pool, she spends most of her time staring down at the tiles on the patio with that dreamy, faraway look in her eyes again. But the dream has soured and there is no waking refuge from it.

'It is just surreal, just a bad dream,' she says. Then adds in a quieter tone, 'How did we get in this mess?'

The answer to that question is a combination of misfortune and recklessness, although back in the days of a booming property market their behaviour would not have seemed all that reckless. Millions of Americans did what the Coffmans did; they took out huge loans against the rising value of their house and spent it as if the boom would be a permanent feature of their lives.

At least the Coffmans used the money for legitimate purposes, taking out loans to expand their house and make room for their six grandchildren. Then, in 2005, John's radiator-repair business got into trouble and the Coffmans borrowed a little over $550,000 from America's biggest home lender, Countrywide Financial. The radiator shop continued to falter and when John got sick, Grayce wound up the business. The couple were left with no assets and a mountain of debt. Despite making a total of $50,000 in payments, their debt to Countrywide grew to $590,000 within two years. In a desperate bid to keep up with their payments, they borrowed more money and sank deeper into a hole of their own making.

Grayce knows how badly they screwed up, but she still feels that her family has been trapped by the devil in the detail of the loans they took out. She says there was no reasonable way that she or her husband could have known how quickly their debts would rise, as unpaid interest was added on to the rapidly increasing principal.

'It started out at $550,000, then it became $558,000 and then it was $560,000. We couldn't understand it. We take some of the blame for this, but the people making the loans should have taken the blame as well.'

'We have been to bankruptcy lawyers and property lawyers,' John says, 'and they all say, "We don't understand this loan", so how would we?'

The Coffmans' last hope comes in the form of Connie Der Torossian, who works for the Fair Housing Council of Orange County. She is a former mortgage adviser who now mediates between homeowners facing repossession and the companies from which they borrowed. Her office has been overwhelmed by a surge of enquiries from families in big trouble, but the Coffmans seem to have found a special place in her heart.

The Coffmans greet her like a favourite daughter when she arrives at their house and she responds in kind. But anger rises to her face as she begins to talk. Connie says the big lenders are working flat-out to cope with the nightmare they helped to create, but she can't believe that they didn't see the warnings. The loans they offered were often designed to confuse borrowers. In many cases, loans were made to people with no earthly way of carrying the long-term burden. And yet no one shouted stop.

'This is an expensive place to buy and sub-prime mortgages opened up the market to first-time buyers who couldn't really afford houses selling in the $600,000s. It just couldn't go on.'

When Connie is asked why no one spoke up, she laughs, quickly and bitterly, before speaking at a higher pitch. 'I did. I could see this was going to happen.'

So why didn't they listen?

'Because things were good,' she says, regaining her calm. 'People were making a lot of money.'

Then she pauses, as if she is about to cross some invisible barrier.

'Greed played a part in all this.'

Connie's home turf is ground zero for the sub-prime crisis that has shaken America. Almost half of the 20 biggest sub-prime lenders in the United States were based in Orange County. They targeted aspiring homeowners who were considered to be too great a risk to get loans from mainstream banks, and for a while their business was unbelievably good, especially in their own backyard. One in five houses bought in Orange County in 2006 was bought with sub-prime mortgage funds and some began referring to the suburbs south of Los Angeles as 'mortgage alley'.

There was a nasty, brutish edge to the sub-prime boom in the working-class neighbourhoods of Orange County, where lenders targeted Latino neighbourhoods that they knew had been shunned by the mainstream financial institutions. The highest concentration of sub-prime loans in the county was in the poor, ethnic districts of Santa Ana where 75 per cent of the home loans were sub-prime. The easy money had a name in these neighbourhoods: *la droga*. The narcotic thrill of owning a house with no money down masked the ugly realities of 'piggyback loans', low teaser payments, adjustable-rate loans and prepayment penalties. You got the money, but you would never understand the terms, particularly if English was your second language.

The sub-prime contagion spread across the Sunbelt, turning the property game into a new gold rush. At one point, it was estimated that one in every 53 adults in California had a real-estate licence. In Las Vegas, such was the demand for the services of mortgage brokers that 'every stripper, waiter and bartender on the Strip had a broker's licence', according to one such part-time broker.

One of the driving forces behind the property boom was speculation. A house was not something to be lived in; it was something to be bought and sold quickly, to be 'flipped'. At the height of the madness, there was a TV show called *Flip that House* and a website called condoflip.com with the motto 'Bubbles are for Bathtubs.'

The property gold rush helped sustain the American economy in the testing times that followed 9/11. Between 2001 and 2005, 40 per cent of all jobs created in the US were related to housing. At its height, the property boom was creating 30,000 jobs every month.

As homeowners watched house prices head towards the stratosphere, they began to do what the Coffmans did and borrow against the rising value of their homes; the house would play the role of ATM, providing a ready source of cash that was as safe as, well, houses. Again, the temptation was strongest in Sunbelt states such as California and Nevada where this 'home equity finance' provided an estimated 20 per cent of all disposable income at the end of 2006. In fact, sources in the auto industry reported that 30 per cent of cars sold in California in 2006 were financed with home-equity loans.

Americans had become the most prolific borrowers on earth and no one in power seemed the slightest bit concerned. The financial gurus in New York and Washington were too busy crowing about the unprecedented stability of the American economy. Ben Bernanke, the man who would go on to lead the US Federal Reserve, had a name for it: 'the Great Moderation'. Somebody forgot to tell the homeowners and car buyers and part-time mortgage brokers of the Sunbelt about the moderation part of the equation.

The web of sub-prime insanity began to unravel in early 2007 as repayments began to bite and house prices started to fall. The number of people losing their homes through foreclosure in Orange County rose to its highest level in at least 20 years in the first quarter of 2008. A consumer watchdog called the Center for Responsible Lending estimated that almost one in four sub-prime mortgages made in Orange County in 2007 would end in foreclosure, which would represent 7 per cent of all the homes bought in the county that year.

Right across the Sunbelt, the price of houses nosedived, particularly in the once booming market of Phoenix, which had been a magnet for investors trying to 'flip' properties for a quick buck. By the spring of 2008, one estate agent in the Phoenix suburb of Goodyear was so desperate for business that she was offering a limo tour of investment properties and a free brunch to follow. In Las Vegas, a group of eternally optimistic property dealers created a sightseeing tour called the 'Vegas Foreclosure Express' which gave potential investors a chance to view repossessed houses which had been put back on the market.

The great property rush may have ended in farce but it brought incalculable pain. For citizens' advocates like Connie Der Torossian, it inspires deep, abiding anger. But if Connie has big questions to pose, Grayce and John Coffman don't. They understand that millions of other Americans like them were seduced into high-risk borrowing. They know that an ever-expanding pool of homeowners face foreclosure, just like them. But they are not as mad as hell. When asked why such a thing could happen, in this day and age, John seems confused.

'Really,' he says, shaking his head, 'that is a good question: How is it happening to so many people?'

John might just as well be talking about a flood or a storm, some natural disaster. There is not a trace of anger in his voice when he speaks. Grayce is equally lacking in resentment. Her eyes betray the crushing burden of her ordeal as they drift towards the middle distance; they even teared up briefly when Connie arrived at the door. But she refuses to be riled, since she cannot afford anything but the most uncomplicated emotions. Ask her why she refuses to give in to resentment and she says, 'Anger is not going to get us anywhere. Anyway, when your silences are filled with worry, there is no room for faith.'

John and Grayce seem puzzled by questions about their political views. They come across as conservative but non-judgemental and Republican in the vaguest sense. They are disconnected rather than apathetic. They draw no moral or political lesson from their slide into despair; they seek no help from politicians. When John is asked if his troubles have made him more interested in the presidential election (which is still months away when I meet them), he offers a strangely emphatic 'no', as if he can't bear the thought of false hope. Grayce is only slightly more optimistic.

'Politicians are politicians,' she says, lowering her eyes and throwing a little ironic glance towards her husband, 'but if they do what they promise, we will get back on track.'

'This is going to be a wait-and-see situation,' John says with finality. 'Just really don't know.'

Of all the sad things about the Coffmans' ordeal, the saddest is their profound sense of isolation. Despite Connie Der Torrosian's intervention, they seem to really believe that they are alone and so have ordered their emotions around that fact. Anger would be a wasted energy. Just as it would be pointless to rage against a departing storm that tore your roof off, it makes no sense to the Coffmans to ask bitter questions about an economic system that could sanction predatory lending and encourage reckless borrowing. The Coffmans are at one with their suffering because they believe they will eventually prevail. If not, they will just get on with it. There is no one to blame.

The Coffmans may be naïve in their faith, but they did not deserve the tidal wave of viciousness that would come their way. The *Orange County Register* published their story just before Christmas 2007, setting off a nasty wave of commentary across the United States. Within hours of the *Register* article being published, one of America's leading conservative bloggers, Michelle Malkin, had posted her response, in which she said acidly that if this 'story doesn't send your blood pressure through the roof and have you shouting "Boo Freaking Hoo!" at the top of your lungs, I don't know what will.' Within weeks, the Coffmans were featured on a nationally syndicated list of the 'Top 5 Most Ridiculous Mortgage Borrower Stories of 2007'.

The *Orange County Register* website received almost 100 responses to the original article and almost every one was negative. What these critics chose to see was a big family on social welfare who had made reckless choices and now wanted sympathy. Their story was 'bogus heart-tugging drivel' said one commentator. 'Geez, the entire story just makes me sick!' said another. Clearly having gorged on the milk of human kindness, one contributor asked how anyone could 'feel sorry for these incredibly shallow, shortsighted, immature, nonthinking knuckleheads'.

As the commentary focused on John and Grayce's decision to take custody of their grandchildren, the tone got darker. One contributor wrote a 'six-point to do' list for the Coffmans which included advice to 'get off the government dole; we're tired of paying for your kids, loser!!!'. 'I have no sympathy for these folks. NONE,' read another posting. 'I have no doubt they failed to teach their own children responsibility, which is why they have so many adopted grandchildren.'

With varying degrees of outrage, the contributors advised the

Coffmans to get a job and give up their house (or be forced out) to pay for the debt. A constant theme was a fierce resistance to any state aid for the family. 'I'll be damned if a penny of my tax goes to help these kinds of family out!' said one contributor, while another warned that 'if they get bailed out by some bleeding hearts, that will just really get under my skin'.

Once again, we are reminded of what it is like to live in a Frontier society which worships self-reliance. Good things happen to good people. Failure is a reminder that you are not trying hard enough. This is easy to believe in the good times, but when times get tough, failure is harder to rationalise. When someone just as decent and hard-working as you gets into difficulty, obvious questions arise. Did they fail or did the system fail them? Can people like me really have faith in the American dream?

It is easier to cope with doubt if you can blame bad times on the personal short-comings of weak people. The more you believe in their failure, the more secure you become about your own security and personal virtue. Take the Coffmans as an example: by focusing on their recklessness, the critics turned this family tragedy into a morality tale. It served to reassure us that bad things like foreclosure happen only to bad people.

With their bitter words, the critics dispelled any lingering doubts about the American dream. 'This country offers Life, Liberty and the Pursuit of Happiness,' wrote one of the Coffmans' critics, 'not three hots and a cot. Maybe the children WILL learn from this experience IF the family is displaced. We work for what we have and respect the property of others.'

By heaping condemnation on the Coffmans, the critics removed the need to answer the other troubling questions posed by this family's misfortune: what kind of company would extend such dangerous loans? What kind of financial system would encourage such lending? By attacking the Coffmans, the critics vented pent-up rage at the unfolding sub-prime insanity in a way that would not cast doubt over the unregulated economic freedom that spawned it.

What was significant about the backlash was the absence of solidarity from other struggling middle-class homeowners. Perhaps the most unsettling comment came from a woman who described herself as 'a single mommy'. She said she would love the resources the Coffmans had access to: 'This story makes me madder every time I read it. I am glad they are not my neighbours because I really don't think I would be able to keep my mouth shut.'

This is the dark side of America's egalitarian impulse. People desperately need to feel that they are competing on a level playing field, so there is an enormous opposition to any group which demands an extra advantage, for whatever reason. That fierce resistance comes in many forms, including objections to preferences for racial minorities, and it seems to intensify in times of recession. The harder you have to struggle, the more you resent handouts to others.

It is not that Americans are less generous than other nationalities – 70 per cent of American households make charitable contributions every year, donating an average of 3.5 per cent of their income. Total charitable giving in the United States now stands at $260 billion a year, which is double what it was in 1995. But while Americans are more philanthropic than ever, they pay less tax and their government spends less on social programmes than most other developed nations. Individuals still want to have a say in who is deserving, rather than leaving it to the collective to make the decision.

In the Coffmans' case, the verdict was swift and brutal. The family were easy targets for resentment and rage, but they were also the wrong targets. They made mistakes, but they are a decent, generous and honourable family. There was no calculation in their decision to go public with their story. They asked for nothing, not charity and not a government handout. They were not complainers, just the opposite; in their eyes, endurance was the ultimate virtue.

Just occasionally a ray of light shone on the dark portrait painted by the critics. A former neighbour of the Coffmans wrote to the *Orange County Register* and described them as 'the most giving people in the universe!'. 'They have never asked for charity or any type of financial bailout from anyone and have always tried to simply make ends meet! Even they will admit that they have made some financial mistakes along the way, but to suggest that they did so out of greed is simply ridiculous.' This tribute to the Coffmans was the exception: scorn was the rule.

What happened to this family points to an historic volatility in American public life. The people of the United States 'are liable to swift and vehement outbursts of feeling', wrote the great Belfast-born historian James Bryce in the late 19th century. 'Americans have what chemists call low specific heat; they grow warm suddenly and cool as suddenly.'

Bad times tend to lead to outbursts of moral panic. Tremendous energy is spent searching for villains and heroes, which tends to weaken the common ground between normal, flawed mortals. Americans are encouraged to cling to the certainties of their lives, like nationalism or race. Tribal loyalties become more important. Society divides into sub-sets. Sympathy is rationed. Prejudice flourishes.

You can see that tendency in the way people reacted to the Coffmans, but can we draw a broader conclusion here? Does the bitter, anti-social impulse we have just seen at work in Orange County threaten to overwhelm the renewal of America's civic instincts we have witnessed all across the Sunbelt Frontier? Because if it did, all our talk of reinvention and realignment would be premature. We need to work out just how bad the bad times really are and just how much they will change the perpetual certainties of American life.

—•—

America has only two social classes: the middle class and the rich. There is no upper class, lower middle class, nouveau riche, bourgeoisie or peasantry. Most emphatically, there is no working class. If you strive, you are middle class, whether you live in a trailer park in Kentucky or a big suburban house in Arizona.

But the definition of rich became a lot more elastic in the years before the crash of 2008. In the old days, if you could afford luxury without feeling pain, then you were rich. But luxury became a mass market, and you needed a lot more money to feel special. In 2005 alone, 227,000 Americans became millionaires. At about the same time, there were as many millionaires in North Carolina (population 8:8 million) as there were in India (population 1,130 million). Not even $1 billion bought you exclusivity any more. Back in 1985, there were just 13 billionaires in the United States. By the tail end of the Bush years, there were more than a 1,000.

Spare a sympathetic thought for the genuinely rich American. Their luxury yacht was no longer the biggest in the marina and their private jet had to jostle for a parking space. What they really needed was a smaller and more exclusive club to become members of. According to Robert Frank of the *Wall Street Journal* that club has became its own country. In his bestseller, *Richistan*, he said that the wealthiest Americans were 'building a self-contained world, with its own health-care system (concierge doctors), travel system (private jets, destination clubs) and language. ("Who's your household manager?") They had created their own breakaway republic – one I called Richistan.'

During his travels in Richistan, Frank came across companies selling $600,000 watches and $320,000 cars and $47 million private jets. He met a property billionaire who had two identical Rolls Royces in his driveway. 'The two-ton one, that's my restaurant car,' the billionaire told Frank. 'You get a better parking space [from the valets].' All told, Frank said, America's richest 0.5 per cent were spending $650 billion a year in the first decade of the 21st century, which was about equal to total household spending in Italy.

So, Richistan was doing pretty well. But what about those left behind in that middle-class nation called America? According to the US census, prosperity touched the lives of almost all Americans between 1993 and 2003. During that decade, the bottom fifth of US society saw their average income rise by 13 per cent, but, apart from a slight drop in poverty in 2006, the good news ended there.

By almost every measure, the gap between rich and poor in the United States has widened by an historic degree in recent decades. If you were in the top fifth of earners in 1973, you earned 10 times as much as someone in the bottom fifth. By 2003, you would be earning almost 15 times as much.

But it was among the super-rich that things began to get crazy. By the time Wall Street reached its peak, the richest 1 per cent of Americans earned roughly 20 per cent of all income and controlled 33 per cent of all the wealth. In fact, they had more money and assets than the bottom 90 per cent of Americans put together. The last time there was such a concentration of wealth in the hands of America's super-rich was at the tail end of the 'Gilded Age', just after the First World War.

The citizens of Richistan did very well out of the drive towards privatisation, deregulation and free markets which characterised the so-called Great Moderation. Chief executives and hedge-fund managers became the new Rockefellers and Vanderbilts, and they kept much more of their income thanks to the tax breaks of the Bush years. The breathtaking inequality of all this was exposed by Warren Buffet, the world's third-richest man, during a speech in June 2007. He revealed he had paid 18 per cent tax on his income the previous year. His secretary paid 30 per cent. He earned $46 million; his secretary had an income of $60,000. Could this be the same America which President Lincoln promised in the Gettysburg Address would be 'dedicated to the proposition that all men are created equal'?

In any other Western nation, such a yawning chasm between rich and poor would have led to reform, if not rebellion. There have been some stirrings of a populist revolt in Washington. One of the most effective American political speeches of recent years came from Virginia Senator Jim Webb in January 2007. In the Democratic response to President Bush's State of the Union address, he said that the average corporate chief executive made 20 times what the average worker did when Webb graduated from college – but now it's nearly 400 times more.

North Carolina Senator John Edwards staked his presidential ambitions in 2008 on the notion that there were 'two Americas'. He cast the election as 'a choice between corporate power and the power of democracy'. He told middle-class Americans that they were being ravaged by corporate abuse: 'The truth is that corporate greed is stealing your children's future as sure as I'm standing here.' The fact that a mainstream Democratic candidate like Edwards would adopt such challenging rhetoric is a sign of the growing appetite for change in America. But Edwards departed early from the 2008 presidential race, proving that there are big obstacles to any populist uprising.

Traditionally, the first limitation is the American definition of inequality. What is traditionally meant by 'equality' in the US is equality of opportunity. In other words, every citizen is entitled to an equal shot at the American dream but not necessarily an equal share of America's wealth.

Rich people are an inspiration in the United States in a way they will never be in Europe. They are reminders that all the striving and pursuing has a tangible pay-off. In the words of tycoon Ted Turner, 'life is a game and money is how we keep score'. By that definition, the visible gap between rich and poor becomes a running total that can be changed during the course of the game as long as you think like a champion.

Less than one in three Americans think that the state should reduce income disparities, and that is because they tend to see inequality as a matter of individual performance rather than a system failure. But before we pronounce the populist cause dead, it is worth looking at the fine print of the American definition of equality. Remember, Americans do not believe in equality of outcome, but they do believe passionately in equality of opportunity: everyone must get an equal shot. The gap between rich and poor is acceptable only if the poor have a chance of catching up.

This is what we mean when we talk of an American dream: the notion that the United States is a land of opportunity where each successive generation will do better than the last. The dream is, in the words of Texas political scientist Cal Jillson, the 'gyroscope of American life'. If, for some reason, this guarantee of upward mobility was removed from life, America would be diminished. And what would happen then? Would the players demand a change in the way the game was played?

There are signs that the American dream has reached a roadblock. The statistics reveal that social mobility has begun to suffer as the gap between rich and poor has widened. Millions of poor Americans still climb out of the ranks of poverty each year but not enough to validate the grand aspirations of the dream. In 2008, the Pew Foundation released a groundbreaking report on economic mobility and found that the United States is now less economically mobile than many other rich countries.

The capacity of the poorest children to do better than their parents is now considerably weaker in America than it is in Denmark, Norway, Finland, Sweden and the United Kingdom. In America, there is a 42 per cent chance that if a father is stuck in the bottom fifth of earners, his son will get stuck there too. In Denmark, the equivalent odds are 25 per cent; in Britain, it's 30 per cent.

No matter how you define equality, no matter how you view success or failure, there is undeniably a weakness at the heart of the American dream, and with the advent of economic crisis, more and more Americans realise it.

Even before the financial and property crash, a CBS/*New York Times* opinion poll found that more Americans believed their country was off track than at any time since the question had first been asked in 1991. Buried in the detail of the survey were answers that cast doubt over the prevalence of the American dream. Just 46 per cent of parents said that they expected their children to enjoy a better standard of living than they had, a 10 per cent drop since 2005. When asked in general terms about prospects for the next generation, just one in three of all those surveyed said that they would live better than people do today.

This growing sense of pessimism looks like it could be the beginning of a shift in American priorities. Whatever the Coffman case told us, the opinion polls suggest that Americans are beginning to reconsider their relationship with failure and inequality.

We know that the critics in Orange County firmly opposed government handouts for homeowners burdened with debt. But in that CBS/*New York Times* poll in 2008, 53 per cent said that the government should help those coping with rising interest rates. There were also signs in the same survey that attitudes to government were shifting: 58 per cent of those surveyed said that households making more than $250,000 should pay more tax; while 43 per cent of those surveyed said that they would prefer a larger government that provided more services (the number supporting that idea has never been higher).

As you might expect, the trends are most pronounced among the Millennials, who have become increasingly worried about economic decline (the economy ranked well above Iraq as the number one issue for young people in the early stages of the 2008 presidential election). In a poll published in the summer of 2007, just one in four 17- to 29-year-olds said that their generation would be better off than their parents.

If there is fear of an uncertain future among Millennials, you do not hear angry populist rhetoric from this generation. Instead, the priority is adaptation. Where previous generations lusted after well-paid, secure jobs that would last a lifetime, the Millennials' career path is, in the words of one commentator, 'more like a maze than a straight line'. Where Baby Boomers felt betrayed by the disappearance of lifetime guarantees, Millennials accept that as a starting point.

What young Americans are becoming increasingly intolerant of are poverty and inequality. In contrast to previous generations, they know more about, and care more about, these problems. In a 2004 poll, 84 per cent of Millennials said that the gap between rich and poor had grown over the previous two decades, and 94 per cent thought that was a bad thing.

Just as 9/11 was a defining event in the lives of Millennials, so was Hurricane Katrina, which brutally exposed the fault lines of race and poverty. It was a media spectacle without parallel and the fifth most closely followed story of the past 20 years in the United States. It was an event which, according to an editorial in the *Los Angeles Times*, might well prove to be 'a watershed in the debate over poverty, largely because it provided a window into the life of the poor that was more visceral and intimate than most Americans ever witness'.

The abject failure of state agencies in New Orleans may have further degraded faith in government among some Americans, but not among the Millennials. It only seems to have increased their appetite for an official response to poverty and inequality. A year after Katrina, a survey found that 'transitional Millennials' (those between the ages of 18 and 22) were more likely than any other age group to favour governmental action to reduce economic differences among Americans.

With each successive poll of young Americans, there is fresh evidence that we are at a turning point. Millennials are just as self-reliant as previous generations, if not more so, but they want collective solutions to problems long ignored by their leaders. That's great news for liberal groups such as the Center for American Progress, which published a remarkable poll in May 2008. Among many other questions, it asked if the government should spend more on health care and education and other social services, even if that meant rising taxes. The Millennials said yes by margins not seen in the 20 years these questions have featured in opinion polls. The study also found that the number of young people who wanted the government to provide more services had jumped by 25 per cent in the space of a decade.

The surveys confirm what we already knew about the Millennials: they want civic solutions to America's problems. They may worry about the long-term health of their nation but have none of the caustic fear which has eaten away at America during past crises. In their particular balance of Frontier and Ritual, self-reliance and solidarity pose no contradictions.

Sooner or later the Millennial instincts will eventually collide with the fearful streak in the American psyche. Probably sooner. To understand the speed and momentum of the unfolding transformation, we have to set the potential of the Millennials

189

against competing instincts that linger in America's subconscious. And we have to come to terms with the existential rage that contaminates its psyche in the midst of an economic storm.

—•—

The Coffmans eventually negotiated a deal with their mortgage providers. At time of writing, they still live in Fullerton with their six grandchildren, two dachshunds and a goldfish called Jaws.

On the other side of America, on Florida's Atlantic Coast, there is no happy ending for the occupants of 3301 Community Drive. The house is set halfway down a pristine row, in a freshly minted development in the rejuvenated tropical suburb of Jupiter.

Real-estate agent Peggy Berkoff is waiting for us in the morning sun. She wears a south Florida smile which cheers you the moment it is flashed in your general direction. She is an unlikely spokesperson for the economic pain of an increasing number of Americans, but also an authentic eyewitness to the angry pandemic of foreclosure.

Peggy is speaking in the dying days of the 2008 election, but she says the bitterness has yet to fully percolate through the political consciousness of her nation. 'People are angry at the lenders and people are angry at the government,' she tells me. 'And I think some people are angry at themselves that they allowed themselves to get into a property that they just couldn't afford. People didn't realise that eventually the music was going to stop and they were going to be left without the chair.'

Peggy brings us up the pathway of 3301 Community Drive and opens the black plastic padlock on the door. As the door swings open, and the November light streams in, the mayhem is immediately apparent. The rug in the front room is covered in dark stains, clothes, food cartons and cigarette boxes. Peggy warns me not to go near the kitchen. This is good advice. It smells of putrefied food and rage.

The former occupant was the owner of a small business who couldn't afford his mortgage payments. He was forced to hand the house back to the bank, which is now 'short selling': getting rid of the house at a vastly reduced price (in this case as much as $250,000 less than its $400,000 peak value).

All around is evidence of a happy family torn asunder. On the ground in the master bedroom are anniversary cards and a register of wedding guests. Peggy tells me the owner's wife left him shortly before he left the house. He lived here with his three children. And they still haunt this place. On the ground in an upstairs bedroom is a schoolbag with the name 'Shawn' written on it. In the other bedroom, a mirror has been wrenched from its hinges and broken.

'I could show you a dozen of these houses with all levels of destruction,' she says. 'We've gone into houses where they have taken hammers to the walls.' Peggy pauses to look around the bedroom at the detritus of a life and says wearily, 'It's sad. It's really sad.'

In the hallway between bedrooms, there are portraits of the two eldest children at Disney World. In one photo, the little girl is hugging Minnie Mouse. In a far corner of the front bedroom, there is a half-used bag of nappies and a changing mat. I think of my own children and feel like running as far as I can from that house. But you can't run from 3301 Community Drive. There is nowhere to run. Perhaps only a small proportion of Americans will face foreclosure, but every single person has a story of economic hurt. Just ask Peggy Berkoff.

'My brother told me a story of a woman crying at the gas station as she was filling her tank. Ordinary people are trying to figure out how to buy groceries, how to make their housing

191

payments, how to provide health care to their families. Politicians are out of touch. They just really don't understand.'

Obama understood well enough to win the presidency. He did so by persuading enough insecure people that the only way to find sanctuary from their economic woes was to embrace change. Now that he is in power, he shoulders an enormous burden. If he doesn't live up to his promise, the putrid rage in that house on Community Drive, and the violent ill-will that washed over the Coffmans, will surely overwhelm him.

In a strange way, Obama needs words, not just action. He needs to find language to express the bitterness that comes with an economic reckoning, just as Franklin Roosevelt did back in 1933. In his inaugural address, FDR channelled popular resentment of the economic elite during the Great Depression, railing against the 'incompetence' of the money-changers 'who have fled their high seats in the temple of civilization'.

As Obama began his term in office, Americans were losing homes, jobs, retirement funds and confidence in the American dream. But at the very same time, they were reading headlines about the continuing excess of the crumbling economic elite: $18 billion in bonuses to Wall Street executives in 2008; $35,000 spent on a chest of drawers for the Merrill Lynch CEO; private jets ferrying car manufacturers to Washington for a taxpayer bailout.

During his inaugural address, Barack Obama briefly mentioned 'greed and irresponsibility', but he framed the recession as a 'collective failure to make hard choices'. It was a restrained response, full of the soothing spirit of Ritual, spoken in the temperate tone of the Millennial generation. And yet these are intemperate times for those on a bitterly cold Frontier. Obama would do well to consider the sharp edge of the American psyche and to learn a lesson from history: a leader must channel the anger of his people or ultimately fall victim to it.

9.
Tombstone – Stirring the Melting Pot

Carmen Mercer is itching to go. Lunch service is over at the O.K. Café and she is ready to get the hell out of Tombstone. By day, she serves up half-pound buffalo burgers and by night she defends freedom on the boundary with Mexico.

Carmen pulls her silver Chevy pick-up out of its parking space and winds her way through the streets of this legendary Arizona town. 'The town too tough to die' has been consumed by make-believe. Just a few blocks along Allen Street, between the O.K. Corral and Big Nose Kate's saloon, the actors recreate gunfights from frontier days for the benefit of the tourists. Carmen drives away from the staged drama with a real-life Colt .45 holstered in her custom leather gun belt.

Carmer Mercer is vice-president of a self-appointed border militia, the Minutemen, and also their chief fundraiser and national recruiter. She is a big noise in the movement against illegal immigration but seems to relish the chance to be just another volunteer patrolling that border. After all, that is what the Minutemen are all about: putting patriotic bodies on that frontier, to raise an alarm, to call attention to the invasion of America. Ultimately, Carmen feels that the federal government will be forced to build a tall wall along the entire 2,000-mile border from the Pacific Ocean to the Gulf of Mexico. But for now, she knows her place, and it is in that silver Chevy driving towards Mexico.

'It's not the immigration we are against, it is the illegal side of it.'

Carmen is dressed in a black Minutemen T-shirt and blue jeans. She is small and has a boyish blonde haircut. She is in her early fifties but has the air of a studious teenager.

'How can you come into a country, sneak into a country, and then expect that you can have that American dream?'

There is something about the clipped, efficient way Carmen pronounces the letter 's' which gives her away. She is not from around these parts. She was born and raised in a small town near Cologne in Germany. She came to Ohio as a 17-year-old student in the 1970s, and after meeting the US soldier who would become her husband, she moved from base to base, from Florida to North Carolina to New Mexico and then to Arizona.

Eventually Carmen divorced and moved to Tombstone in 1992, taking over the O.K. Café a couple of years later. She had no hard and fast plans to become a US citizen until she got involved in local town politics. She was naturalised in 1999, almost a quarter of a century after coming to America.

'For me, part of my gratitude to the American people is to do something about this illegal immigration.'

If Carmen still feels like an outsider in this country, she doesn't show it. She smiles with the confidence of a woman who has found her calling. Her voice overflows with the positive energy of gratitude and born-again patriotism. There is no rage when she talks, no audible resentment.

'This is still a wonderful country. I know. I work with patriots every day.'

Carmen's destination is a ridge overlooking the border near an unofficial fence that the Minutemen have erected at their own expense. Carmen gets out of the pick-up with her binoculars in her hand and her Colt .45 hanging from her hip. She stares down the ugly gash ripping through the verdant desert foliage which separates the United States from Mexico.

'This is where we did our first operation, right here on this very line. We stayed here for 30 days and got incredible attention.'

She is smiling wistfully, as if the memory of a childhood romance has just popped into her head.

'It's been a battle, but a rewarding battle.'

The battle began just after 9/11 when Carmen and another Tombstone businessman founded a neighbourhood-watch group to beef up border security.

'All of a sudden people realised what was happening. We realised how many people were breaking into this country.'

Within a couple of years, Carmen's group had 400 members. They eventually became the Minutemen and membership soared to 9,000. As her volunteers spread out across the border with their lawn chairs and binoculars, Carmen became involved in lobbying against an immigration-reform bill which would have given illegal immigrants a path to amnesty. She spent five weeks in Washington with a coalition of conservative and anti-immigrant groups successfully campaigning for its defeat.

Carmen doesn't have the same bipolar quality you often notice in right-wing activists, that same low specific heat moving from instant boil to sudden freeze. Perhaps it is the Teutonic blood in her veins which enables her to express her thoughts in a steady, temperate tone. Yet when you try to pin down the impulses that motivate her, a chill creeps into the conversation.

Carmen doesn't spend a lot of time making the economic argument against immigration; there are no angry declarations that Mexicans are taking American jobs. Instead, the images of 9/11 persist. Carmen sees illegal immigration as part of a broader attack on the United States, not just on its borders but on its way of life.

'When people came to Ellis Island they were registered. I

believe this wave of immigration is different. Because they sneak in illegally, I believe they will not respect our laws and will not respect the traditions that made this country.'

Carmen's even-tempered veneer hides something darker. She begins to speak with disturbing certainty about tales of sickness and disease. For example, she says, the growing use of pacemakers is linked to an illness carried by immigrants: 'I waited two years to become a citizen. I went through a thorough health check and, believe you me, none of these illegals have gone through these checks. We have diseases entering this country again which are very deadly. We have strains of TB which can't be treated with a simple antibiotic. We have parasites that enter the person's heart and kill them. I have five grandkids and I am very passionate about health, so these issues are very important to me.'

And as we stare at the border in the late-afternoon sun, we travel through Carmen's deepest fears, from pandemic all the way through to terrorism.

'We know that al-Qaeda members have been stopped trying to get into this country, so the threat is there, absolutely.'

Looking towards that border, that straight line through the dirt, it becomes clear what it must look like to Carmen. It is a vortex spewing out all the evil that threatens her idealised version of America. On the other side, there is dark matter waiting to assume human shape and burrow its way into the very foundations of the shining city. Carmen spent her whole life searching for her sanctuary. She cannot bear to see her dream soiled, contaminated, by the sum of all her fears. And so she stands there on the frontier, waving her arms, flying a flag, making enough noise to attract the attention of a slumbering city behind her.

A helicopter comes out of nowhere. A flash of blue and white passing over Carmen's silver Chevy, following that dirt-brown gash in the desert. As she stares into her binoculars like a jumpy sentry, an ambulance drives by, kicking up a cloud of dirt and filling it with luminous red and blue lights. There is no siren, which suggests that this is not yet an emergency. There may still be time to find out what's going on.

At an even speed, Carmen follows the straight line of the border until she sees the helicopter resting in a clearing beside the ambulance and a vehicle with the green and white livery of the official Border Patrol. The aircraft's rotors are still turning quickly, but there is no sign of activity.

Carmen gets out of her pick-up and saunters into the brush to find someone to talk to but returns within a couple of minutes.

'I don't know what's happening. He's not telling me. We found a water bottle so it must involve illegal aliens.'

The helicopter has started to shift slightly on the ground and within seconds it jerks skyward, falling into a broad sweeping turn away from the border and towards the thick desert vegetation. The pilot is looking for something, or someone.

Carmen has no more fearful stories to tell now. She speaks with some sympathy about the plight of the individuals she wants to keep out of her country, about those exploited by the human smugglers, the coyotes.

'They are dropped here by the *coyotes* and told that Tucson is over the hill. But it's still 120 miles away and all they have with them is a half-bottle of water.'

When she is asked for a specific case which might illustrate the dangers, her eyes seem to flicker a little as if she is running through a rolling index of horror.

'Our group has found a lot of dead bodies. Just recently we came across a couple. The man was an amputee. He had been left wandering for days and had blisters on the stump where his prosthesis used to be.'

197

It is not the savagery of the image which shocks most. It is the coexistence of compassion and fear in Carmen's monologue. She and her volunteers see such evil in that border; they imagine mortal danger in those who cross it; they rage against the politicians who will not build a wall to keep them out. And yet at the very same time they see themselves as saviours, both of a nation's integrity and the lives of those who would soil it.

'We always carry water and food and have saved about 350 lives.'

There is that wistful smile on Carmen's face again, as if such acts of humanity help the Minutemen as much as the illegals.

'This is the rewarding part. When you can help save lives.'

—•—

About 100 miles west of Tombstone, just south of Tucson, the hard tarmac has just given way to the soft sand of a desert track. As far as the eye will take you there are creosote bushes and saguaro and cholla cacti pushing all the way to the shimmering outline of mountains and presumably Mexico.

At the wheel of the heavy blue truck is Pastor Robin Hoover, singing slowly to himself to the tune of 'Rawhide': 'Rollin' Rollin' Rollin', boy, my ass is swollen.'

He is that kind of man of God, profane and passionate. In spite of his rough mouth and his simple workshirt and baseball cap, the pastor carries himself with pride and distinction. As we bounce over the pockmarked track, he leans forward on the steering wheel until his pale beard and dark glasses are almost touching the windscreen.

'I'm looking for the station, which should be right around … '

He leans back with resignation on his face.

'Somebody has obviously taken the flag down.'

Pastor Robin Hoover is the founder of and guiding light for

an organisation called Humane Borders, which maintains a network of emergency water stations in the desert. Each station contains two 58-gallon drums of water and has a blue flag on a 30-foot pole to indicate its position. They are dotted along Arizona's Avara Valley, which leads all the way to the Mexican city of Altar, the main staging post for people trying to cross the border. 'More people will successfully cross through this valley every year,' says the pastor, 'than live in the city of Tucson, which has over 600,000 people.' This desolate, scorched stretch of desert is what the pastor calls the 'Grand Central Station' of migration.

The pastor pulls his vehicle to a stop on the soft verge of the desert track and leans towards the passenger window to get a better look.

'Ha, ha, ha …' He laughs with emphatic bitterness and then says in a rough, Texan accent: 'It's gone.'

The pastor gets out and unlocks the back of his blue truck where he keeps the replacement equipment.

'There's another station up here a couple of miles and I think we are going to experience the same thing. It's hunting season so we've had hundreds of people through here in the last couple of days.'

There is nothing where the water station used to be except for the word 'bitches', which the vandals have scrawled in the sand. The pastor chooses not to dwell on the destruction, and with another volunteer called Paul, he unloads two empty water drums and starts to draw the hose out of the back of the truck to fill them.

'Out here, water is like gold. It is the most valuable commodity there is,' he says. But too many people find that out the hard way. 'Many of these migrants have no knowledge of the desert before they get here. People say they should know better. Well, it's not in their lived experience to be in a place like this, to walk for four hours and not see another human being, or water for that matter.'

The pastor holds the metal-tipped head of the hose a few inches from the mouth of the barrel and a dappled column of water flows through the plastic opening. Humane Borders supplies 30,000 gallons of water to undocumented immigrants trekking through the Avara Valley every year.

'Every day between January and May, 6,500 people begin a trek into Arizona alone. During the summer, the number falls to 600 but that is when most of the water is drunk. That is when someone dies out here every day.'

The pastor says that back in 1995 there were no recorded deaths on the Arizona border but, in 2007, 300 people will die crossing the frontier. They are victims of an immigration policy that seems to lurch back and forth like a punch-drunk boxer, pummelled from one side by angry appeals for a crack-down and clobbered from another by the impossible demands of a vast, porous border.

Back in the 1990s, the authorities came up with a compromise: they would pour all their resources into a blockade of illegal crossings in Texas and California. That would solve the bigger problem since no one would be foolish enough to try to cross through the hellish conditions of Arizona's Sonora Desert, where temperatures can reach 50°C during summer days and fall far below freezing on winter nights. But they obviously didn't understand the *coyotes*. The smuggler gangs switched routes and began to channel hundreds of thousands of men, women and children across the Arizona frontier. The result is that 3,100 people have died along this stretch of border country since 1998.

Looking back, the authorities either dangerously underestimated the desperation that drives the migrants or wilfully decided to raise the price of admission to America. Pastor Hoover pulls no punches when he describes the surge of migration through his valley. 'They have been pushed here by the policies of law enforcement,' he says. 'Policy-makers have deliberately chosen tactics that will lead to the death of many migrants.'

The official figures speak of a quiet carnage. The Government Accountability Office has said the number of migrants who died crossing the US border with Mexico reached a high of 472 in 2005. But in Pima County, which includes the Tucson area, the death toll continues to rise. The county's medical examiner dealt with the deaths of 177 people crossing the border in the first eight months of 2007, more than the same period in 2005. His office spends up to $200,000 every year and deploys ten staff to care for and identify the bodies of those who die. In the summer of 2005, there were so many bodies they had to buy an 18-wheeler truck to store them. Since then, the county has built a refrigerated mortuary.

Pastor Hoover spends a lot of the time talking in cold figures but occasionally there is a searing flash of anger. 'This is a phenomenal human tragedy,' he says with feeling. 'These are not numbers; they are human beings.'

The pastor founded Humane Borders back in 2000 out of the church that he runs in Tucson. There had been a rash of migrant deaths in the desert outside town and the pastor was moved in particular by the story of one young woman who gave the last of her water to her infant child. She died but her child survived.

Now Humane Borders has more than 63 trained drivers and 8,000 volunteers who maintain 87 water stations on both sides of the border. The group distributes maps in Mexico and Central America that show the location of water stations and emergency beacons. It also marks the sites of migrant deaths and carries a warning: 'Don't do it. There's not enough water. Don't pay the penalty.'

Ultimately, the group is driven forward by the potent technicolour personality of Pastor Robin Hoover. He is perfectly suited to the savagery of this hidden border war. He grew up in the West Texas town of Big Spring and is full of the contradictions that shape that harsh corner of America. On the one hand, he is a plain-spoken working man who has held jobs in nursing, photography and construction. But he is also a social activist; before he moved to Tucson, he ministered to border communities in the Rio Grande Valley. At the very same time he is an uncompromising intellectual with three university degrees, including a doctorate in political science.

He is both hero and villain and seems to enjoy both personae. He speaks with pride about the Human Rights award he received from the Mexican President Felipe Calderón. But he also seems to draw energy from the hatred directed his way by the Minutemen, who accuse him of 'sedition' and 'aiding and abetting criminal activity'.

There is a touch of the bare-knuckle bruiser about him. You quickly realise it is very easy to get on his wrong side, which is a cold and scary place. 'I'm a religious man but I am not a pious man,' he says, steering his truck through the desert. 'I will call a chicken fucker a chicken fucker.' He grew up just a half-hour's drive from George W. Bush's hometown of Midland, but he is a million miles from its narrow conservatism. 'Bush is all West Texas,' he says. 'There is no blood in him.'

Language is clearly important to Pastor Hoover. He prefers to call the phenomenal surge of people across that border 'migration' rather than 'immigration'. He refuses to use the word 'illegal' to describe the people who cross. And when it comes to his views of the Minutemen, he resists the urge to utter obscenities and chooses to call them 'vigilantes of fear'.

The pastor accepts that the trigger for the current wave of anti-immigrant sentiment in America was 9/11, but he has no time for the powerful existential vulnerability that came with it. Instead, he chooses to focus on the Machiavellian urge of leaders who manipulated the surge of nationalism that followed the attack on the Twin Towers.

'This is a resistance fuelled by cultural imperialism. But, more importantly, it is being fuelled by politicians who feel that anti-migrant sentiment is good for their electoral prospects.'

While you don't hear much talk of economics from Carmen Mercer, the pastor believes that people like her are searching for scapegoats at a time of increasing uncertainty. They blame the migrants from Mexico without even understanding who they are. 'These are not just the poorest of the poor,' he says. 'Not all of them come for low-wage jobs. These are people making a significant contribution to our economy.'

Look at the border through the eyes of Pastor Robin Hoover and you see that it offers no protection. It is an impediment, a blockage in an otherwise healthy artery, bringing nothing but pain to the heart of American life.

'If you want to increase national security, if you are worried by the illegal side of it, just give them a visa.'

It took the pastor a single step to get to that conclusion. He has little time for anyone who can't make the same leap of faith, especially the likes of Carmen Mercer.

'There are people who come down here and sit on their lawn chairs and strap on their .45s and talk big. They have been run over by globalisation and don't know what else to do.'

If only it were that simple.

—•—

Carmen Mercer has her video camera held just far enough from her face so that she can see the screen sticking out from the side. She is well pleased with what she sees.

'It seems like it is double panels and they are very tight together. Very effective.'

Carmen sounds like a teacher praising a model student. She walks towards the new stretch of government-built fence, holding her camera as she goes, providing a running commentary.

'And I would say it is almost 15 feet high also.'

The fence is made up of tall black plastic poles and narrow mesh. It looks fragile but not to Carmen.

'That's concrete at the base, so they can't dig underneath, so it's, eh … a good construction.'

The evening sun warms Carmen's face. She looks as if she is close to tears. The new stretch of wall will run for 30 miles of that 2,000-mile frontier.

'I am glad to see it … finally happening. Absolutely.'

—•—

E pluribus unum. It is the most important phrase in the American lexicon: out of many, one. You'll find the phrase on the dollar bill and the humble cent as a gentle reminder to the common people of the United States that there is strength in difference. But it is also a warning that without a regular transfusion of fresh blood, America would not be America.

Immigration brings constant renewal but also the clash of opposites which makes the US such an unnerving spectacle. To better understand the American experience of immigration, it helps to revisit our hidden code, that tension between Frontier and Ritual. To become an American, the immigrant must play the role of pioneer and make the journey across the frontier. Once safely across, they must immerse themselves in the rituals which transform a foreigner into an American, a pioneer into a settler. But at both stages of this process, there are recurring problems with each successive wave of immigration. The first point of conflict is described best by Andro Linklater in *The Fabric of America*. He sums up American history as a dynamic and difficult interaction between 'those already inside the frontier who naturally wish to preserve what is there, and those who want to cross the frontier and will inevitably alter the existing state of things'.

The second recurring battle arises from the impact of immigration on the rituals that form the American identity. By its very nature, immigration is a process of creative destruction in which old rituals are pushed aside in favour of new ones. What strikes one observer as a fine blend of cultures will look like an unappetising mess to another. Irish poet and songwriter Thomas Moore visited the United States in the early years of the 19th century and was repelled by what he saw:

> Tis one dull chaos, one unfertile strife
> Betwixt half-polish'd and half-barbarous life;
> Where every ill the ancient world could brew
> Is mix'd with every grossness of the new.

If that is what the melting pot looks like to an outsider, what does it feel like to be up to your neck in its slow simmer? According to historian Michael Kammen, Americans have always 'vacillated between self-praise for being a nation of immigrants and self-hate for the stations of restless locomotion through which we daily pass'.

The self-hate has been most intense during the three great waves of immigration that have changed American history, in the 1850s, 1880s and early years of the 20th century. That first great wave is the one with which the Irish are most familiar, since it coincides with our own post-Famine exodus. Historians record the first mention of immigration as a source of party political controversy in 1848 and, within a few years, America has its first explicitly anti-immigrant movement, the Know Nothings.

By the end of 1854, two million Irish had arrived in the United States and many more were to follow. In 1856, the Know Nothing candidate, Millard Fillmore, won more than a fifth of all the votes cast in that year's presidential election. Anti-immigrant forces were so strong that it looked as if they might take control of the emerging Republican Party. But, in the end, the Republicans became the party of Abraham Lincoln and other, more pressing issues, like civil war, removed immigration from the political agenda. This cycle seems to repeat itself with each successive wave of immigration. A surge in new arrivals triggers a rise in anti-immigrant sentiment. The panic eventually peaks and then wanes, while the new immigrants settle down and change America for the better.

What we are witnessing today is a fourth great wave of immigration surging onto American shores. The US Census Bureau calculates that one American is born every 7 seconds, one dies every 13 seconds and an immigrant arrives every 31 seconds. America is expected to add another 100 million to its population during the next 40 years and a growing share of the new citizens will have been born somewhere else. Back in 1970, new immigrants accounted for 5 per cent of the US population. Today, it is 12 per cent and rising; if trends continue, there will be a record-breaking proportion of foreign-born Americans by 2025.

These figures alone point to a literal reinvention of the United States. But there is also the possibility that change could be retarded by the anti-immigrant sentiment bubbling away in Arizona and beyond. History tells us that this period of nativist panic will eventually tire itself out and those new immigrants will quietly renew and refresh the American identity. But after spending time with Carmen Mercer and Pastor Hoover, you have to ask if we can we safely make that assumption.

There are clear parallels between the current conflict over immigration and what has come before. It is still a conflict between those who guard the frontier and those who wish to pass it, between those who wish to preserve American rituals and those bound to change them. But we need to be mindful of what is dangerously unique about the conflict we are witnessing on that border.

To begin with, the war of words over immigration is enmeshed in a far wider struggle. This wave of new migrants began arriving at the tail-end of the 'culture war' for control of America's identity, fought between liberals and conservatives. Immigration is just another flash point between two very different world views which emerged from the convulsions of the 1960s. On one side are the liberal, educated cosmopolitans who, in the words of commentator David Brooks, 'valued diversity and embraced a sense of national identity that rested on openness and global integration'. Out of this group came the Moses generation of which Barack Obama spoke, the pioneers who pushed back the frontiers of social and racial justice, who fought to tame the uncivilised instincts of the American psyche. Their high ideals are reflected still in the uncompromising principles of Pastor Robin Hoover.

But their challenge to the established order created a backlash among those who valued American rituals as they were, who placed community above the individual, tradition above change. 'Members of this class came to feel that America's identity and culture were under threat,' writes David Brooks, 'from people who didn't understand what made America united and distinct.' Today, you will feel the hard edge of that backlash on the US–Mexican border. You will hear it in Carmen Mercer's fearful rhetoric and see it in human form resting on a lawn chair with a Colt .45.

The culture war absorbs many different debates into a single, all-encompassing clash of opposing world views. That tends to strengthen the hand of the immigration zealots. Hardliners on that border would have far less sway were they not symbols of the broader resistance against a cosmopolitan elite who do not understand the real America. Carmen Mercer is the antidote to those urban liberals who look beyond their big cities and see nothing but rednecks, blue collars and white trash.

The traditionalists feel besieged by the liberals and so tend to make simplistic judgements about them. They ignore the fact that among the agents of change are God-fearing, small-town Americans like Pastor Robin Hoover. But at the very same time, open-minded and educated men like the pastor can be brutally dismissive of those who disagree with them. Granted, there is not a lot of room for nuance in a life and death struggle like his, but too few people with the pastor's views have addressed the causes of the deep-rooted fear that drives so many to resist immigration.

The Minutemen occupy the political fringe, but many Americans will accept the central premise of their argument: that America is a rare elixir to be shared out among those who play by the rules. Any sudden uncontrolled influx of people and that American elixir is diluted for ever. This very same visceral fear has ebbed and flowed through American history. During each great wave of immigration, Americans face the same challenge and ultimately, sometimes reluctantly, pass the same test. They eventually come to see the truth in those words: *E pluribus unum*.

But Carmen Mercer says this time it's different. What is happening on the southwest frontier of the United States has no parallel in American history. In at least one sense, she is right. The life of an immigrant had far more value when the Irish were flocking to America more than a century ago. There will be no memorials and statues at those staging points for the illegals, no statues to commemorate the thousands who never made it along the way. They once used an old pioneer motto to describe new arrivals on American shores: 'The cowards never started and the weak died on the way.' They would not dare use it now.

Of course, this is not the difference that Carmen had in mind. What she would like Americans to focus on is the fact that the fourth wave of immigration is predominantly from one source: Latin America. Unlike the broad range of nationalities and cultures represented in previous waves of immigration, Spanish speakers dominate this wave, with Latinos expected to make up one-quarter of the US population by 2050. If the anti-immigrant activist had two favourite facts, it is that salsa replaced ketchup as the most popular condiment in America right about the time Jose became the most popular name in California and Texas.

Previous waves of migrants came from far across the sea, not from next door. Traditionalist academics such as Samuel Huntington note that the income gap between the US and Mexico is the largest between any two adjoining countries in the world. This creates the perfect condition for a long-term invasion of migrants from 'a poor contiguous country, with more than a third of the population of the United States, who come across a two-thousand-mile border marked historically simply by a line in the ground and a shallow river'.

The critics say that another distinguishing feature of this wave of new arrivals is the number of 'illegals' among them. By one estimate, the number of undocumented immigrants grew by 770,000 per year in the 1990s, and kept coming at a rate of more than half a million in each of the first years of the 21st century.

You could argue that the biggest danger here is that illegal immigrants will be trapped in the shadows of American life, never having the chance to truly assimilate as others have done before them.

Without assimilation, immigration is a force for division, not renewal. In his book *Who Are We?*, Samuel Huntington argues that the current wave of Latino immigrants is proving hard to integrate into American life, partly because they are more likely to retain citizenship of their country of origin. 'With dual citizenship, American identity is no longer distinctive and exceptional,' Huntington writes. 'American citizenship becomes simply an add-on to another citizenship.'

Huntington and other traditionalists rely heavily on statistics which suggest that Spanish-speaking new arrivals from Latin America are slower to integrate than other kinds of immigrants, statistics which prove that this wave of immigration is different, and presumably more dangerous. But there is a weakness in their perspective, a failure to appreciate the growing importance of immigration in America's developing transformation.

In the first place, the critics of immigration suffer from what demographer Dowell Myers calls the 'Peter Pan Fallacy'. They seem fixated on only the very latest arrivals and assume that all immigrants remain 'forever frozen in their status as newcomers, never ageing, never advancing economically, and never assimilating'. They focus on the fact that just a third of Latino immigrants who have been in America for less than ten years speak English well. But they seem to ignore the fact that nine of out ten children of immigrants speak the language well and the figure rises to 97 per cent among their grandchildren.

Previous waves of immigrants did integrate more quickly, mainly because more of them had English as a first language, but the long-term trends for this batch of new arrivals are encouraging. In May 2008, the Manhattan Institute published a report showing that the rate of assimilation has substantially quickened in recent decades.

Alarmist predictions about illegal immigration may also have fallen behind the curve of a deepening recession. There is growing evidence that fewer people are making that potentially deadly crossing across the desert, since there are fewer jobs on the other side. The Pew Hispanic Center estimates that the number of illegal immigrants in the United States fell by half a million between 2007 and 2008.

Perhaps the greatest mistake the traditionalists make is to assume that they continue to speak for the majority of Americans on immigration. To be fair, they could be forgiven for thinking that they do. After all, hard-line positions on immigration played well in the early stage of the 2008 presidential campaign. When it comes to public opinion, a CBS News poll in 2007 found that 69 per cent of people wanted illegal immigrants deported.

But the same CBS poll revealed an interesting love-hate attitude to immigration. When people were offered an alternative to deportation for illegal immigrants who had been in American for more than two years, 62 per cent took it. The poll also found a declining hostility to immigrants, 57 per cent saying that most recent immigrants contributed to this country (up 23 points from 1986) and just 28 per cent saying that most immigrants caused problems (a drop of 16 per cent). Another telling expression of (conservative) public opinion was the nomination of John McCain, the Republican who annoyed the anti-immigration lobby most.

The fourth great wave of immigration is not yet over, but it seems that the usual rise in anti-immigrant sentiment may have passed its peak. There is just one remaining cloud on the horizon and that is the apparent weakness of the American economy. If economic insecurity is the driving force behind anti-immigrant sentiment, then you would expect a renewed surge of resistance during a recession. And what if the United States was entering a period of long-term stagnation? What if immigration no longer promised renewal but an added burden on a nation in decline?

The omens do not seem good. The United States has

borrowed, spent and imported far beyond its means. Its financial system has been laid low by the sub-prime fiasco and its economy is beginning to face stiff competition from surging economies such as China and India. And yet there are good reasons to believe that rumours of America's demise have been greatly exaggerated.

Here's the delicious irony: the very thing that will save the United States from the bitter wages of economic decline is immigration. What you often forget, as you listen to all the angry talk about a broken border, is that the US has successfully absorbed more than 20 million legal immigrants over the past quarter-century. The population of the United States is expected to grow from around 300 million in 2005 to 438 million by 2050, and 82 per cent of that growth will come from new arrivals or their offspring. No other country has ever enjoyed such an invigorating injection of human capital.

While other countries get older and less productive, America will be kept vibrant and youthful if, as expected, there continues to be rising fertility and surging immigration. In 2050, the average American will be under 40, while the average European and Japanese will be more than a decade older. And what of China, America's greatest potential rival? Its median age will rise from 33 in 2005 to 45 in 2050. While other countries are getting more pensioners, the US will be creating more workers.

A younger, more dynamic society is also a more innovative society. The World Economic Forum continues to rate the United States first in technology and innovation, first in spending for research and technology and first in the quality of its research institutions. The US produces one-third of the world's scientific papers, employs two-thirds of the world's Nobel Prize winners, has seven or eight of the world's top ten universities (depending on which ranking you choose) and leads the world in the education of computer scientists.

And guess what? Immigration will keep the United States on the cutting edge. It spends more than twice as much on higher education than Europe, which helps it to attract 30 per cent of students around the world who study in another country. Foreign students and immigrants do remarkably well after they arrive in the US, getting 65 per cent of all computer science PhDs awarded by American colleges. Once they graduate, these tech-savvy immigrants tend to put down roots: half of all start-up companies in Silicon Valley had at least one founder who was foreign born.

It is hard to argue with Fareed Zakaria of *Newsweek* when he says, 'the United States' potential new burst of productivity, its edge in nano technology and biotechnology, its ability to invent the future – all rest on its immigration policies'. In other words, the unfolding transformation of the United States cannot be sustained unless the new arrivals keep coming in overwhelming, invigorating numbers. Of course, native-born Americans must find a way of coping with the upheaval that brings.

The challenge is to find common purpose on immigration, to overcome both the paranoid and the legitimate fears that come with millions of new arrivals. An important first step will be an end to that 'culture war'. As long as America is divided into tribes of zealous traditionalists and hard-edged idealists, you struggle to see how there can be a rational debate about broken borders or the problems of integration. The rise of the Joshua generation is the best hope of ending tribal political warfare. But that would be a first step, not a final solution. Ultimately, it all comes down to that age-old tension between Frontier and Ritual.

So far, we have discovered that the reinvention of America involves a decisive shift towards Ritual and the rise of a new civic and collective ethic. But some elements of transformation require Americans to rediscover Frontier. Immigration is one of them. It demands the qualities of innovation and change, dislocation and danger, which energised the original pioneers. After all, it is that dangerous, dynamic frontier ethic which keeps the immigrants coming, which keeps renewing America. The motto *E pluribus unum* sits on the Frontier side of the equation.

But this is a hard sell in an era of doubt. Ritual is a safe place to be when times get hard. One of the most difficult parts of America's reinvention is persuading the born-again patriots, the struggling blue-collar workers and the pious young boomburb families that they should embrace reinvention and all the creative destruction it involves.

At certain moments in their history, Americans have risen to a challenge and confronted their problems head-on. At others, they have retreated behind the walls of their 'city on the hill' to find sanctuary. These competing instincts are at work in that angry conflict over immigration, but they are also shaping a fearful debate about America's wider role in global affairs. Which brings us to our last big question: how do you reinvent a nation that fears the world as much as the world fears it?

10.
Titan – The Boomburb Empire

'This was ground zero for at least one missile.'

When our guide Harry says these words, he finally sounds as if he has a soul. We all breathe a little easier, even though he's talking about nuclear holocaust.

Harry has spent the last 20 minutes describing the features of this former Titan II missile base as if he were an affable salesman in a suburban car showroom pointing out the finer points of fuel efficiency, anti-lock brakes and skid control.

Under a corrugated metal roof, he showed our tour group the engine that would have sent the 103-foot missile on its 6,000-mile journey towards the Apocalypse. He told us it would have powered up for just five minutes of the 35-minute flight to the Soviet Union. The rest of the trip would have been an intercontinental glide. He also gave a flawless explanation of the composition of the coolant agent and the boiling point of the propellant, or maybe it was the other way round. Memory is an unreliable guide at this point; it was impossible not to be distracted by the fact that Harry's white hard-hat was the same colour as his shorts and his blue polo shirt matched the socks around his ankles.

But now, as we stand right by the half-open silo roof, we are gripped by each and every word he utters. Harry has just pointed out that on Doomsday, the Soviets would have surely chosen this flat, featureless piece of Arizona desert, just over the ridge from the small town of Sahuarita, as a target for nuclear attack.

For the first time, this no longer feels like a museum; it is the frontline of the Cold War at the moment of its potentially catastrophic climax. With a few words, Harry has transported us back to the early 1960s. This is now one of 18 active missile bases dotted along the outer edges of Tucson, Arizona. Inside the single silo, on the tip of that missile is the largest nuclear device ever deployed by the United States: a nine-megaton W-53 warhead with the explosive power of 600 Hiroshimas. The warhead is designed to detonate as a 'groundburst', which would take out a reinforced military target, or an 'airburst', which would have annihilated a Soviet city. If and when Doomsday arrives, our warhead will explode in a groundburst. The news brings with it a disorienting jolt of relief.

From the outset of the tour, the guides at the Titan Missile Museum had encouraged us look for shades of grey in the black and white reality of Mutually Assured Destruction. The museum does not simply illustrate history, it also provides an explanation, occasionally even a justification. Before we left on our hour-long tour with Harry, we were shown a video in the briefing room presented by the museum's archivist, Chuck Penson. With his long ponytail and nerdy charm, he was an unlikely but compelling spokesman for the doctrine of 'peace through deterrence'. Penson played the role of a US Air Force 'missileer' arriving at the command bunker for a 24-hour shift, picking up the chunky, old telephone receiver and reading the secret code that will gain him entry. As he turned back to the camera to explain the base's security procedures, he pulled a lighter out of his pocket and set fire to the piece of paper carrying the code he had just read. Having hooked us with his amateur dramatics, Chuck delivered the punchline, telling us, 'Peace isn't won. It is kept, from moment to moment.'

Penson's troubling logic stays with us as we finally get our chance to descend into the command bunker. But it is not half as disturbing as the sign at the bottom of the first set of stairs warning us to look out for rattlesnakes. Harry explains that serpents occasionally seek refuge from the unforgiving desert heat on the cool, shaded concrete at the entrance to the bunker.

There are just 55 steps between ground level and the door of the command post. That doesn't put a lot of distance between us and the thermo-nuclear fireball that may be about to consume this corner of Arizona. But Harry is waiting there with another thick sliver of comfort: a four-foot-thick steel door which he has manfully wrenched open.

He explains that almost everything in the bunker is mounted on springs, from the light fixtures to the missile itself. This would protect us from blast waves, assuming those crazy Soviet bastards dropped the big one on Sahuarita first (these are not Harry's exact words but you must realise we are emotionally invested in his tour at this point).

We are finally led to the control room, which is a minimalist copy of the bridge of the Starship *Enterprise*. If this really was 1962, the walls of blinking lights, the surgical green steel panelling and the rows of buttons and keys on the commander's console would be unbearably futuristic. But in 2008, it's amusingly retro. The spell is broken, momentarily.

Harry is off again, talking about gizmos and gadgets, and the members of the group are now furtively checking each other out. In the close proximity of the control room, it becomes apparent just how diverse the people on this tour are. We are in the middle of a scary movie surrounded by the comforting faces of everyday America. A black father has brought his two kids. One of them is an adorable young boy, not much older than seven or eight, whom Harry invites to sit in the commander's grey plastic chair.

Right behind are two contrasting couples. One young man

and woman look suspiciously like honeymooners, all tactile gestures and private jokes. Sitting on a bench beside them is an elderly couple. The husband is a former military man, a sergeant. We know this because his wife asks a question which turns into a bitter complaint about the treatment of young servicemen.

Lurking in the back is a refined sixty-something couple who are travelling with their adult son. He has a hipster's light scraggly beard and is wearing a flat cap, long camouflage shorts and a T-shirt advertising the attractions of San Francisco. He seems ill at ease and holds his big camera close to his side, loaded and ready to use.

Harry returns to the juicy detail. He is about to explain the launch procedure. A charge of nervous excitement runs through the room, but some of us also have a hint of something bitter on our tongues. It tastes of revulsion.

Before Harry begins, he points out the warning stencilled in big red letters on the walls at various points around the command bunker: 'No lone zone. Two man policy mandatory.' During their 24-hour shift (and presumably the duration of the Apocalypse) the two missileers on duty would do virtually everything in plain sight of each either just in case one of them went whack-a-doodle.

Harry points to the red safe in the corner of the control room which contained the codes that would have had to be verified before the launch. Then he tells us he will need an assistant; after all, this is a 'no lone zone'. Before anyone has a chance to volunteer, Harry picks the little boy sitting in the commander's seat. He points to the keys sitting in the two consoles and explains that both missileers would have to insert their keys at the very same moment and turn them simultaneously to initiate the launch sequence.

Harry and the young boy turn their keys together. Now it's intimate all over again. That bitter taste is getting stronger. The room is on edge despite the calm, mechanical tone in Harry's voice. We try to keep up with it but his words are a jumble. An alarm bell goes off without warning. Feet leave the ground. Blood drains. Harry smiles. His understated presence gives us more room to ponder the terrifying potential of the clinical routine we are witnessing.

It takes 58 seconds from the moment the keys are inserted to the moment that the Titan missile starts to climb out of the silo.

There are loose ends we would have liked to have cleared up before we sent our missile on its way. Do we know the actual location of the target? Does it have a name? Can we see it on a map? What value does it have as a target? What was the purpose of destroying it? Why there?

You can see how easily you would tie yourself in knots with that kind of thinking. The clear imperative in this bunker was to execute one routine after another. Worry about the daily grind of a 24-hour shift. You are a soldier. A technician. Just do your damn job like the professional you are and let someone above your pay grade do the deep thinking.

Still, it would have been very hard not to think deep mortal thoughts. We passed through that four-foot steel door but are still worried about the odds of survival down here. After all, we are a mere 55 steps from ground zero. For the first time, Harry seems a little sheepish. He admits that the missileers would not have survived an attack by a Soviet nuclear missile if it had landed in close proximity. Even if they had survived the brutal, definitive exchange of missiles, they would have faced an impossible choice. They had enough food to last a month but enough air for only a week or so.

'After ten days,' Harry says, 'they would have a choice whether to suffocate down here or go back up and face that new world.'

It is time we saw that missile, if only to make sure it is still in place and the world is as we left it a few minutes ago. Harry leads us down a long, bright corridor and warns the taller gentleman among us to watch out for the low roof. The corridor ends at a half-open green metal door with the red-stencil 'lone zone' warning on it. Behind it, two mannequins in space suits strike a pose as if filling the rocket with something (it's either propellant or coolant, but we dare not ask).

As we inch closer and Harry begins talking about the shock-absorbing tiles around the walls of the silo the eye is drawn to the gentle patterns on the panels of the mid-section of the missile. The rivets run in a pointed arc across the copper surface like the windows of a medieval Arabian citadel. Perhaps not everyone will see the resemblance.

Harry encourages us to spread out and take advantage of the glass windows that wrap around the circular girth of the Titan. After the twilight of the bunker, it is a shock to see the torrent of natural desert light flooding down the silo. The roof is permanently half open. It is mandated by the Arms Control Treaties which ended the Titan programme. The Soviets and the Americans wanted to be able to peer into the silos with their satellites to make sure that they remained decommissioned.

The vaguely Islamic design of the missile's mid-section is countered by the shape of the top of the missile, which brings to mind a copper-clad church steeple before it is ravaged by the rain and wind. It seems natural to be in a religious frame of mind as we stare at that tower of awesome destruction. After all, we are standing in front of mankind's best effort yet to appropriate the vengeful wrath of God.

Harry is coming to the end of his time with us. There are a few questions still to be asked but none that an ordinary mortal, even one so genial and accomplished as Harry, could answer to anyone's satisfaction.

We shall take those questions with us as we go back up the stairs, into the dry heat, and retreat to the gift shop, where we peel away wordlessly from the group and become individuals again, stirred, if not shaken.

Just a few hundred yards from the main gate of the museum is a familiar cluster of light-brown stucco homes, a sign for a golf club and then an upmarket trailer park. While we were down in that bunker, the suburbs crept south along Route 19 past Tucson airport all the way up to the gates of the Apocalypse.

If you are a glass-half-full type of person, you will draw comfort from this. Weapons of global destruction are becoming just another suburban attraction, wedged between the water park and the new Circuit City. The days of the Evil Empire are over. Welcome to life in the Boomburb Empire. This is a comforting thought: odd, but comforting.

Yet that hour in the bunker is a disturbing reminder that America's greatest contradictions outlived the Cold War: the United States was created to spread the values of liberty, justice and equality. But to defend its land and promote its values, it has resorted to destructive power on a scale without parallel in history. Americans are full of ambition for the world and yet they seem so frightened by it.

The ring of nuclear weaponry surrounding Tucson was designed to keep the young men of the American heartland from fighting other people's wars in distant lands. It offered the United States a chance to shape the world without leaving its shores. It was the riskiest game of roulette ever played, and many Americans clearly believe the gamble paid off.

The doctrine of 'peace through deterrence' is an exhibit in a museum, but its combination of fear and idealism, risk and safety, belief and delusion still battle for the soul of America. The tension between Frontier and Ritual has always shaped American foreign policy. It still does today, even in this era of reinvention.

—•—

Back when the United States was a lovable, snotty-nosed cherub of a nation, George Washington described it as 'infant empire'. And if Washington was to be the emperor, he resolved to follow the lead of the great Roman consul Lucius Quinctius Cincinnatus. Cincinnatus was prevailed upon to leave his farm and take the reins of absolute power during a wartime emergency. He saved the empire, returned power to the Senate and went back to ploughing his fields. Washington wanted much the same thing: win the Revolutionary War, oversee the birth of a republic and return to a life of farming on his beloved estate at Mount Vernon.

Washington was not the only founding father to be influenced by Cincinnatus. Some of the early American revolutionaries founded the Society of Cincinnati, pledging to defend the 'exalted rights and liberties of human nature' and the 'future dignity of the American empire'.

This early cult of Cincinnatus contains the seeds of Frontier and Ritual. Like a later generation of pioneers, those early patriots sacrificed for the dream of self-reliance and independence. But once they had conquered, they sought to return to the comfort of their homestead.

The tension between Frontier and Ritual, essentially the same duality which defined Cincinnatus, has shaped US foreign policy from Washington to Bush. Each president has struggled to advance America's cause while never straying too far from the collective homestead.

Balancing those competing urges was never going to be easy. American presidents have generally chosen the instinct which suited their time. The early idealists like Thomas Jefferson declared the United States to be an 'empire of liberty'. Isolationists like John Quincy Adams said America 'does not go abroad in search of monsters to destroy'. America tends to drift between these competing poles, allowing Frontier to dominate for a while and then veering back to Ritual. America has been outlaw and sheriff, idealist and isolationist, actor and audience, aggressor and protector.

It is easy to see which role occupied America in its early days of expansion. As the great Irish philosopher Bishop Berkeley put it: 'Westward the course of empire takes its way.' What would begin as an ugly, chaotic rush for land and riches on the Western frontier was given a divine, missionary edge by the Irish American journalist John L. Sullivan in 1845 when he wrote: 'Our manifest destiny [is] to overspread the continent allotted by Providence for the free development of our yearly multiplying millions.' In that phrase 'manifest destiny' was a doctrine of conquest that would influence American foreign policy directly or indirectly for decades to come.

While this was clearly a Frontier philosophy, it was borne of a familiar longing for Ritual, as a popular song of the era reveals:

> All I want in God's Creation
> Is a pretty little wife and a big plantation
> Way up north in the Cherokee Nation.

President Andrew Jackson led the charge against the Native Americans. President James Polk waged war on Mexico. Polk was responsible for the second-largest expansion of American territory and would have tried to take all of Mexico had it not been for Southern politicians who were afraid of polluting white America with too many Mexicans (if only they could have lived to see the Latino wave of the 21st century).

Manifest Destiny eventually fell out of favour but it was not long before the onset of a second imperial phase. The closing years of the 19th century brought the Spanish–American War and the conquest of Cuba, Puerto Rico and Guam. In 1898, President William McKinley launched an attack on the

Philippines after going down on bended knee and seeking guidance from God. The resulting war would claim the lives of as many as 250,000 Filipino and 4,000 US troops.

McKinley's successor, Teddy Roosevelt, carried a big stick and talked loudly about America's right to intervene anywhere in Latin American (this was known as the Monroe Doctrine). His claim that 'aggressive fighting for the right is the noblest sport the world affords' was engraved on a plaque on Donald Rumsfeld's desk a century later.

For all his machismo, Roosevelt realised that an imperial-style foreign policy brought imperial-sized burdens. He came to believe that the war in the Philippines was a mistake, and when confronted with the prospect of intervening in the Dominican Republic, he said he had 'about the same desire to annex it as a gorged boa constrictor might have to swallow a porcupine wrong-end-to'.

After Roosevelt, the appetite for foreign intervention waned, and eventually an anti-imperial instinct began to assert itself. In truth, it had been there for some time. Abraham Lincoln had been a fierce critic of that first war with Mexico, urging his countrymen to 'put a check upon this lust of dominion'.

The first president to live up to America's founding promise to the world was Woodrow Wilson, who pursued the notion of 'collective security' among a broad family of nations. It was an innovation dismissed as naïve by many European leaders, but it would ultimately become a cornerstone of global diplomacy.

At home, Wilson was bitterly attacked by a powerful isolationist lobby who wanted the United States to return home after the First World War. But his idealistic vision would eventually be revived by Franklin Delano Roosevelt, who forged consensus around a new foreign policy that was assertive yet anti-imperial. His brand of 'liberal internationalism' used military power to preserve stability, but also sought out partnerships in pursuit of American ideals. This blend of Ritual and Frontier would help to win the Second World War, rebuild Europe, create global institutions and galvanise Western democracy. This was the America which aspired to be umpire, not empire.

The United States was still capable of throwing its weight around, as it did in South and Central America and Indonesia, and its war in Vietnam brought failure and domestic dissent. Just as these dirty little battles reminded the US of the folly of empire, the nuclear stand-off with the Soviets limited its capacity to act at will.

By the time the Berlin Wall fell in 1989, the United States was the lynchpin of a global system of law and order. But it was also the global sheriff with more fire power than any nation in the history of the world. By the turn of the 21st century, it had more than 700 bases in more than 30 countries. It was an anti-imperial empire in search of a purpose.

President Bill Clinton earned a reputation as a global peacemaker, but he did his fair share of fighting, launching military action in the Balkans, Sudan, Iraq, Afghanistan, Haiti and Somalia. His Secretary of State, Madeleine Albright, summed up the administration's approach when she said Americans must be 'authors of the history of our age'.

This was the backdrop against which George W. Bush entered from stage right. He was a man with little knowledge of the world, but what he knew convinced him that America should mind its own business. He promised humility and said he would not tell other nations, 'We do it this way, so should you.' As he told a crowd at the Ronald Reagan library in California in 1999:

> America has never been an empire. Let us reject the blinders of isolationism, just as we refuse the crown of empire. Let us not dominate others with our power – or betray them with our indifference.

225

> And let us have an American foreign policy that
> reflects American character. The modesty of true
> strength. The humility of real greatness.

A lot more Ritual. A little less Frontier. That was what George Bush promised before the planes hit the Twin Towers.

Too many people talk about 9/11 without appreciating the existential shift it forced on individual Americans. The physical distance between foreign wars and the homestead was erased in an instant. The attacks on New York and Washington ended centuries of free security: a happy accident of geography based on what the historian C. Vann Woodward describes as 'nature's gift of three vast bodies of water interposed between this country and any other power that might constitute a serious menace to its safety'. Like a fast car hitting a wall, America lost that free security in an instant. It was that abrupt breach which Woodward says explains the 'faltering and bewildered way in which America faced its new peril'.

Bewilderment and confusion would soon give way to clarity inside the White House. George Bush abandoned the soft layer of Ritual which helped to get him elected and embraced his tense, edgy Frontier instincts. He also turned to a group of policy makers who had seen an opportunity to test a theory. Neo-conservatism was not triggered by 9/11; it was a reaction to the fall of the Berlin Wall. The Neo-Cons believed that the collapse of the Soviet Union gave America an opportunity to reshape the world in the name of freedom and democracy, an opportunity they claim that Bill Clinton squandered.

They were not imperialists in the classic sense; they were not driven by a thirst for conquest or dominion. But when they got their chance, they were not afraid of America's imperial potential. The journalist Ron Suskind has written the single most illuminating account of their thinking. 'We're an empire now, and when we act, we create our own reality,' a senior Bush adviser told Suskind in the year after 9/11. 'We're history's actors … and you, all of you, will be left to just study what we do.'

The world knows exactly what the Neo-Cons did and it will be up to history to deliver the ultimate judgement. But here is the more immediate challenge: predicting America's next uncertain steps in the world. As its people continue to cope with the slow-release shock of 9/11 and the trauma of Iraq, they have turned their back on the Neo-Con experiment. But as they scramble for an alternative, will they opt for the reinvention of their foreign policy? What instinct guides them most right now: Frontier or Ritual?

—•—

It is hard to know what a president with a different personality would have made of the existential shock of 9/11. What if he or she had seen an opportunity? What if he had persuaded Americans that survival depended on a more profound engagement with the world? Questions that begin with the words 'what if' often end in madness, so no more of that.

Rather than predicting how things could have been, let's see how the American world view actually evolved from the end of the Cold War to now. What is striking about public opinion in the years before George Bush became president was how much Americans wanted to retreat from the role of global sheriff. In two successive polls in the mid-1990s, just one in eight Americans said they thought the United States should be the single leader of the world.

The more things changed the more they stayed the same, at least when it came to public opinion. For all the patriotic fervour that followed 9/11, and the initial support for the invasion in Iraq, the American people remained convinced that they should play a limited role in the world. In his inaugural address in January 2005, George Bush told his people, 'The best hope for peace in our world is the expansion of freedom in all the world.' But the following month, an opinion poll found just 31 per cent of Americans believed that building democracy abroad should be a very important goal of their foreign policy. That figure would fall to 27 per cent in September of the same year.

From time to time, the American people will be led overseas in the name of freedom or security, or both. But they must be mightily inspired, manipulated or threatened before they will rouse themselves from the homestead.

We should never assume that the ambitions of American leaders are the same as the preferences of their people. Fundamentally, ordinary Americans have overwhelming pride in their country but have no interest in forcing others to live like them. Most tend to assume that when people are truly free they will choose to live the American way. In the meantime, their default position towards the world is indifference.

A nation that celebrates self-reliance has a hard time working out why others would rely on it. Perhaps the foreign leader who understood this best was former British Prime Minister, Tony Blair. A few months after the invasion of Iraq, during a speech to the US Congress, he addressed Americans who were sceptical of their country's overseas commitments:

> And I know it's hard on America, and in some small corner of this vast country, out in Nevada or Idaho or these places I've never been to, but always wanted to go, I know out there there's a guy getting on with his life, perfectly happily, minding his own business, saying to you, the political leaders of this country, 'Why me? And why us? And why America?'

In retrospect, what is intriguing about Blair's comment is how alienated the people of Idaho and Nevada became from the answers they were given. There is arguably no more Republican state than Idaho. It was consistently the most pro-Bush state in America, but even in Idaho the president's approval rating dropped below 50 per cent in 2007 (his rating in Nevada fell into negative territory as far back as 2005).

Frustration with Bush's foreign policy was a key factor in this growing disillusionment. As the 2008 presidential election campaign spread across the American heartland, from Idaho to Nevada, the extent to which America's battered reputation came up on the hustings was truly remarkable. Apart from the human suffering of war, what rankled most among voters in small towns and suburbs was that the United States was now perceived as a bully.

Ordinary Americans no longer recognise themselves in their country's global image. This is a good sign for those who are hoping for a reinvention of American foreign policy. Another encouraging sign was the occasional similarities between the two main candidates. Obama and McCain differed in their approach to so-called rogue regimes, but on the general need for more international co-operation they were at one.

Straight off the blocks, Barack Obama promised a radically different approach to foreign policy, a consistent balance between Frontier and Ritual. 'America cannot meet the threats of this century alone,' he said in his first big foreign-policy speech, 'but the world cannot meet them without America. We must neither retreat from the world nor try to bully it into submission – we must lead the world, by deed and example.'

John McCain disagreed with aspects of George Bush's foreign policy but seemed to share some of the president's assumptions about the world. Yet within weeks of securing the Republican nomination, he travelled to Europe to outline a

229

distinct change in style. He spoke about the need to fight global warming, denounced torture and promised a new era of co-operation between the US and its allies. 'When we believe that international action is necessary ... we will try to persuade our friends that we are right,' he said. 'But we, in return, must also be willing to be persuaded by them.' Hawk or no hawk, McCain was no George Bush.

The desire for co-operation we have heard in the 2008 campaign certainly reflected the views of a critical mass, the Millennial generation. Opinion polls show that 18- to 25-year-olds were much more likely than their elders to support compromise with America's allies. A majority said that the lesson of 9/11 was that the US needed to be more connected to the world, and a similar majority said that human rights was a very important goal of American foreign policy. Millennials are also more likely to have seen the world: 59 per cent of 18- to 24-year-olds have travelled outside the United States (whereas just one in five Americans of all ages made a foreign trip between 1997 and 2002). All told, 241,000 Americans were studying abroad in 2007, almost two and half times the number a decade earlier.

Everything we have heard from Barack Obama and the Millennials points to reinvention. But it's not that simple. Perhaps more than any other facet of American life, foreign policy is where Americans are hopelessly adrift.

Even the Millennials are confused by the challenges ahead. For example, there is a surprisingly hawkish tendency among young people. Just before the invasion of Iraq, Millennials were more supportive of the impending war than other age groups, and one poll found that a narrow majority of young Americans favoured unilateral action against Iran.

Those mixed messages reflect a broader confusion among Americans in general. Polls show that they are capable of simultaneously holding two opposing views. One survey back in 2004 showed majority support for the notion of pre-emptive military action by the US. But in the same poll, voters said they wanted their leaders to listen to their allies rather than go it alone.

The ability to see equal truth in two contradictory positions is what the psychologists call cognitive dissonance, a phrase that aptly describes the age-old duality behind US foreign policy. But the balance between the competing instincts of Frontier and Ritual is not static; there is movement between the two. And for all the concern about America's global reputation, the trend tells us that Americans are retreating to the safety of the homestead. 52 per cent of people surveyed by CBS News in December 2006 thought the United States 'should mind its own business internationally'. At the darkest days of the Vietnam War, just 36 per cent of Americans held the same view.

This trend is not led by some isolationist vanguard. Instead, we are seeing a great cloak of perplexed indifference settle over the American heartland. After years of war and terror, people there have become desensitised to images of chaos in the world. They have found the best way to overcome the loss of free security is to pretend that it still exists. Americans still feel vulnerable, but they cope with their doubts by retreating behind the walls of their promised land.

The public has a willing ally in the American media, which continues to cut back their coverage of world events after a post-9/11 glut. You can't blame them when you see the ratings foreign news gets these days. When CBS News sent its anchor Katie Couric to Iraq for their evening show, the ratings plunged to an historic low.

In days gone by, the American public had a more direct connection to military conflict. Many more families from the heartland were directly involved in those far-off wars. During the Second World War, more than one in ten Americans served in the US military. In the course of the war in Iraq, it is down to one out of every 100.

The future of the United States is still intertwined with the future of the world – more so in this post-9/11 globalised world – but the American way of life acts increasingly like a shield protecting its followers from the outside world. In a strangely un-American way, it rewards them for not looking towards the horizon. But it is hard to be 'mankind's last best hope' if you can't see over the walls of that shining city.

—•—

In all the food courts in all the shopping malls in all of America, there is the same sense of refuge. But in the Arizona boomburb of Glendale, the experience is just that little bit more intense.

Outside, the temperature is somewhere in the region of 40 to 45°C. It's been the hottest summer on record in the Valley of the Sun. The brisk walk across the black asphalt surface of the car park is enough to singe your mortal soul. Up ahead are the doors of the Arrowhead shopping mall, catching the light like water on an oasis.

The first gust of air-conditioned relief marks the onset of a Zen-like state of contentment. It will stay with you throughout your visit, like some spectral personal shopper. All around is abundance and movement – but also calm. After all, there is enough stuff for everyone.

But first, the food court and tasty treats from all across the planet: Japanese at Hibachi-san or Chinese at Panda Express or Italian at Sbarro or Mexican at Taco del Mar and Chevy's or all-American at A&W or Cajun at the Bourbon Street Grill.

This is a place to feel worldly without the intimidating presence of foreignness. It is also a place to gather. The food court offers you the chance to linger among your fellow consumer-citizens in a vague approximation of what they used to do once upon a time in market squares. Actually, this not just the Arrowhead shopping mall, it is the Arrowhead Towne Center. That is *towne* with an 'e', as in Merry *Olde* England.

Two older ladies in tracksuits power-walk by the food court. Moments later, a middle-aged woman passes in the opposite direction at a similar pace. She is wearing running clothes and has a mini-disc player strapped to her arm and a water bottle in her hand. You can't help but notice there is a definite scarcity of obesity around here: a tell-tale mark of affluence.

The troubles of the world are very far away until you get up to leave the food court. Two tables away is an elderly man wearing a baseball cap which says 'World War II Veteran'. A few steps later and you see that a slightly younger, plumper man is wearing a hat with the words 'Vietnam War Veteran'.

What are the odds?

Pretty good actually, if what you are looking for is the remembrance of past wars. But what about the other type of war: the one being fought right now? The White House continues to declare, 'We are a nation at war,' but this doesn't feel like a nation at war.

Apparently, there is a Marine Recruiting Office somewhere in the mall. This seems strange. How many kids at the mall make the impulsive decision to become a 'jarhead'? Buy a pair of Oakley shades maybe, but not a one-way ticket to Iraq. It just seems unlikely with all this loveliness around.

'What problems … what problems we got?' That's what high-school principal Herman Serignese told us that first Friday night at Saguaro. The words bounce off the glass and steel walls of this 'towne' centre and sweep out the door into the endless expanse of the Boomburb Empire.

Empires are weakened by indulgence. But not the United

States. George Bush told his fellow Americans to go shopping after 9/11. Go out and cultivate the brands that bewitch the world, revel in the contentment of your local shopping mall, remind yourself how America earned its 'soft power': the ability to influence people without bombing them. Wasn't it FDR, the great internationalist, who once joked that the way to persuade the Soviets of America's superiority was to drop Sears catalogues on them?

All this talk of shopping and war brings a radical comparison to mind: Arrowhead Towne Center and the Titan Missile Base have a lot in common. They both speak of the same desire to shape the world without ever having to leave home. In both places, there is the same desperate need for sanctuary and similar traces of manipulation.

But here's the big difference: things were clearer back then. During the Cold War, the United States had an obvious enemy, a clear mission and a categorical imperative to make friends and keep friends. It had no choice but to maintain a disciplined balance between Ritual and Frontier. There was no room for drift when it took just 58 seconds to initiate the Apocalypse.

Today, the Obama administration has quietly shelved the 'war on terror' but for ordinary Americans it still feels like the enemy is everywhere and nowhere. They would like to make things right, but what they hear from beyond the walls of their shining city is the low-level hum of a hostile crowd. It feels like a good time to retreat to the stucco house in the desert, to work, to live, to be happy, to be American. To forget.

Americans spent a good part of the last decade coping with life on the Frontier; now they yearn for the warm embrace of Ritual. They are drifting towards a state of profound detachment, which will complicate Obama's desire to recast US foreign policy. Above all, the president needs to convince Americans that the security of their Shining City requires more involvement with the world, not less. This was his opening salvo on a sunny day in Washington in January 2008.

> And so to all other peoples and governments who are watching today, from the grandest capitals to the small village where my father was born: know that America is a friend of each nation and every man, woman and child who seeks a future of peace and dignity, and that we are ready to lead once more.

The spirit of renewal and re-engagement that flowed through Barack Obama's inaugural address has animated billions around the world. But what really matters is whether the fine words of one man can rouse America from its restless slumber among the sunlit homesteads of Idaho and Nevada.

Conclusion: The Future

With hope and virtue, let us brave once more the icy
currents, and endure what storms may come. Let it be
said by our children's children that when we were tested
we refused to let this journey end, that we did not turn
back nor did we falter; and with eyes fixed on the
horizon and God's grace upon us, we carried forth
that great gift of freedom and delivered it
safely to future generations.

President Barack Obama, 'Inaugural address', 20 January 2009

11. Henderson – The City Shines On

Frank Sinatra said that the colour that gave him most peace was the cobalt hue of the eastern sky just before sunrise. He called it 'Five O'Clock Vegas Blue'. Sadly, whatever solace there is in the pre-dawn sky over Las Vegas, it is burned to a cinder by lunchtime.

Viewed from the top of a nearby suburban hill, the city is an untidy clutter of building blocks littering a pristine desert valley. The Vegas Strip is shrouded in a grimy vanilla mist that seems impermeable to everything but the occasional airplane taking off or landing at McCarran airport. The sky doesn't turn blue again until it is well clear of the Strip's signature landmark, the Stratosphere Tower.

Here on the hill, there is another city, where the air is clear and the sun shines bright. This is Sin City's wholesome half-brother, Henderson. You have a casual fling with Las Vegas. You marry Henderson.

You can get a decent view of the Vegas Strip from the manicured lawns of Henderson's open air 'lifestyle center', the District at Green Valley Ranch. The District offers you a chance to channel the mystical spirit of some long-lost small town. It describes itself as 'a place to meet friends for a cup of coffee, to stroll along a tree-lined main street, to read a book under a tree, or enjoy an afternoon picnic'. The words 'organic', 'vibrant' and 'diverse' leap out from the centre's website. Its official slogan is:

'Shop, dine, live' – which certainly beats the alternative: 'Sell, starve, die.'

At the heart of the District is a pedestrian shopping street. At one end is a vintage carousel for the kids. At the other is the Green Valley Ranch casino for the adults. As you walk the length of the street, inoffensive music wafts from speakers hidden in the foliage around the trees, setting a mood of absent-minded contentment.

The street is wide. It channels the breeze rising from the floor of the valley. But by the time it swirls around the District, the grimy air of the Strip has been purified through an unseen filter of affluence. You can tell you are in the 'monied burbs' because there are three boutiques selling kids' fashion, a surplus of stores selling home furnishings in dark wood and a choice of specialty breads, teas and wellness products.

There is also an element of contrived wilderness, just to remind you that you are on a 21st-century frontier. The outdoor activity shop on the corner of Main Street has the words 'camp', 'climb', 'cycle', 'paddle', 'travel', painted in big letters above its window. The freeze-dried meals in the camping section include an organic section. Red-pesto pasta. Just add water.

The urban style of the District invites comparison but not so much that it would trouble you. There is something vaguely old and East Coast about the main street, a hint of Brooklyn or Boston about the row houses that frame it. The taste of the past, however, is not strong enough to compete with the rich colours and smooth surfaces. The signs of ageing have been removed by an injection of architectural Botox.

One of the great ironies of American life at this time of reinvention is that the nostalgia for times past is most intense in places that burn with ambition and drive. Henderson is one such place. The city was created during the Second World War to supply the magnesium used in munitions and aircraft. When the war ended, the town was quite literally surplus to requirements and, in 1947, the US government offered Henderson for sale.

The town was rescued by a group of local businessmen who saw potential in the hillside community. More than half a century later, Henderson is the second largest city in Nevada and has just emerged from a period of staggering growth. The city is officially a boomburb, and not too long ago, its top officials were predicting the population would rise from 275,000 to over 500,000 by 2030.

Henderson started out making products, but now the city itself is the product. The 'Henderson Lifestyle' pitches itself at the higher end of the market and offers a selection of premium residential developments laid out across the gently sloping black volcanic earth of the McCullough Mountain Range. Their names speak of superior aspirations: Anthem, Black Mountain Vistas, Calico Ridge, Champion Village, Madeira Canyon, Seven Hills and Tuscany Village.

The city's official slogan is: 'Henderson – a Place to Call Home'. The man responsible for keeping the promise during the boom years was outgoing Mayor James Gibson, a clean-cut lawyer who speaks in reassuring bass tones.

'Back in 1990, Henderson had a population of 64,000,' he told me at our first meeting on a scalding September afternoon in 2007. 'Today, we are approaching 280,000 people. The kind of growth we are experiencing is mind-numbing. We open more than one school every month in this county.'

Other Sunbelt cities have had similar growth spurts, but Henderson has reached a higher stage of suburban evolution. Social innovation is at the heart of its expansion, making Henderson the kind of cosmopolitan brand that cities like Gilbert and Surprise aspire to be.

The Mayor and I had our first meeting on a pathway that winds around the back of the city's open-air auditorium, the largest in Nevada. It's a scenic spot offering panoramic views of Las Vegas and the upper reaches of Henderson, but it also gave the Mayor a chance to underscore his city's refinement.

In the auditorium the night before, the Moscow Ballet concluded a series of performances of *The Nutcracker*. The Henderson Symphony Orchestra was about to return to its stage to perform Beethoven's Sixth Symphony. The venue has since celebrated its tenth annual festival of 'Shakespeare in the Park'.

Henderson's pursuit of high culture stems from a ferociously acquisitive instinct, an obsessive desire to stand out. It has the only bird preserve in Nevada, the biggest recreational facility and more parkland per capita than any other city in the state. It is rated the sixth best walking city in America, and, in 2006, it was ranked 20th in the CNN/*Money* list of the top 100 places to live in the US.

We already know that the best way to locate the soul of a modern American community is to check out the social-networking site Meetup.com. A quick glance at the listings for the Henderson area reveals an ethereal trend that you wouldn't expect from the usual suburb, with three different Vegan societies, a Consciousness and Awareness group and a Compassionate Fashion Collective. Most telling is the fact that Henderson's Wine Meetup group has 412 members against the 200 who belong to the Beer Lovers! group.

Wine over beer; new age versus old age; walking not driving; the trends of the new American suburb have a faddish quality about them, as if conjured up by a marketing department in some shiny, glass building somewhere. Here's how David Brooks sums up the style-obsessed residents of 'monied burbs' in his classy trend-watching tome *On Paradise Drive*:

> They want places where they can offer disquisitions
> on the reliability of the risotto, where the pre-

dinner complimentary bread slices look like they were baked by Burgundian monks, and where they can top off their dinner with a self-righteous carrot smoothie.

But Brooks is also wise enough to see the consequential trends behind the exaggerated sophistication of the boomburbs. He is the writer who popularised the use of the phrase 'The Great Dispersal' to describe the exodus to the Sunbelt. Now, he is one of the first American public intellectuals to chart the impact of young migrants with big-city instincts on the metropolitan fringe. Brooks believes there has been an evolution in tastes from the first frenetic generation of boomburb pioneers to today's 'lifestyle'-oriented settlers.

> If you asked people in that age of go-go suburbia what they wanted in their new housing developments, they often said they wanted a golf course. But the culture has changed. If you ask people today what they want, they're more likely to say coffee shops, hiking trails and community centers.

The closest anyone has come to labelling these instincts is Joel Kotkin, the author of *The New Geography*. He has described the nesting instinct on the modern suburban frontier as 'New Localism'. Not the most original two words but a vital phenomenon nonetheless.

The growing force of New Localism in boomburbs like Henderson is driven by the migration of highly educated 'creatives' away from their natural urban habitats. The Las Vegas metropolitan area, for example, saw its graduate population rise by over 20 per cent in the late 1990s. As the cultured, creative, educated and young professional class travels, so too do the trappings of a cosmopolitan community.

The rise of this 'creative class' and their migration to the burbs coincides with a great environmental awakening among Americans, particularly those farther up the income ladder. We talked earlier about the 'beiging' of America. We may also be witnessing the 'greening' of America. Not a moment too soon.

—•—

Morning has broken. The sky is clear. The sun is burning bright. So why do you feel like Dorothy, lost in the Emerald City?

You are standing in the north tower of a hotel shaped like a pyramid looking out at a hotel shaped like a cartoon castle, its blue and red turrets standing guard over the perpetual motion of Highway 15 which communes briefly with Las Vegas, collecting its automotive waste before returning to the Mojave Desert.

In the background, the television is tuned to the *Today* programme.

'I'm Matt Lauer and I'm reporting from the town of Ilulissat, third-largest town in Greenland. The noise you hear in the background is the halibut processing factory …'

NBC's flagship morning show has sent its hosts to the 'ends of the earth' to report on the impact of climate change. Matt Lauer is close to the North Pole, his colleague Anne Currie is near the South Pole and weather man Al Roker is broadcasting from the Equator.

Back in studio, the reserve anchor is interviewing Chip Giller, the author of a new book called *Wake Up and Smell the Planet*. In four minutes, he gives seven hints on how to fight global warming, one person at a time. Among his suggestions are skipping meat once a week and ditching the car occasionally.

Back in that Las Vegas hotel room, Chip is competing with the drone of Highway 15 and the siren song of the breakfast buffet.

Down in the restaurant, the waitress is an elegant lady in late middle age with a strained look on her face. She wears a badge on her chest that advertises the hotel's topless cabaret. In the nearby bar, two young women dressed in colourful 1950s-style cocktail dresses sit giggling at the bar as they polish off the remains of a bottle of something bubbly.

It is just shy of 9 a.m.

At the junction of Tropicana and Las Vegas Boulevard, elderly couples taking a morning stroll choose to ignore the detritus of the night before – the fag ends and the cards advertising prostitutes – as they cross the street. The yellow newspaper stands are stuffed full of booklets with titles like *Sundown*, *After Dark* and *Little Darlings*, advertising women over 40 with manipulated anatomies and *Asian Barely Legal Blondes* with disguised ethnicities.

Fatburger is open 24 hours a day. So is a bar advertising 'Margarita by the yard' and an obscene T-shirt shop with all manner of slogans and symbols inviting or offering oral sex. A Porsche Boxter sits outside a luxury car rental shop with a sign in the front window saying 'Rent Me'.

The distinguished Las Vegas historian Hal Rothman described his city as a 'liberation from the burden of sin'. Rothman suggests that Las Vegas is a refuge from the puritan instinct in American life, but what if it was also window to a deeply embedded delusion?

If you time it right, you will arrive at the Bellagio Hotel just as the show is about to begin. All around the eight-acre replica of Lake Como, *Viva Las Vegas* seeps from unseen speakers and the fountains begin to bubble gently. Within seconds they explode high into the Vegas sky, obscuring the fake Eiffel Tower just across the water.

This city gets just four inches of rainfall every year – making it the driest urban area in America – but it has the highest rate of water consumption of any big US city. The mammoth hotels on the Strip are symbols of this shortfall, but they are not the cause; 70 per cent of the water used in southern Nevada comes out of water sprinklers, working desperately to stop suburban lawns from turning into sand.

In 2006, at the very peak of that Great Dispersal, a new resident was arriving in Vegas every six minutes and a new house was being built every 19 minutes. The fresh arrivals didn't come for the smorgasbord of excess along the Strip, but there was a touch of fantasy in the way they wanted to live.

In those sprawling Vegas suburbs, the pursuit of happiness is in danger of becoming a catastrophic environmental delusion. The United States will gain roughly 120 million people during the coming three decades and they will have to live somewhere. Just one in ten Americans wants to live in a city; half of them want to move to settle down in suburbs. The problem is that they keep flooding to suburbs that have been carved out of desert, like North Las Vegas or its sister boomburb, Henderson.

Under the scorching sun, the new arrivals lay a carpet of concrete and asphalt creating what scientists call 'urban heat islands' which send temperatures soaring to record-breaking heights. People put up with the heat because they have air conditioning, but to keep the air cool, they need to use enormous amounts of energy. According to one independent energy watchdog, air conditioning in the US now accounts for 8 per cent of the world's total electricity supply.

More energy is needed to power bigger houses. Americans now occupy about 20 per cent more developed land per capita than they did 20 years ago. Public transport has never been a feature of these desert boomburbs so everything revolves around the private car. Since 1980, the number of miles driven by Americans has increased three times faster than the number of Americans.

The American dream has never been lived on this scale, and it is impossible to find any scenario in which it can continue in this form. This turbo-charged pursuit of happiness is a relic of a different time, when oil was plentiful and cheap, when reservoirs were full and when climate change was science fiction. The Sunbelt boomburbs tell us that the American dream must reinvent itself or face a potentially lethal collision with environmental and economic reality.

—•—

They seem to get the message out in Henderson. In part, because they understand their frontier roots. Mayor Jim Gibson speaks with evangelical passion about the need to conserve Henderson's delicate relationship with the desert. He wants people to remember that they live on the edge, the meeting point between humanity and wilderness. He speaks with sadness about the growing scarcity of water in the region and the obstacle it poses to the onwards march of his city.

Barack Obama won in this county by a record-breaking margin and Jim Gibson believes that represents a shift in consciousness, not simply a political preference. 'The increased registration of Democrats is also reflective of something,' he told me in the wake of Obama's election. 'Much of what we hear suggests that people are more attuned to an environmentalist perspective, or at least a conservationist perspective.'

The flowering 'green' consciousness is also fuelled – with a neat twist – by the rising price of fuel. In March 2008, as prices at the petrol pump spiralled to record highs, Americans drove 11 billion fewer miles than in the same month in 2007, which was the biggest monthly fall in driving in America since records began in 1942. Mayor Gibson says this inflicted a long-term shock to the system for people in Henderson: 'They are anxious not to ever have to see $4.11 gasoline again.'

Across the United States, consumers are moving away from petrol-guzzling mega-cars, with sales of Hummers plummeting and sales of the fuel-efficient hybrid Toyota Prius soaring. 'I think this is a permanent shift in attitude,' says the mayor. 'You can buy a Prius for a whole lot less than you can buy a larger car and you can certainly drive them for less.'

Something is happening in America and the country's politicians know it. Governor Arnold Schwarzenegger has committed California to cutting carbon emissions by 25 per cent before 2020. New York is replacing its entire fleet of 13,000 yellow cabs with hybrid cars and one of President Obama's first acts was to sign executive orders improving fuel economy and setting stricter emissions standards.

Out in those Las Vegas suburbs, many new housing developments have been fitted with water conservation and energy-saving innovations, while those wasteful lawns are being ripped up and replanted with desert foliage, saving huge amounts of water. Las Vegas even has 'water police', who enforce strict water-rationing codes and impose heavy fines on rule-breakers.

There is also a trend towards sustainable development. The buzz-phrases among boomburb planners are 'New Urbanist neighbourhoods' (with more walking and cycling), 'transit-oriented development' (building around public transport hubs) and 'more neighbourhood and less sprawl'.

Mayor Gibson echoes the themes of the New Urbanist movement: 'It's real important to have open space and parks and trail systems. We also try and locate schools, shopping and parks within new developments so that we don't have to bus kids to schools across the valley.'

The mayor worked closely with a group of private developers

to create Nevada's first large-scale New Urbanist development. The name of the project says it all: Inspirada. It was designed to be one of the largest communities of its kind in the US, with 26,000 residents, 300 acres of park land and more than 20 miles of trails for walking and biking.

The development involved seven individual villages, each with a theme drawn from music, art, athletics, dance, exploration, painting and science. The villages would be built around a central square with schools, police stations and fire stations. Houses would be built closer to streets, cars would be parked in hidden garages, and balconies, porches and patios would make a return to suburban life. Gone were the rows and rows of identical stucco mansions. Instead, neighbourhoods would have distinct character to set them apart from each other.

'We fell in love with our cars and fell out of love with our neighbours,' says John Ritter, the leader of the consortium developing Inspirada. 'The street ends up looking like a line of garages.'

The developers at Inspirada planned to build light rail stations so that if Henderson develops a mass transit system in the future, Inspirada will be the first community to be connected.

Henderson has embraced New Urbanism as a logical extension of its prized autonomy, its burning desire to be different. 'It's all our decisions,' said the mayor. 'It's all about trying to do it the way we do it in Henderson, the Henderson way, the fiercely independent way. This is the place where the American dream really comes full circle. That's how we see it.'

The mayor is a genuine visionary. But he makes one mistake. He talks of the American dream as if it had a single destination. It's not. It's an everlasting journey with countless different detours – and the occasional shuddering stop.

—•—

It is the week before Christmas. A freak blizzard swept through Clark County a few days ago and there is still snow on the ground in the rolling hills around Henderson. A cutting wind races down the pedestrian street at the District, but there are no pedestrians to stop it before it crashes up against the Green Valley Casino.

Patrick Coolican and Mike Mishak work nearby at the Las Vegas *Sun* and they have agreed to meet in a faux-Irish bar inside the casino called Quinn's. Over pints of Newcastle Brown Ale, they explain how Las Vegas and its boomburbs fell off an economic cliff.

Unemployment is heading towards 10 per cent this Christmas and the Vegas boom they said could never end has just ended. 'Local economists and analysts keep saying there is light at the end of the tunnel,' says Patrick, 'and they just keep getting it wrong.' The engines of the local economy – tourism and gambling – have slowed down. An economy based almost exclusively on what Patrick calls a 'marketing idea' is in freefall.

'They just thought it would go on forever and ever. The $6 cocktail became the $8 cocktail became the $10 cocktail and soon people were spending $800 for a magnum of vodka at a club. What is that?'

Mike chimes in with what seems, in retrospect, a crazy notion. 'There was seemingly no shortage of people willing to pay.'

There is now.

Many of those high-rollers with the platinum cards and gold-plated delusions deserted Las Vegas, cutting the local economy off at the knees. And the recession hit just as the property market in Clark County collapsed, along with the dreams of countless people.

By the close of 2008, the home-foreclosure rate in Nevada had been the worst for any American state for more than 18 months. In October 2008, it was more than seven times the national average, with one in every 60 homes being foreclosed.

The worst thing was the speed with which a stunning boom became a crippling bust. In 2004, house prices in Vegas rose by 52 per cent. In 2008, prices fell by 30 per cent, leaving half of all homes in the Vegas area worth less than the loans owed on them.

Remember, a little earlier we heard the half-joking observation that every stripper in Vegas had a real-estate licence? Well, a leading official in the local Realtor's Association offered the *Washington Post* a variation on that theme. As he was parking his car at a local casino, the valet told him he was selling one of his houses for $1.2 million. Just one of them, mind. That was when the realtor understood the market was sunk.

The sickness spread all the way out to Henderson. The day after meeting Patrick and Mike, I drive to see Mayor Gibson, who is about to leave office after more than a decade in City Hall. On the way, I see plenty of Prius cars but also a scary number of foreclosure signs, rocking silently in the cold wind outside impressive McMansions. The city of Henderson has suffered a 10 per cent drop in property tax and is slashing its five-year spending plan by $50 million. No wonder Mayor Jim Gibson looks more sombre than at our first meeting.

'We're just hoping we get to the bottom of the trough,' he says, with an ironic smile. 'Because the decline is something that none of us have been able to quantify with any accuracy. All we know is that it is steepening monthly.'

There are some optimists left in Clark County willing to repeat the old mantra: 'People lose a lot of money betting against Vegas.' Local business leaders say new hotel developments on the Vegas strip will create 130,000 new jobs by 2012. This is about the only hope left for local political leaders like Mayor Jim Gibson. 'As gaming goes,' he says philosophically, 'so most everything goes.'

It is exactly that dependence on gambling which has brought Las Vegas to its knees. During the good times, the city failed to invest in education and seemed incapable of diversifying its economy. It just assumed the good times were a permanent feature of life. In so many ways, Las Vegas is a cartoon version of a wider reality. Excess and delusion are more deeply embedded in Vegas but they have also been facts of American life.

A growing number of Americans has woken up to the delusion at the heart of their turbo-charged dream. They have elected a new leader and are seeking out a new way of doing things and a new 'lifestyle' consistent with the world they live in and the environment they have been entrusted with. You see the potential of this powerful current in 'monied burbs' like Henderson. But these communities also reveal, with frightening clarity, the crippling legacy of past delusions.

—•—

The grip on the steering wheel becomes incrementally tighter the closer you get to those mountains. The journey towards Henderson's outer limits brings that familiar feeling of approaching world's end.

Coming off the highway, at the turn for the city's executive airport, the wind comes at the car in ever strengthening waves. There are no stucco walls or shopping mall to stand in its way. The city is behind you. The frontier is ahead.

Beyond Henderson airport, the road is reduced to a single lane in each direction. On either side, there are fields of levelled rubble, some divided in rectangular plots waiting silently for development that will not come. That Metropolitan Fringe feels very different here in the winter. The soft contours of the hills to the right are stained by snow, running across the soft folds like patches of grey on the hairline of a middle-aged man.

The sign rushes by too quickly to catch all the detail. But the important word registers: Inspirada.

The houses stick up from the horizon with more confidence than the other tracts of light-brown bungalows around them. At the edges of the development, the houses are little more than wooden ribcages. Some sit with expectant, neat piles of brown tiles on their exposed roofs. Others seem fully formed and contented.

Inspirada is the work of several different developers, each responsible for a slice of the overall project. The first portion you approach has an Italian theme. To get to it, you leave Volunteer Road at Via Firenze. The next turn brings you on to Foro Romano Street and eventually you reach Stella Cliento Square.

This is New Urbanism made flesh, or at least bricks and canvas. The centrepiece of the square is a colourful plastic and wood playground under a flapping, white marquee, providing shade in summer and catching wind in winter. At the next square, Solista Park, the playground is even bigger and so is the marquee.

The houses around the square are sturdy, as if they have been built with eternity in mind. There is more individual style and sophistication in this one street than in entire boomburb developments. There is plenty of vegetation: light gorse-like bushes and evergreen hedges and skinny desert trees. But there is no grass. This is the desert after all. An environment to be sustained, communed with, rather than conquered.

Which begs the question: what is that four-storey building doing here, the one with the sign advertising 'New York-style' loft apartments?

And why have all the Italian names suddenly disappeared, gobbled up by the artistic sensibilities of another developer.

Brush Stroke Street leads you to Canvas Edge Drive which skirts past Monet Sunrise Street, Degas Tapestry Avenue and

Color Palette Drive. The street names pass by at a surprising clip, which is another innovation at Inspirada. Everything is closer together. Streets are bordered by pavements which lead down alleyways and into squares. Angles. There are plenty of angles. Gone is that endless curve which gives the average American suburb its peculiarly disorienting feel.

A wrong turn leads into a neighbouring 'Old Urbanist' development. In this vintage suburban plot, the houses are almost identical. A narrow white strip of concrete runs along the edge of lush grassy gardens. It is not a pavement so much as a kerb. The curved streets all seem to end in culs-de-sac. You are lost, even though you can see Inspirada on the other side of the high railings in the middle-distance. You can see the bicycle track winding around the back of the houses. You want to be there, not here. You want that future, not this present.

Eventually, you find a way out and are soon back in Inspirada, cruising contentedly up Brush Stroke Drive.

It's only then you discover the problem.

Inspirada is over before it has actually begun.

The streets at the edge of the development come to an end without warning, turning instantly from asphalt to dirt. Behind a row of half-finished houses at the boundary, there is nothing but a vast expanse of angular dirt plots. There are two bulldozers sitting empty and unused and a couple of workmen with pick-up trucks going through the snag-list on some of the just-finished properties.

Tuning back into the completed portion of the development, you notice that only a fraction of the houses are occupied. It's just four days before Christmas. In most American housing developments that would mean a forest of lights and decorations but here there is nothing but an occasional seasonal wreath on a door, a smattering of plastic candy canes rising out of one gravelled yard.

Inspirada has run out of inspiration.

Back in City Hall, a bitter smile plays on Mayor Gibson's face when he is asked why work on Inspirada seems to have stopped. Before the question is over, he laughs in a way that tells you there is a long, complicated story behind this. But instead of a long, complicated answer, he says simply, 'Stopped in its tracks.'

So it has been suspended?

'I think there is product out there which isn't selling.'

Inspirada didn't seem like a product. It was an ethos. It was New Urbanism.

'Our hope and goal is that we will still get that kind of project out of it but a lot depends on what happens in the marketplace.'

As the mayor speaks, it becomes clear the dream at Inspirada has fallen victim to the reality of recession. New Urbanism requires more planning, more amenities and more money. It comes at a higher cost to developers.

'If it turns out that the developers begin to feel they need a slightly different product, we are not going to turn a deaf ear to it because we are not in a position to do that.'

Inspirada was supposed to be a symbol of change in the United States. It was supposed to represent the aspiration of a New America for sustainable, progressive communities in touch with reality. But reality bit back. In hard times, marketing trumped values. 'Right now there is no market.' The Mayor laughs again, this time with a tired, humourless chuckle.

—•—

Each time you think you have resolved a contradiction in American life, another comes along to replace it. So it seems with the complicated reinvention of American life.

The Great Dispersal has been the engine of change in the new America. In those exurbs, suburbs and boomburbs, in all their youthful diversity, a new generation of pioneers created a very modern balance between Frontier and Ritual. But the Sunbelt has also been a breeding ground for insatiable appetites and lingering fears that now threaten to cripple the forces of progress.

Not too long ago, it seemed the Great Dispersal would last forever. In 2006, real-estate professors at Wharton College in Pennsylvania predicted that Nevada's Clark County would grow by a little over 80 per cent between 2000 and 2020, adding almost one million new residents. They also forecast that the fastest-growing cities would continue to be in the Southwest. 'Prospective real estate developers,' they advised, 'had better buy a good pair of sunglasses and some sunblock.'

Then came the crash.

The state of Nevada attracted less than 46,000 new residents between July 2007 and July 2008, a population increase of just 1.8 per cent and the smallest expansion in a generation. Nevada had been the fastest-growing state in the US for 18 out of 23 years and had never been out of the top four. Suddenly, it dropped to sixth. The news was worse around Las Vegas. Clark County's population declined by about 10,000 in 2008, an estimate based on the growing number of vacant houses. Nationally, that surge in migration which reshaped America tapered off as the economy tanked. Just 12 per cent of Americans moved home between 2007 and 2008, the lowest figure since the government records began in the late 1940s.

The obvious conclusion is that the reinvention of America is now over. How could it continue when the turbo-charged engine of transformation had run out of fuel? But on closer examination, the dynamism that helped create the new America is still there, if not necessarily with the same numerical force. Americans who choose to move are still looking to the Sunbelt. A survey of the ten most popular cities to live in, released in early 2009, showed all ten were in the South and West, with Denver taking the top spot (the ten least-popular cities were all in the Northeast and Midwest). While Nevada may no longer count among the top four fastest-growing states, Utah, Texas and Arizona do.

The hard times of recent years will certainly moderate the explosive growth of the new America but it shows no sign of diluting its youth or its breathtaking diversity. And this is what makes the transformation of America an unstoppable force.

Just imagine it is 2050. About 438 million people now live in America (up from 296 million in 2005). If you are white, you are now officially a minority. One out of every five people passing you on the street was born in another country (double the number in 2005). Close to one in three of those faces is Hispanic (double the number in 2005). One in ten is Asian American, and 27 million Americans are a combination of two or more races.

You will notice that a lot more people are over 65, about twice as many. In fact, the first-born Millennials are reaching retirement. They have had a good run, after controlling American politics for close on four decades (they became eligible to run for president way back in 2013). There may be many more older people, but immigration has kept America young in comparison with the rest of the Western world. Back in Europe, the median age has climbed to over 50. Here in America, it is barely 40, and one in four people on that average street are teenagers.

As for the politics of this new America, it is harder to make certain predictions. But if we are right in assuming continued growth for those Sunbelt suburbs, we can also expect the moderating trend in American discourse to be sustained.

The sprawling communities we have visited in this book are the political thermostat of the new America. The people who live in the boomburbs are optimistic and positive, and they retreat from extremism. They want politicians to talk about quality-of-life issues such as job growth, climate and water, and not wedge issues such as gay marriage and abortion. They are bucking the dysfunctional trends that have crippled American political life for the past three decades.

As their cities settle, and they forge deeper civic bonds, tribal loyalties matter less to boomburb voters. They are no longer a partisan base ready to be fired up with explosive moral code words. They are looking for practical solutions and common ground. If it were up to voters in the Sunbelt to set the national agenda, the era of hyper-polarised politics would end tomorrow. The good news from the 2008 election is that Sunbelt voters *are* increasingly setting the agenda.

The civic preferences of boomburbs are taking the hard edge from ideological conflict in the new America. It is hard to overestimate the importance of this post-partisan trend. Three decades of culture war paralysed the political process in the United States. 'A can-do country is now saddled with a do-nothing political process,' said *Newsweek*'s Fareed Zakaria before the 2008 election, 'designed for partisan battle rather than problem solving.'

The rush to the practical centre in American life represents a renewal of the spirit of Ritual. It is to be welcomed after years of disorder and imbalance. But with every great correction in American life, there is a danger of over-correction.

At its best, America is a balance of Ritual *and* Frontier. My fear for the years ahead is that Americans will forget that the spirit of the pioneer defines them as much as the spirit of the settler. There are signs that an increasing number of Americans now equate reinvention with retreat. You can understand why. As a rising tide of war and recession threatened their lives, they sought refuge in their shining cities, behind increasingly imposing walls, where the problems of the world seemed very far away.

The next chapter in American history will be defined by

tension between the pioneers who embrace change and the settlers who run from it. You can see the outlines of those distinct groups in a survey of attitudes released by the Pew Research Center in January 2009. It found that a majority of Americans wanted to live in racially diverse communities. By a margin of two to one, those surveyed said they would also rather live in a community where people have a mix of political views. Virtually every social and ethnic group preferred diversity in their surroundings, but the pioneering preference was stronger among those with money, education and liberal views.

Yet, there is worrying evidence that a substantial minority of Americans is seeking refuge from diversity. In the 2008 election, there was a growth in the number of like-minded enclaves with radically diverging preferences: 48 per cent of votes in the election were cast in counties that went for John McCain or Barack Obama by a margin of at least 20 per cent. In 1976, only 27 per cent of voters lived in such 'landslide counties'.

In essence, we may be seeing a new rivalry between competing life experiences. Millennial voters have known nothing but high immigration, good times and rapid technological change. Older voters have lived through war, recession and social upheaval. One generation seeks change and another craves security. 'So the older generation may be convinced of the younger generation's naiveté,' writes columnist Ellen Goodman, 'the younger may complain of their elders' time warp.'

The generations also have completely different experiences of racial identity. Four out of ten Millennials are minorities, compared with two out of ten senior citizens. To put it bluntly, young Americans are the most racially diverse generation alive, while the oldest Americans are the whitest.

Millions of young and diverse Americans are drawn to the Sunbelt, leaving the Northern and Midwestern states with slower growing, ageing white populations. Many older, white Americans live in the Rustbelt, which has suffered sharp economic decline in recent decades, so that racial-generational divide is sharpened by geography and economics.

Generational tension may ease as the Millennials begin to grow old; race may become less divisive in a future where every American is a minority. But it is harder to see how the cultural tensions between the new America and that mythical 'real' America can be resolved any time soon. If anything, they are likely to deepen, as blue collars feel increasingly marginalised, as they coalesce around a glorified notion of 'the way things were'.

The reinvention of America cannot be stopped, but it is certain to be a tense, faltering process. Americans may have embraced a living symbol of change in Barack Obama, but their future will still be shaped by the eternal contradictions of their past.

—•—

'I was there, where you were you? What size are you, Ma'am?'

The sound of a salesman hawking T-shirts drifts across the wide-eyed mass of people creeping forward on D Street. It's too cold for T-shirts, almost too cold for the words printed on them. The sun has broken through the scrappy layer of cloud above Washington but the millions pushing towards the National Mall have heeded the official warnings to layer up and keep warm.

The inauguration is still three hours away but the crowd on D Street is caught in a bottleneck with no obvious way forward. There is the first inkling of fear in the eyes of parents beside me. 'Stay close, dear,' a woman says to the young child in her embrace, her voice cracking ever so slightly.

My route takes me away from the crush, but as I turn the corner on the crowd, there is a policeman by the side of the road, trying to resuscitate a man lying on his back. People stream by, unaware of the small, tragic drama being acted out beside them. On a day of fresh beginnings and high expectations, Washington is also a city of sirens and police marksmen and National Guardsmen on street corners. But strangely, that does not feel like an impossible contradiction.

This moment means the world to the crowd churning impatiently all around me, precisely because they know what it feels like to doubt. Today there is a surplus of hope here but no hubris. If you look closely, you will see sobriety in the faces of those who have come to celebrate. The Obama fairy tale has its demons, just like the American dream. People have come to Washington on this inauguration day to pool their collective fears in the hope they will be raised above them. Obama knows what is expected of him today. He is just moments into his inaugural address when he speaks of the darkness.

'Forty-four Americans have now taken the presidential oath. The words have been spoken during rising tides of prosperity and the still waters of peace. Yet, every so often, the oath is taken amidst gathering clouds and raging storms. At these moments, America has carried on not simply because of the skill or vision of those in high office, but because we 'the People' have remained faithful to the ideals of our forebears, and true to our founding documents. So it has been. So it must be with this generation.'

He is speaking about that Obama generation and its collective instincts and its patriotism. But, today, he must also speak to those who do not possess the innate optimism of youth.

'Today I say to you that the challenges we face are real. They are serious and they are many. They will not be met easily or in a short span of time. But know this, America – they will be met.'

The speech surges through the ceremonial heart of America's capital city with the force of a storm surge breaching a coastal wall. It radiates from the Capitol in relentless waves, gathering strength from rolling cheers all the way to the Washington Monument. By the time one rhetorical flourish has run its course, Obama has begun another.

'On this day, we come to proclaim an end to the petty grievances and false promises, the recriminations and worn out dogmas, that for far too long have strangled our politics.'

Each fresh applause line collides with the backwash of sound rebounding from stately government buildings. Their grand stone alcoves capture and then expel the echoes of Obama's sombre cadence. The air over Washington is a foaming sea of elegant but discordant words. Joy. Heartbreak. Pride. Responsibility. Maturity. Callow youth.

'We remain a young nation, but in the words of Scripture, the time has come to set aside childish things.'

This will be the line that defines Obama's inaugural address. It is a warning to the outlaw pioneers of the boom times and the ordinary Americans infected by gold-rush delusions. It eventually turns into an appeal for more Ritual, for a renewal of personal discipline and a rebirth of civic life.

'What is required of us now is a new era of responsibility – a recognition, on the part of every American, that we have duties to ourselves, our nation and the world; duties that we do not grudgingly accept but rather seize gladly, firm in the knowledge that there is nothing so satisfying to the spirit, so defining of our character, than giving our all to a difficult task.'

In the new America, the pendulum has shifted away from Frontier and towards Ritual. But the danger is that a necessary correction will turn into a full-blown retreat. Frontier certainly inspired the ugliness of sub-prime lending and delusional sprawl. But it is also the constant motion of Friday-night football, the rugged courage of the fire fighter, the energy of the Freestyle Evangelical and the vision of the New Urbanist. The new America could not be sustained without the spirit of the pioneer.

It's what inspired millions to make a new life in America, what created the Sunbelt boomburbs and what drives the social technology that shapes the Obama generation. The United States needs the pioneer, now more than ever.

'Our journey has never been one of shortcuts or settling for less. It has not been the path for the faint-hearted – for those who prefer leisure over work, or seek only the pleasures of riches and fame. Rather, it has been the risk-takers, the doers, the makers of things – some celebrated but more often men and women obscure in their labour, who have carried us up the long, rugged path towards prosperity and freedom.'

This speech did not warm the heart. It offered no single phrase to the folk memory of future generations. But it was all the better for that lack of showmanship. This was a moment for a sober reminder of the secret of change, the true genius of America: the constant battle between hope and fear, between Ritual and Frontier.

'Starting today, we must pick ourselves up, dust ourselves off and begin again the work of remaking America.'

The work had already begun. This is America. The work never stops. Obama is proof of that.

Bibliographical Note

The central themes of this book emerged while I was researching and writing the documentary series *American Dream: Dead or Alive*, broadcast on RTÉ in February 2008. The series was directed by Ruan Megan, produced by Adrian Lynch of Animo productions and filmed by Colm Whelan. I am very grateful to them for supplying me with DVD copies of original interviews and footage filmed during our travels on the Sunbelt in the autumn and winter of 2007 (particular thanks to Colm for his photographs). The detailed accounts of my conversations and encounters in Saguaro High School, Orangewood Elementary, Radiant Church, on the US–Mexican border and other locations in Surprise, Gilbert, Henderson, Phoenix and Las Vegas are largely drawn from the video record of that journey.

This revised edition of *The New America* contains my own first-hand experiences of the climax of the presidential election campaign of 2008. All events from Florida, Colorado and New Mexico were as I witnessed them, as was my account of election night in Washington DC and the inauguration of Barack Obama.

I returned to Las Vegas and Henderson just before Christmas of 2008 to chart the impact of the economic crisis on the New America. I am grateful to Patrick Coolican and Mike Mishak of the *Las Vegas Sun* for their fine reporting and their generosity and warmth during our meeting in Henderson in December 2008.

For the historical background to Radiant Church, I relied on a *New York Times* article written by Jonathan Mahler in March

2005. I learned about the background to the creation of Ladera Ranch from an April 2006 article in the *Washington Post* written by Stephanie McCrummen. A series of articles in the *Las Vegas Review Journal* provided information about the development of Inspirada in Henderson.

The details of my encounters with the Lucio Family in Brownsville, the Coffmans in Fullerton and all other scenes in Orange County, Los Angeles and Texas are drawn from my personal notes and video footage filmed by RTÉ cameramen Nick Dolan and Cedric Culliton, during coverage of the 2008 presidential primaries. I relied on personal notes and photographs to help me write the account of my visit to the Titan Missile Base in spring 2008.

In setting out to examine the life of the new American suburb, I have been inspired by the work of *New York Times* columnist and author David Brooks, in particular by his book *On Paradise Drive*. By far the most informed observer of the boomburb phenomenon is Professor Robert E. Lang, the founder of the Metropolitan Institute at Virginia Tech. With Jennifer LeFurgy, he wrote *Boomburbs*, which is an essential reference book for anyone seeking to chart America's future (LeFurgy's 2005 paper for the Metropolitan Institute on voting patterns in the Boomburbs was also an important source in this book).

In trying to understand the history of the suburb I found Kenneth Jackson's *Crabgrass Frontier* to be an invaluable guide. J. Eric Oliver provides a critical assessment of politics in the suburbs in *Democracy in Suburbia*, while New Urbanist planners Andres Duany, Elizabeth Plater-Zyberk and Jeff Speck deliver a fascinating and challenging critique of past failures in their book *Suburban Nation*.

Several authors guided me as I tried to frame those central themes of Frontier and Ritual. I was particularly impressed by historian Michael Kammen's stylish classic *People of Paradox*. My favourite books on the history of the American West are *Frontiers* by Robert V. Hine and John Mack Faragher and *The Fabric of America* by Andro Linklater. Myles Dungan has skilfully recorded the Irish role on the American frontier in *How the Irish Won the West*. The essential guide to the history of American conservativism is *The Right Nation* by John Micklethwait and Adrian Wooldridge. Anatol Lieven provides an edgy, provocative history of American nationalism and the Jacksonian tradition in *America Right or Wrong*.

It is impossible to gauge American attitudes to the rest of the world by listening to US politicians. Instead, buy a copy of *America against the World* by Andrew Kohut and Bruce Stokes. It is a distillation of some of the most important surveys of US and world opinion conducted by the Pew Centers and has been an essential reference for this book. For anyone who is still confounded by the worldview of the Bush administration, I highly recommend *The One Per Cent Doctrine* by Ron Suskind.

In trying to assess the role of the imperial instinct in American history, I have turned to Niall Ferguson and his book *Collossus*, Josef Joffe's *Überpower* and *Are We Rome?* by Cullen Murphy. For a partial but provocative view of the immigration debate in the United States it is well worth reading Samuel Huntington's *Who Are We?* To illustrate the long-term benefits of immigration for the United States, I relied heavily on the work of Fareed Zakaria, in particular his essay 'The Future of American Power', published in the May/June 2008 edition of *Foreign Affairs*.

Robert Frank illustrates the growing economic disparities in America in a very colourful way in *Richistan*. For a deeper understanding of the future of the American dream, it is worth following the ongoing research of the Economic Mobility Project at the Brookings Institution in Washington, particularly its February 2008 report, which informed my thinking on social mobility.

In order to put the 2008 presidential election in context, I dipped into some of the best political biographies and memoirs of recent years. Barack Obama's second book, *The Audacity of Hope*, is helpful enough, but the first, *Dreams from My Father*, is far superior in explaining what makes this man tick. To understand the depth of John McCain's appeal, it is well worth reading the book he wrote with his long-time adviser Mark Salter, *Faith of My Fathers*. For a better understanding of the mixture of hope and doubt which characterised the Clinton dynasty, I would recommend *A Woman in Charge* by Carl Bernstein and *My Life* by Bill Clinton.

The best commentary on the rise of the Millennial generation is *Millenials Rising*, written by Neil Howe and William Strauss. Morley Winograd and Michael D. Hais have written an important book about the political potential of this generation in *Millennial Makeover*, as has Michael Connery in *Youth to Power*. For a hugely entertaining and critical take on the Millennials, I highly recommend *X Saves the World* by Jeff Gordiner. Among the reports I consulted while researching the Millennials were *The Progressive Generation*, published by the Center for American Progress in May 2008, and a survey of Youth Voter Turnout, compiled by Rock the Vote during the 2008 presidential primary season.

Any book about change in American society must contain some reference to the work of William H. Frey of the Brookings Institution and the University of Michigan. He is by far the most important demographer in the United States and during my research I kept coming back to his record of the dramatic evolution of American society, in particular his paper on *Race, Immigration and America's Changing Electorate*, published by Brookings in February 2008, and his report *The Racial Generation Gap*, published by the Milken Institute in 2007.

One of the most rewarding discoveries of my research was a book about the history of the all-American corporation U-Haul, called *A Noble Function*, by Luke Krueger. I was also happy to return to the pages of *The Long Tail* by Chris Anderson, which remains one of the most important books of the Internet age. It was also a joy to dip back into two all-time favourites, *The Great Gatsby* by F. Scott Fitzgerald and *American Pastoral* by Philip Roth.

Finally, this book is a product of its age and relied heavily on the research tools of the Internet. I would have been lost without the city-data website, which provided information on everything from political affiliations in US cities and towns to their racial composition. Zillow.com provided details on property values in the communities featured in this book and Meetup.com was an entertaining guide to their hidden social life. The Census bureau was an essential source in almost every chapter. RealClearPolitics and Politico provided an invaluable running commentary on the 2008 presidential election and a surprisingly diverse range of other subjects. As for Wikipedia and YouTube ... words can't express my gratitude.

Index